The Law Regulating Unmanned Aircraft Systems in the United States, South Africa and Kenya

Manana Wanyonyi Rodgers

The Law Regulating Unmanned Aircraft Systems in the United States, South Africa and Kenya

A Civil Aviation Perspective

Springer

Manana Wanyonyi Rodgers
International Air Law, Aviation Security
Kenya Airports Authority
Law Society of Kenya
and East Africa Law Society
Nairobi, Kenya

ISBN 978-3-031-49926-5 ISBN 978-3-031-49927-2 (eBook)
https://doi.org/10.1007/978-3-031-49927-2

This Springer imprint is published by the registered company Springer Nature Switzerland AG
The registered company address is: Gewerbestrasse 11, 6330 Cham, Switzerland

Paper in this product is recyclable.

This book is dedicated to my beloved family. Firstly, to my late mother, Doris Nabaloyo (RIP), who for over half a century doggedly trudged through abject deprivation to raise her eight children and give them an education. Secondly, to my amiable wife, Catherine Kagendo (CK), who has steadfastly stood by my side all through my advanced study. Thirdly, I wish to dedicate it to our lovely children Michelle Manakhe, Abigail Nafula, Hope Nabwire and Neema Nabalayo. Finally, to my siblings Peter Wamalwa, Santos Barasa, Gallas Wafula, Collins Wanyama and Brian Malali, and their families.

Foreword

This book, *The Law Regulating Unmanned Aircraft Systems (UAS) in the United States, South Africa and Kenya*, is based on a PhD thesis by Rodgers Manana completed in 2020, for which I served as external supervisor.

The book addresses a very important topic, namely how unmanned aircrafts are to be integrated into the civil aviation airspace. The importance of the subject is obvious. Unmanned aircrafts serve many useful functions relating to commercial, recreational, scientific, agricultural, environmental monitoring and research undertakings, security and law enforcement amongst many other functions. They can be used to save lives! Yet, at the same time unmanned aircrafts are not without their problems. Unmanned aircraft can pose safety concerns in the sense of accidents in the airspace. Unmanned aircrafts can also pose threats to the security of a State. Finally, it should come as no surprise that unmanned aircrafts can pose a threat to the privacy of individuals.

This tension, between the benefits of unmanned aircrafts, on the one hand, and the dangers and risks posed, on the other hand, is what is explored in the book. The key point in the book is that while international law does not provide ready-made answers for resolving this tension, there are tools in the toolbox—if only we open it—that can be used. Through his comparative analysis of three States, South Africa, Kenya and the United States, he shows usefully how those tools could be used, but also some of the missed opportunities in this respect.

Technology is always far ahead of law and law is always struggling to catch up. This growth in the literature on cyber-related issues and the law is a testament to this. This phenomenon of law lagging behind technology is equally true of unmanned aircraft systems and the law. Yet, this topic has not generated nearly as much literature as other cyber-related topics have.

I applaud Rodgers Manana for taking up the baton. Having worked in the area for such a long time, he is well positioned to provide insights, and I hope this book will not be his last contribution to the field.

University of Pretoria & International
Court of Justice (ICJ), South Africa
4 September 2023

Dire Tladi

Preface

This book is a practical guide to international air law with specific focus on emerging technology of unmanned aircraft systems (UAS). The emphasis of the law regulating UAS in the United States, South Africa and Kenya presents an overview of international air law and specific States' domestic law responses towards integration of UAS into civil airspace. The law regulating UAS is the concern of governments and private agencies, hence the urgent need for effective international, State legislation and compliance. It need not be overemphasized that the book is a pioneering work in this field in Africa and, therefore, is unique in sharing best practices and experiences. It provides real-time recommendations for concerned parties such as the international community, civil aviation agencies, governments, universities, continental and sub-regional blocks, private agencies, manufacturers, users, exporters, importers and non-State actors.

The book is derived from doctoral thesis, and its publication is deemed quite opportune as it addresses a topic that is close to the hearts of many people and companies across the globe.

Nairobi, Kenya — Manana Wanyonyi Rodgers

Acknowledgements

It is imperative to note right at the outset that the writing of this book is from a purely practical lens given the vast experience and exposure to the aviation industry. I am grateful to my initial doctoral supervisor Professor Casper Waschefort, a former lecturer and professor of International Law at the University of South Africa, now based in the United Kingdom. Professor Waschefort closely walked with me and was instrumental at the formative stages. I salute you Professor for your invaluable guidance. You were constantly by my side as I swam through unchartered waters, and I am all too glad to make original contributions to the body of knowledge and study.

I am similarly indebted to Professor Van Der Bijl, my Master of Laws (LLM) supervisor who encouraged me to enrol for doctoral studies. Her wisdom and encouragement emboldened me day after day to take up the challenge. Her scholarly insights shaped my legal mind to appreciate the diversity of legal research.

In equal measure, I wish to pay special tribute to my ultimate doctoral supervisor Professor Dire Tladi, Professor of International Law at the Department of Public Law and Institute for International and Comparative Law in Africa, University of Pretoria; former member of the International Law Commission; and currently, a Judge at the International Court of Justice (ICJ). I shall forever be grateful to you for your selfless commitment and sharp legal mind that in a huge way helped to hone my intellectual and critical approach to legal issues. You have steadfastly stood by me in providing timely feedback and offering impeccable guidance including providing preface for this book. Words cannot express my gratitude, but please accept my most humble word of thanks.

Mention also must be made this early of my family, especially my beloved wife Catherine Kagendo (CK), who once legitimately complained that I had become a career student in the first 15 years of our matrimony. Dear, you would empathize with me and wish I could take a break and create more time for family. I will be forever grateful for your unflinching understanding. To our four little girls, Michelle, Abigail, Hope and Neema: thank you for being disciplined and sympathizing with

Dad whenever he was under intense pressure to meet stringent timelines. May you all grow to be scholars of repute!

To my late mother, Doris Nabalayo (RIP): thank you Mum for being such an inspiration to many even as you battled cancer. It was my earnest prayer that you could live long to see the fruits of your selfless labour. As for my siblings Peter, Robert, Gellas, Collins and Brian, the late Mildred and Frank, I salute each one of you for supporting me and always standing shoulder to shoulder in our pursuit to quench the urge for knowledge in the midst of lack. Together we have made it. Let us keep the fire burning. To our cousin, Priscilla: thank you for babysitting and taking good care of us during our tender years. Bravo to our dear father, Josephat Manana, for being such a reassuring father figure. To former Provincial Commissioner Mzee Maurice Makhanu, thank you for holding my hand to KPC where I gained immense experience in a plethora of disciplines.

Special tribute goes to my teachers at St. Antony Boys' Sirisia High School, Sabwami Keya (SK), Weresia, Mwaturo, Mutundu, Wakachala, Barasa, Melemele, Kwarula (RIP), Masafu, Kasili, Lukhanyu, Wakoli, Grace and Wangusi, amongst others, and my classmates Inno, Sikuku, Wafula, Sululu, Tenge, Muliro, Imosha, Mutoro, Nabiswa, Manyasi, Lumbasi (RIP), Isaiah Sitati, Olaho, Lukhale and Owen, amongst others. Thank you, folks, for fundraising to enable me to enrol for the Kenya Certificate of Secondary Education (KCSE). Thank you Brother Peter Joe Wamalwa for aiding Mum in paying part of my school fees. I am also grateful to friends and well-wishers who, again, raised funds that saw me pursue Law at the University of Nairobi. Special thanks to the team that organized the fundraiser at the Law School, University of Nairobi, led by Wambaya, Ann Muchiri, Lillian, Jane, Nyambane, Betty, Caro, Cate Kagendo, Kivuva, Tsombe, Muli, Nancy, Makundas, Wilybroda Nasimiyu, Joseph and Richard Wataka, Joseph Wafula, George, Kundu, Wanyonyi, Saleh Chemsweat, Kirimi, Pauline, Nancy Nyatiti, Patrick Wanjuki, Arwings, Nilesh Shaa, Nderi, Titus, Chepseba, Ombati, Mohamed Wangusi and Mr and Mrs Francis Ndiema, amongst others, and another team in the United States led by Ian Wetzel, Andy Garbe and Ali Nusbaum (presently Attorneys in the USA): bravo buddies for your unrivalled generosity and kindness.

To the families of Matthew Barasa Wamalwa, Joy Mwende, John Mukholi and Ian Werunga, thank you for offering me shelter during the hour of need. To my friend Agina, my learned friends Francis Wanjia, Emily Muthoni, Bosire, Wakiaga, Leonard Sang, Zandoko Amboko, Nelson Otieno, Don Kevin and Dr. Ken Obura and my former roommate at the University of Nairobi, Kennedy Siboe: thank you all for accepting to review and critique my work.

To Professor F.D.P. Situma of the University of Nairobi's Law School: I thank you profoundly for agreeing to read and critique the original draft that pushed me into more research to refine this work. I equally appreciate Professor Tom Ojienda, for finding time to peer-review this work and offering valuable critique. Thank you too Professor Kithure Kindiki for your scholarly advice, mentorship and encouragement.

To my undergraduate contemporaries at the University of Nairobi's Law School, Faith Simiyu, Dr. Lyla Latif (formerly of Cardiff University), Dr. Ogendi (formerly

University of Pretoria), Dr. Felix Odhiambo (formerly UDSM), S. Jakakimba, Dr. Asala (University of Nairobi), Dr. Francis Kariuki (Strathmore University), Tom Bifwoli of ICC with the family and Harriette Chiggai former LSK VP, thank you buddies for the unwavering support and encouragement during the whole doctoral academic journey. To all those who took good care of me while on academic trips to South Africa, such as Lindiwe, Meluleki (MM), Ken and Raj, please receive my heartfelt appreciation.

I wish to most sincerely recognize my current employer the Kenya Airports Authority and specifically former and current colleagues: George Muhoho (former Managing Director), Matthew Wamalwa (former Deputy Managing Director), Stanley Mutungi (former Head of Aviation Security & Safety, who recommended my employment), Ken Kaunda, Agnes Owour, Judy Kerich, John Tito, Victor Arika, Joy Nyaga, Munene, Matthew Kabetu, George, Grace Munga, Sirai, Yatich Kangugo, Amos Chena, Rombo, Peter Miano, Esman, Patrick Nyoki, Langat, Shahin Mastu, Harrison Machio, Naphtali Oseko, Shivoko, Kaumbutho, Maloba, Lavene Esiaba, Rashid, Victor Njeru, Caro Muthinja, Nancy Karanja, Joseph, Amutala, Kithuka, Ombete, Willy Biwott, Wala, Gertrude, Seline Adoch, Evelyn Muriithi, Margret Okello, Ndirangu, Muchugu, Salim Bush, Nancy, Henry Ogoye, Joash, Mathews, Paulyne, Luseka, Wakoli, Lusweti, Emma, Margret, Wafula, Ngigi, Fred, Mwenda, Rose, Lucy Ndiko, Jecinta, Adasa, Wasike, Malemo, Kisang, Karanja George, Opondo, Dr. Chewa, Mohamed, Kiraithe, Brig (Rtd) Ofulah, Col. Kaleli, Dr. Kalai, Dr. Koros, Dr. Namanda, Jonah, Njagi, Chemeli (currently at ICAO HQ in Montreal, Canada) and Justus Kabaka (of ICAO Regional Office in Nairobi) amongst others; present and former friends at Kenya Civil Aviation Authority (KCAA), namely, Emile Arao (DG), Capt Kibe (former DG), James Kandere, Millicent Henga, Wanja, Chweya, Nakasanga, Hellen, Kuchio, Ogola, Malanga, Lawrence Amukono, Muthoni (RIP), Denis and Cyril. Please accept a special mention for being wonderful colleagues and orienting me into the exciting aviation industry. Thank you Agaba Arnold and Artur Energ of McGill University in Canada for hospitality in Montreal during my guest lecture to the Institute of Air and Space Law.

To the late Harvey Agumba (RIP), my Bachelor of Laws (LLB) dissertation supervisor: I pay special accolade to you for sharpening my legal research skills. To my friends Matias Adasa, Lillian, June and Lucy Ndiko: thank you for your unrivalled ICT skills, which you gladly rendered whenever required. To my learned friend, Allen Mukuki: thank you for introducing me to Professor Dr. Wolf Muller-Rostin, Professor of Air and Space Law in Europe, who provided me with numerous academic literature on International Aviation Law. Professor Muller-Rostin, please accept my profound gratitude for your scholarly advice and referral to Dr. Benjamyn Scott, of the Institute of Air and Space Law at Leiden University, who equally offered professional advice in a field that admittedly has few experts at doctoral level.

Special gratitude also goes to Captain Gilbert Kibe, former Director General of Kenya Civil Aviation Authority, for granting my interview request, from which the impetus to compile this book received a massive boost. Distinct mention goes to members of staff at the East Africa School of Aviation (EASA) library. Thank you, Nick and your colleagues for maintaining a habitable learning environment. Equally, much appreciation to the management of Ethiopian Airlines' Kenya office, for offering me rebate on air tickets to travel frequently to South Africa for my Summer School and Conferences. To my home county mentors such as Rt. Hon. Dr. Moses Wetang'ula and Hon. Tim Wetang'ula, bravo for being role models in the profession.

Finally, I am grateful to David Ndung'u, Cosmas Butunyi, Lawrence Amukono and Laura Hofmann for giving this work the much-needed editorial touch. Patrick Nyoki, thank you for acceding to read the entire manuscript. You are all dear to me, and I thank you most immensely. God bless you all.

List of Instruments

Domestic Instruments

Kenya

- Civil Aviation (Air Operator Certification and Administration) Regulations of 2013
- Civil Aviation (Airworthiness) Regulations of 2013
- Civil Aviation (Operation of Aircraft) Regulations of 2013
- Civil Aviation (Personnel Licensing) Regulations of 2013
- Civil Aviation (Remotely Piloted Aircraft Systems) Regulations of 2017 (annulled)
- Civil Aviation (Rules of the Air) Regulations of 2013
- Civil Aviation (Safety Management) Regulations of 2018
- Civil Aviation (Security) Regulations of 2015 as amended in 2020
- Civil Aviation (Unmanned Aircraft Systems) Regulations of 2020
- Legal Notice No. 133—The Civil Aviation (Surveillance and Collision Avoidance Systems) Regulations, 2018
- Legal Notice No. 129—The Civil Aviation (Certification, Licensing and Registration of Aerodromes) Regulations, 2018
- Legal Notice No. 91—The Civil Aviation (Safety Management) Regulations, 2018
- Legal Notice No. 94—The Civil Aviation (Aircraft Nationality and Registration Marks) Regulations, 2018
- The Civil Aviation (Security) Regulations, 2020
- Civil Aviation Authority Strategic Plan 2012/13–2016/17
- Government of Kenya Vision 2030 of 2007

South Africa

- Civil Aviation Regulations, 2011
- Eighth Amendment of the Civil Aviation Regulations of 2015

- SACAA Aeronautical Information Circular No. 008/2015 of 23 July 2015
- South African Civil Aviation Authority Technical Guidance Material for RPAS of 2015

United States (US)

- FAA Reauthorization Act 2018
- FAA Advisory Circular 91-57A.
- FAA Advisory Circular on Certification process for Agricultural Aircraft Operators Document Information No. 137-1B.
- FAA Advisory Circular on Exemption for Limited Recreational Operations of Unmanned Aircraft No. 91-57B.
- FAA Advisory Circular on Foreign Air Carrier Security No. 129-3.
- FAA Advisory Circular on Federal Aviation Administration No. 150/5000-16.
- FAA Advisory Circular on Propeller Instructions for Continued Airworthiness No. 35.4-1.
- FAA Order on Air traffic Control No. JO 7110.65 and FAA Order on Facility Operation and Administration No. JO 7210.
- FAA Order on Airworthiness and Certification of Unmanned Aircraft Systems and Optionally Piloted Aircraft No. 8130.34D.
- FAA Order on Unmanned Aircraft Operations in the National Airspace System (NAS) No. N JO 7210.846.
- FAA Strategic Plan for the Financial Year 2019–2022.
- Mississippi Criminal Code of 2013.
- Official Code of Georgia of 2017.
- The Academy of Model Aeronautics Safety Code of 2018.
- The National Strategy for Aviation Security of 2018.
- US Code of Federal Regulations, Title 14.
- US Code of Federal Regulations, Title 49.
- US Integration of Civil Unmanned Aircraft Systems in the National Airspace System Roadmap of 2013.

Regional Instruments

- Africa Union (AU) Protocol to the African Charter on Human and People's Rights on the Rights of Women of 21 July 2003 (entered into force in 2005)
- Constitutive Act of the African Union of 2001
- Constitution of the Africa Civil Aviation Commission of 17 January 1969 (entered into force on 17 March 1972)
- EASA Policy Statement Airworthiness Certification of Unmanned Aircraft Systems of 2009
- ECOWAS Supplementary Act 1/1/10 of 2007

- European Commission (EC) Regulation on Common Rules in the field of Civil Aviation, 2008
- Protocol to African Charter on Human and People's Rights 216 of 2003
- SADC Model Law on Data Protection of 2010
- Treaty for the Establishment of the East African Community of 1999 (entered into force in 2000)

International Instruments

Conventions

- Beijing Convention of 1 July 2020
- Cape Town Convention on International Interests in Mobile Equipment of 16 November 2001 (entered into force on 1 March 2006)
- Convention on Civil Aviation of 7 December 1944 15 UNTS 295 (entered into force on 4 April 1947)
- Convention on Compensation for Damage Caused by Aircraft to Third Parties of May 2009
- Convention on the International Recognition of Rights in Aircraft of 19 June 1948 UNTS 4492 (entered into force on 17 September 1953)
- Convention on Suppression of Unlawful Seizure of Aircraft, Convention relating to Unlawful Acts Relating to International Civil Aviation of 10 September 2010 (entered into force on 1 July 2018)
- Convention on Unification of Certain Rules Relating to International Air Carriage of 28 May 1999
- Convention relating to the Regulation on Aerial Navigation of 13 October 1919 (entered into force on 15 June 1929)
- Convention on the Law of the Sea of 1982 1833 UNTS 397
- Convention Supplementary to the Warsaw Convention for the Unification of Certain Rules Relating to International Carriage by Air Performed by a Person other than the Contracting Carrier of 12 October 1929 (entered into force on 1 May 1964)
- Convention for the Unification of Certain Rules Relating to International Carriage by Air of 12 October 1929 2242 UNTS 309 (entered into force on 13 February 1933)
- Convention for the Suppression of Unlawful Seizure of Aircraft of 16 December
- 1970 860 UNTS 105 (entered into force on 14 October 1971)
- Convention on Offences and Certain Other Acts Committed on Board Aircraft of
- 14 September 1963 (entered into force on 4 December 1969)
- The Paris Convention of 1919 or Convention Relating to the Regulation of Aerial Navigation signed on 13 October 1919
- International Covenant on Civil and Political Rights of 16 December 1966 99 UNTS 171 (entered into force on 23 March 1976)

- Protocol to Amend the Convention on Damage Caused by Foreign Aircraft to Third
- Parties on the Surface of 23 September 1978 UNTS 372 (entered into force on 25 July 2002)
- Universal Declaration on Human Rights of 10 December 1948
- United Nations Charter of 26 June 1945 1 UNTS XVI (entered into force on 24 October 1945)
- Vienna Convention on the Law of Treaties of 23 May 1969 UNTS 331 (entered into force on 27 January 1980)

United Nations Resolutions

- UN General Assembly Resolution 217 A (III) of 10 December 1948
- UN General Assembly Resolution A36-13
- UN General Resolution 2200A (XXI) of 16 December 1966 UNTS 171 (entered into force on 23 March 1976)

ICAO Instruments

- International Civil Aviation Organization (ICAO) A Manual on Remotely Piloted Aircraft Systems Doc 10019 AN/507 of 2015
- International Civil Aviation Organization Circular 330 AN/189 on Civil/Military Cooperation in Air Traffic Management of 2011
- International Civil Aviation Organization Circular 328 AN/190 of 2011 on Unmanned Aircraft Systems
- International Civil Aviation Organization Annexes 1–19

Contents

About the Author

Manana Wanyonyi Rodgers holds a Doctor of Laws in Public, Constitutional and International Law from the University of South Africa. His area of interest is International Air Law with focus on emerging technology of Unmanned Aircraft Systems (UAS). He is equally, an advocate of the High Court of Kenya, Commissioner of Oaths, and Certified International Civil Aviation Organization (ICAO) AVSEC Inspector.

List of Abbreviations and Acronyms

AC	Advisory Circular
ACAS	Automated Collision Avoidance System
AFCAC	African Civil Aviation Commission
AFTM	Air Traffic Flow Management
AIC	Aeronautical Information Circular
AIP	Aeronautical Information Publication
AIS	Aeronautical Information Services
AMISOM	African Union Mission in Somalia
ANS	Air Navigation Services
ASAS	Airborne Separation Assurance System
ASL	Air and Space Law
ASSR	Aviation Safety Standards and Regulations
ASTC	Aviation Security Training Centre
ATC	Air Traffic Control
ATM	Air Traffic Management
ATMS	Air Traffic Management Services
ATOs	Approved Training Organizations
AU	African Union
AUVSI	Association for Unmanned Vehicle Systems International
BC	Before Christ
CA	Communications Authority
CAA	Civil Aviation Authority
CASR	Civil Aviation Safety Regulations
CDL	Common Data Link
CFR	Code of Federal Regulations
COA	Certificate of Operations
CCS	Command and Control System
DGPS	Differential Global Positioning System
DHS	Department of Homeland Security

DOD	Department of Defense
Dr.	Doctor
EAC	East African Community
EASA	European Aviation Safety Agency
EASA	East Africa School of Aviation
ECOWAS	Economic Community of West African States
EEZ	Exclusive Economic Zone
EPA	Environmental Protection Agency
EPIC	Electronic Privacy Information Centre
EU	European Union
FAA	Federal Aviation Administration
FAR	Federal Aviation Regulation
FBI	Federal Bureau of Investigations
FINSA	Flight in Non-Segregated Airspace
FIR	Flight Information Region
GPS	Global Positioning System
GNSS	Global Navigation Satellite System
HALE	High Altitude Long Endurance
IBID	*Ibidem*, in the same place (immediately preceding footnote)
IAL	International Air Law
IATA	International Air Transport Association
ICAO	International Civil Aviation Organization
ICCPR	International Covenant on Civil and Political Rights
ICJ	International Court of Justice
ICT	Information and Communication Technology
ICL	International Customary Law
IL	International Law
JAA	Joint Aviation Authority
JKIA	Jomo Kenyatta International Airport
JPDO	Joint Planning and Development Office
KCAA	Kenya Civil Aviation Authority
KDF	Kenya Defence Forces
KG	Kilogram
KJ	Kilojoules
KM/H	Kilometre per hour
KWS	Kenya Wildlife Service
LLB	Bachelor of Laws
LLD	Doctor of Laws
LLM	Master of Laws
MPS	Minimum Performance Standard
NAS	National Airspace System
NCASC	National Civil Aviation Security Committee
NCAQCP	National Civil Aviation Quality Control Programme
NASA	National Aeronautics and Space Administration

NATO	North Atlantic Treaty Organization
NCASP	National Civil Aviation Security Programme
NIS	National Intelligence Service
NCLB	No Country Left Behind
OAS	Organization of American States
OAU	Organization of African Unity
OCGA	Official Code of Georgia Annotated
PANS	Procedures for Air Navigation Services
PhD	Doctor of Philosophy
R&D	Research and Development
RC	Remote Control
RCP	Required Communications Performance
RNP	Required Navigational Performance
ROA	Remotely Operated Aircraft
RPA	Remotely Piloted Aircraft
RPV	Remotely Piloted Vehicles
RTCE	Regional Training Centre of Excellence
SACAA	South Africa Civil Aviation Authority
SADL	Situational Awareness Data Link
SADC	Southern African Development Community
SA-CATS	South African Civil Aviation Technical Standards
SASCASSOA	South African States Civil Aviation Safety and Security Oversight Agency
SARPs	Standards and Recommended Practices
SMM	Safety Management Manual
SMS	Safety Management System
SSP	State Safety Programme
SUPRA	Mentioned above
TSA	Transportation Security Agency
TVET	Technical and Vocational Education and Training
UA	Unmanned Aircraft
UAS	Unmanned Aircraft Systems
UAV	Unmanned Aerial Vehicle
UAVS	Unmanned Aerial Vehicle Systems
UDSM	University of Dar es Salaam
UK	United Kingdom
ULC	Uniform Law Commission
UN	United Nations
US	United States
UTM	Unmanned Traffic Management
USPC	Unmanned Systems Program Committee
UVS	Unmanned Vehicle Systems
VMC	Visual Meteorological Conditions
VHF	Very High Frequency

Abbreviations of Journal Names

AASL	Annals Air & Space Law
ABAJ	American Bar Association Journal
ADR	Africa Defence Review
AFMCE	Atmospheric Flight Mechanics Conference and Exhibit
AJIC	African Journal of Information & Communication
AJME	Australian Journal of Multi-Disciplinary Engineering
ALP	Aviation Law and Policy
AMA	Academy of Model Aeronautics
BIGSPP	BIGS Policy Paper
CJTL	Columbia Journal of Transnational Law
CS	Communications and Strategies
CLSR	Computer Law & Security Review
CTAWP	CTA Working Paper
CYILA	Chinese (Taiwan) Yearbook of International Law and Affairs
DJLJ De	Jure Law Journal
DPLR	DePaul Law Review
ESPIP	European Space Policy Institute Perspectives
HJLPP	Harvard Journal of Law and Public Policy
IAPA	Impact Assessment and Project Appraisal
IJAAA	International Journal of Aviation, Aeronautics and Aerospace
IJAL	International Journal of Air Law
IJAST	International Journal of Applied Science and Technology
IJC	International Journal of Computers
IJCAS	International Journal of Control, Automation and Systems
IJCL	International Journal of Constitutional Law
IJARCET	International Journal of Advanced Research in Computer Engineering & Technology
IJRS	International Journal of Remote Sensing
JAAER	Journal of Aviation/Aerospace Education & Research
JAG	Journal of Public Administration and Governance
JAL	Journal of Air Law
JALC	Journal of Air Law and Communication
JATWW	Journal of Air Transportation World Wide
JFM	Journal of Fluid Mechanics
JIS	Journal of Intelligent Systems
JLIS	Journal of Law of International Sea
JSDD	Journal of System Design and Dynamics
JSS	Journal of Strategic Security
JTEP	Journal of Transport Economics and Policy
JTL	Journal on Transportation and Logistics
JTS	Journal of Transportation Security

KJLJ-JBSD	Kenya Journal of Law and Justice: Justice Be Our Shield and Defender
KLI	Kluwer Law International
McGill LJ	McGill Law Journal
MLR	Michigan Law Review
MNA	Mobile Networks and Applications
NDLR	North Dakota Law Review
PLBIR	Privacy Laws and Business International Report
PPTE	Periodica Polytechnica Transportation Engineering
SL	Scitech Lawyer
SLR	Syracuse Law Review
TAJ	The Aeronautical Journal
TCLJ	The Cambridge Law Journal
TPIA	The Politics of International Aviation
TFSC	Technological Forecasting and Social Change
ULR	Uniform Law Review
YASL	Yearbook of Air and Space Law

List of Figures

List of Tables

Chapter 1
Introduction and Overview of the Book

1.1 Background

International Air Law is a series of rules that govern the use of airspace at international and domestic levels. The rules encompass the relationship between States, service providers, cargo and passengers. They also oversee the impact of aviation on the environment and individuals, its benefits to the public and nations across the globe. Given the vastness of the subject, the scope and focus adopted in this book is the law regulating unmanned aircraft systems into civil aviation with specific study of the US, South Africa and Kenya. Unmanned Aircraft Systems (UAS) are aircraft and their associated elements, which are operated without pilots on-board.[1] UAS also describes a category of remotely-piloted aircraft used for non-recreational purposes and intended for commercial, military, governmental, or scientific purposes.[2] The UAS either fly autonomously or are remotely controlled. As a system, the UAS has four critical elements, namely: the command, control, communication system, and a ground crew who control the aircraft.[3] UAS is not a precise term and is sometimes referred to as unmanned aircraft, Unmanned Aerial Vehicles (UAV), remotely piloted vehicles and remotely operated aircraft or drones.[4]

UAS are variously identified by a number of titles such as Remotely Operated Aircraft (ROA), as previously used by the Federal Aviation Administration (FAA), and the National Aeronautics and Space Administration (NASA), of the United States (US), Unmanned Aircraft (UA) or Drones. Other terms are Remotely Piloted

---

[1] ICAO Circular 328-AN/190 at Glossary on explanation of terms, p. x.

[2] Yenne (2004), p. 13.

[3] US Department of Defense "Army Unmanned Aircraft Systems Roadmap 2010-2035" https://fas.org/irp/program/collect/uas-army.pdf (Date of use: 10 August 2023). See also Nonami et al. (2010), p. 13.

[4] De Garmo (2010), p. 11.

M. Wanyonyi Rodgers, *The Law Regulating Unmanned Aircraft Systems in the United States, South Africa and Kenya*,
https://doi.org/10.1007/978-3-031-49927-2_1

Vehicles (RPVs) as used during the pre-Gulf War times. Remotely Piloted Aircraft (RPA), commonly known as UAV, are used mostly by the military in many European countries.[5] In some instances, the difference in terminology is associated with how UAS are operated. For example, if operated from a remote-control centre, they may be referred to as RPA.[6] However, for purposes of this book and to ensure uniformity, the term UAS is used to represent all pilotless aircraft, except where specific circumstances necessitate an analogous term.

Compared to other countries, the US has a longer history with UAS and is, therefore, the country most likely to have robust provisions and legislative steps on regulation of UAS. Studies suggest, however, that the US still faces challenges with regard to implementation of the existing regulatory framework in areas such as oversight of UAS, Sense and Avoid Technology (capability of UAS to detect other aircraft while airborne and avoid crash), standardization of safe UAS operation, and data collection, among others.[7]

On its part, South Africa has made strides in the development of a robust regulatory framework for UAS, and rates high in the implementation index by the ICAO scheme through incorporation of visibility, provision for extended visual line-of-sight operations and development of technical guidance materials.[8] With this rating, however, the country still faces some serious implementation challenges such as effective enforcement mechanism.[9] Firstly, the registration system does not provide for means of approving and registering UAS models for private operation and operation by community-based organizations. This deficiency leads to loopholes that could expose the South African citizenry to safety and security challenges. [10] Secondly, the South African civil airspace is yet to fully integrate commercial operation of UAS. The South African regulatory framework also has the effect of precluding UAS from eligibility of being certified for commercial operation in airspaces that have not been segregated.[11]

UAS integration into the civil aviation legal framework in Kenya is yet to be fully realised due to their limited use. The Kenya Civil Aviation Authority (KCAA), the government agency responsible for the regulation of the aviation industry, has made significant progress in this endeavour, driven by applications for licenses for the use of robotic aircraft for shooting films, relief services and commercial purposes. In October 2017 KCAA drafted UAS regulations to provide for their licensing, registration as well as make privacy provisions. The regulations, however, were short-

[5]Newcome (2014), p. 20.

[6]Newcome (2014), p. 20.

[7]Shima and Rasmussen (2009), p. xix.

[8]South African Civil Aviation Authority "South African Civil Aviation Authority Technical Guidance Material for RPAS Part 101". http://www.caa.co.za/Pages/RPAS/Remotely%20Piloted%20Aircraft%20Systems.aspx (Date of use: 28 August 2023).

[9]Ingham et al. (2006), pp. 695–699.

[10]Ingham et al. (2006), p. 698.

[11]Ingham et al. (2006), p. 698.

lived as they were declined by Parliament on 26 June 2018 for non-compliance with existing laws. They were also found to fall short of the requisite security provisions, and public participation during their formation was deemed to have been insufficient as per Article 10 of the Constitution of Kenya, 2010, and Section 5 of the Statutory Instruments Act, No 23 of 2013.[12] These deficiencies, together with non-adherence to protection of rights to privacy as enshrined in Article 31 of the Constitution of Kenya, fines and penalties not aligned to the parent Act, have seen Kenya lag behind other African countries such as South Africa in integration and regulation of UAS.[13] It was not until 30 March 2020 that Kenya finally established new UAS regulations.

Therefore, it needn't be overemphasised that the legal frameworks in the three countries have kept the regulation of UAS in a flux and evolution with technological advancement. Consequently, there is need to align domestic regulations with regulatory framework in international law that is comprised mainly of the Chicago Convention, 1944. Others are regulatory instruments adopted by ICAO such as ICAO Annexes, Standards, and Recommended Practices. This book assesses the three countries' experiences and approaches of integrating UAS into the international civil aviation legal framework. It explores current international and domestic regulatory regimes that apply to UAS operations. Specifically, it does highlight safety, security, privacy, and related challenges that are experienced both in the substance and application of the respective domestic legal frameworks. Ultimately, it is hoped that the best models for adoption in the course of achieving safe, full and sustainable integration of UAS in the respective airspaces shall become a reality.

Further case is made that in spite of immense promise that UAS use exhibits, a number of issues have to be comprehensively addressed before they are fully integrated into civilian or commercial use in Kenya. These include the expansion of binding UAS regulation framework, overcoming inherent challenges facing the integration process, harnessing regional initiatives and development of sufficient institutional capacity to deal with safety, security and privacy challenges. The following rationalises the general need for regulation of UAS and introduces various regulatory approaches.

---

[12] Mutai E and Otuki N "MPs annul drones rules over concerns of security, fines" 2018-6-18 *Business Daily* https://www.businessdailyafrica.com/corporate/shipping/KCAA-s-revised-drones-rules-set-for-Parliament/4003122-5135554-vc3c0p/index.html (Date of use: 29 August 2023).

[13] Andae G "Kenya flies behind peers in drones regulation" *2019-9-18 Business Daily* https://www.businessdailyafrica.com/corporate/tech/Kenya-flies-behind-African-peers-in-drones-adoption/4258474-5278452-fvbplqz/index.html (Date of use: 6 August 2023).

1.2 Rationale for UAS Regulation

1.2.1 Overview of UAS Legal Foundation

The Paris Convention on International Civil Aviation was adopted in 1919. It was amended in 1926, introducing provision of pilotless aircraft under Article 15 that contained some requirements such as prohibition of flying pilotless aircraft over a territory of a contracting State without special authorization. The proviso was embraced under Article 8 of the Chicago Convention of 1944 and the ICAO framework of 1969. The reaffirmation of the previous position, coupled with the fact that the adoption of the two Conventions was made under the United Nations (UN), demonstrates a global consensus on the need to regulate UAS and have them integrated into civil aviation. A review of the FAA Modernization and Reform Act of 2012 of the US, South Africa's Civil Aviation Act No. 13 of 2009 as amended in 2015, and Kenya's Civil Aviation Act No. 21 of 2013, as amended in 2016 and UAS regulation in 2020, for example, shows that law reform in civil aviation has increasingly tended towards regulation of UAS. The following section is a discussion on the justification and dimensions of the necessity to regulate UAS.

1.2.2 General Justification

The mode for regulation of UAS varies in terms of the extent and scope of motivation in the individual circumstances of each of the 193 member States of ICAO.

1.2.2.1 Expansion in Use of UAS

While it is debatable whether there was UAS use in the military before the 1920s, there is consensus that the first remotely controlled craft, known as *Sperry Messenger*, was built around this time. This was followed by a phenomenal expansion in UAS use. For example, in the mid-1990s, the first remotely controlled UAS was put into environmental monitoring. Demand for UAS by civilian and commercial users for law enforcement, search and rescue, reconnaissance, intelligence gathering, firefighting, and agriculture, has been on the rise. Other uses are survey, mapping, combating poaching, wildlife preservation, and scientific research.[14]

This rapid growth in use is attributed to the fact UAS are relatively cheaper than manned aircraft in undertaking certain tasks. At the same time, UAS are less prone to factors such as fatigue and the risks that pilots are exposed to when monitoring phenomena like violent crime, hostile environments like volcanic eruptions,

[14]Nunes and Laursen (2004), p. 4.

securing pipelines and oil facilities, and spotting fires.[15] It is no wonder, therefore, that some civil airspaces that were the exclusively the domain of manned aircraft are today under UAS navigation. It is anticipated that the phenomenal growth in UAS use is the hallmark of civil aviation going forward.[16]

It is worth noting that increased UAS use has its drawbacks or challenges. For example, its integration into a busy national airspace raises safety concerns, including the risks of collision and environmental pollution. The sensitive matter of security is also compromised as UAS can be launched from any location. Criminals could easily disguise their intentions and successfully defeat the investigation capacity of any criminal justice system. Equally, UAS provide a rich ground for unauthorised surveillance with potential to violate the right to privacy. Weaponry testing and experimentation could cause loss of life and destruction of property.

It is with these concerns in mind that all aircraft are expected to meet certain minimum safety and regulatory requirements. This calls for development of a regulatory framework that defines approaches and standards, while creating or granting powers to institutions to monitor and implement the same. Such regulatory framework would bespeak that UAS must have ability to avoid collision with other aircraft, or what is known as Sense and Avoid Technology.[17]

The need for UAS regulatory provisions is entrenched by recent trends of UAS' use in land surveying and adjudication. They could as well play a pivotal role in critical activities like documentation of heritage.[18] It naturally follows that increased usage of UAS broadens the regulatory issues around unmanned aircraft, and consequently, how they should be mapped. Also, it evidences the multifaceted interests that must be considered in their regulation.

1.2.2.2 New, Increased Concerns and Associated Challenges in UAS Use

In order to overcome the prevailing challenges in the aviation chain, it is inevitable that regulation of UAS is accorded the attention it deserves. While Chap. 2 provides a comprehensive discussion of these challenges, it does no harm to highlight some of them at this stage. There is first the safety challenges, which arise from design and use of UAS. To begin with, they are prone to accidents, suffer inadequacy in Sense and Avoid Technology, lack of protective frequency spectrum, and prohibitive insurance costs. [19] Despite the increase in UAS number and use, there is lack of adequate Command and Control System (CCS), and a Unified Traffic Management (UTM) amongst developing States. This state of affairs significantly hinders

[15]Polkowska (2012), p. 60.

[16]Farber (2014), p. 11. For instance, Farber had predicted that by the end of 2020, the US could have 30,000 UAS overflying its national airspace.

[17]Marshall (2009), p. 693.

[18]Marshall (2009), p. 693.

[19]Marshall (2009), p. 693.

compliance, meaning that provisions for requirements that are hard to comply with would prove perilous in the long run.

Secondly, there are security challenges that relate to possible misuse or cyber-hacking of data and information owing to capabilities of global positioning system technology in every UAS. The challenges are exacerbated by the potentially dirty, dull and dangerous nature of UAS uses. This is mainly manifest where UAS is used in monitoring or espionage and imaging. That UASs are versatile and can be launched or propelled literally from anywhere, this by itself is a major security concern. Security challenges also abound owing to the nature of air traffic control in the use of UAS, together with the general risk of them falling into private hands.

Thirdly, there are issues of privacy that come to play with regard to UAS use. Assurance of the right to privacy is an extension of the human rights-based approach derived from international human rights treaties.[20] Privacy assurance in the use of UAS has been under attack owing to use of traditional photography, where people can be photographed or observed from the sky without their consent. There is also the matter of UAS flight over residential areas, which unregulated or under-regulated overflight could breach the private life of the public. It is no secret that UAS could be cheaper, quieter, easy-to-access and use. Consequently, it can be a notorious 'eye in the sky' unlike the traditional photographic technologies. The challenge is graver today, given that UAS is increasingly gaining high and sophisticated operational capabilities.

The threat has been the subject of debate in countries like the US where Robert Mueller, a former Federal Investigations Bureau (FBI) Director, told the US Congress that UAS deployed for surveillance and procedures were being developed for use in law enforcement.[21] This is a clear indicator of the need to develop and implement policy guidelines to ensure that such practices do not unduly compromise people's fundamental rights such as right to privacy as enshrined in various constitutions. Such a policy, for instance, contemplate data protection and cybercrimes under principal legislations of States because UAS operation could be manipulated for unauthorised purposes. hence exposing data held by third parties to risk. The regulatory framework should also provide what privacy means and move away from overreliance on the constitutions for protection of the right to privacy.[22]

[20] UN General Assembly, Universal Declaration on Human Rights 10 December 1948, 217 A (III), Article 12 and UN General Assembly, International Covenant on Civil and Political Rights, 16 December 1966 99 UNTS 171, Article 17.

[21] Mattingly P "FBI Chief admits Agency uses Drones in Domestic surveillance" https://www.washingtonpost.com/world/national-security/fbi-uses-drones-in-domestic-surveillance-mueller-says/2013/06/19/d51d40da-d925-11e2-a9f2-42ee3912ae0e_story.html (Date of use: 11 July 2023).

[22] Thompson (2015), p. 6.

1.2.2.3 Technological Advancement

The relationship between law and technology is an interesting one as application of the latter in operation of UAS complicates its regulation, thus necessitating every dynamic rule to contemplate and deal with constantly emerging issues. Whereas the law should ideally govern technology, it seems to lag behind. Rawich, for example, argues that the ongoing development and use of UAS clearly shows that the "law regulating UAS lags behind technology, it does not lead it."[23] This statement is quite apt today regarding UAS regulation owing to computer automation, evolution of the internet, high-definition imagery and smart technology. These advances mean in essence that a lot can be done virtually by remote control.

Global information, communication and transport systems are much ubiquitous and improved today compared to 1944 when the Chicago Convention was enacted. At the formulation and adoption of the Convention, the world relied purely on pre-information technology systems. A lot has changed regarding the design, use and manufacture of UAS and all that appertains to its architecture. For instance, there is increased use of sophisticated computer systems to operate UAS, which seemingly adds to its potential to intrude into people's privacy. The same holds for cyber technology. As such, though the Chicago Convention contemplated regulation of pilotless aircraft, it did not take technology into consideration.

The need to integrate UAS into the civil aviation regime has emerged because its development and use has tremendous potential to completely change the way human beings live, travel, fight and eat.[24] Thus besides the abounding challenges in the incorporation of ICAO-bound Standards, Annexes and Recommended Practices, there is a real likelihood that the law might never catch up with technology. In recognition of this limitation, Article 37 of the Chicago Convention envisages that once an international standard is set, it is up to contracting States to develop their own domestic rules to implement it. The Convention appears to recognize it is only by relying on State action that the law can keep pace with technological advances.

Stocker *et al* state that the envisaged integration can only be achieved formally through adoption of standards developed by ICAO under the provisions of Article 37 of the Chicago Convention.[25] States such as South Africa, and lately Kenya on 30 March 2020, that have successfully tried to incorporate regulation of UAS in accordance with ICAO Annexes, Standards and Recommended Practices continue to grapple with challenges of implementation and enforcement as expounded in Chaps. 5 and 6 of this book. Hence, such authors as Marcontelli opine that most UAS regulatory frameworks are largely conservative.[26] Since each country has its

[23] Rawich (2009), pp. 597–622.

[24] Gupta et al. (2013), p. 1646.

[25] Stocker et al. (2017), p. 459.

[26] Marcontelli D and Douglas S "Why the Use of Drones Still Faces Big Regulatory Hurdles" 2018-9-10 *Forbes* https://www.forbes.com/sites/oliverwyman/2018/09/10/why-the-use-of-drones-still-faces-big-regulatory-hurdles/#529c17ea1c0d (Date of use: August 2023).

own unique steps and experiences in integration of the use of UAS, it suffices to state that advancement in technology leads to new legal issues affecting the aviation industry. This is the drive behind the writing of this book.[27]

1.2.2.4 Failure by Courts to Fill Regulatory Gaps

Surveillance by UAS is always bound to expose citizens to law enforcement agents who are permitted to gather unprecedented amounts of information. It could also be a formidable security threat where States spy on each other. [28] These privacy and security challenges leave the citizenry in a precarious position. Executive arms of States are fond of trying to justify their actions whenever there is a public uproar about security, safety and privacy concerns. In such circumstances, protection of the citizenry can only be assured through judicial intervention. However, as Kerr notes, courts have been slow in assessing constitutional effects of new technology, such as that of UAS.[29]

1.2.3 UAS Regulatory Approaches

From the foregoing discussion, it is apparent that there are three regulatory issues that run through this book. Firstly, whatever the approach, an effective regulatory regime must seek to properly balance and address safety, security and privacy challenges that arise from the use of UAS.

Secondly, redress for the challenges must be balanced to ensure that neither individual nor public interests are arbitrarily compromised. For instance, overemphasis challenges to security has capacity to compromise privacy concerns by members of the public.

Thirdly, in order to adequately regulate UAS, there is the need to ensure a careful balancing of the interests of all stakeholders other than the public-private interests. The stakeholders include flight operators, end-users, aviation authorities, and States. Irrespective of the diverse nature of approaches a State adopts, it is worth considering the inherent regulatory issues.

States adopt different approaches in overall regulation of UAS, a difference that emanates from the fact that they face peculiar struggles in integrating UAS into the civil aviation framework.[30] The approaches are dependent on the extent of regulation

[27] Hayhurst et al. (2006).

[28] McAuliff M "FBI's Robert Mueller: Drones are in use in US" 2013-6-19 *Huffington Post* http://www.huffingtonpost.com (Date of use: 12 August 2023).

[29] Kerr (2004), p. 86.

[30] Jones (2017), pp. vii & 4.

and tools employed, and usually overlap. A number of authors have endorsed a variety of approaches to regulation of UAS[31] as explained here below.

1.2.3.1 Outright Ban

This is where UAS are completely prohibited in the territory under the jurisdiction or control of a State. Under this approach, there is no chance of use or licensing of UAS within the jurisdiction of the State. The approach has been adopted by countries such as Cuba.[32] The practice in most countries, however, is to have total ban apply only to certain types or categories of UAS. For example, the Republic of South Africa banned the use of camera UAS in 2014.[33] The New York City 'aviation' law as adopted in New York City—Administrative Code § 10-126 when read together with New York City Restriction of 2017, makes flying UAS within New York an offence.[34] Members of the public are mandated to report incidents of UAS use to the police.[35] New York City Council members, Paul Vallone and Justin Brannan, made efforts to amend the law in January 2018. Their amendment aimed to legally allow but overly restrict UAS flying in New York City. Considering UAS benefits such as use in marketing, inspection of buildings, recreational and hobbies, perhaps it is time policymakers in New York City had a relook at 'avigation' law, which appears unaffectedly outmoded as there is desire to exempt UAS from such provision.[36] The challenge remains, however, that with such a dense population and tall buildings in New York City, it may be tough for drone operators to comply with FAA's regulation against overflying the population.[37]

1.2.3.2 Effective Ban

This is where a State allows for licencing of the use of UAS but the licensing is restricted to the extent that the end result is akin to an outright ban. The restrictions, however, do not amount to a total ban when there is compliance with the set conditions. The effective ban is designed to give the impression that UAS operation is possible within a jurisdiction, but there are strategic bottlenecks to ensure their use does not materialise. This approach is ideal when a State is transitioning from a total ban as exemplified by the US when it was opening a window for exportation of

---

[31] Jones (2017), p. 6.

[32] Jones (2017), p. vii.

[33] https://www.uasvision.com/2014/06/05/south-africa-civil-aviation-authority-bans-camera-uas/ (Date of use: 16 July 2023).

[34] New York City—Administrative Code § 10-126, Section 6 (c).

[35] New York City—Administrative Code § 10-126, Section 6(3) (g).

[36] According to Collins English dictionary, avigation is defined as aerial navigation.

[37] The US' Federal Aviation Regulations, Part 107 Section 107.39.

weaponed UAS.[38] While licensing and approvals are possible, certain actions such as illegal surveillance are prohibited. Further, the export of the unarmed version under the new policy is limited only to US contractors.[39] The ban need not come from the State or the aviation regulatory authority *per se*. The National Service Park has banned use of the UAS on land and waters under its jurisdiction.[40]

1.2.3.3 Permissive Approach

This approach as the term suggests is liberal, but does not translate to a lack of regulations. It entails a regulatory framework consisting of manuals, policies and rules on licensing, registration and insurance. These are worded in a manner that makes them easy to follow. The permissive approach is divided into full permission or *ad hoc* permission. *Ad hoc* permission allows the State to evaluate applications for certification on a case-by-case basis.

The permissive approach envisages self-explanatory rules and laws that are augmented by adequate State actions in matters of investment in infrastructure, training, UAS-based pilot examinations and insurance. In other words, countries that adopt and apply this approach must do all they can to ensure human and technical skills, and expertise are incorporated.[41]

1.2.3.4 Wait-and-See Approach

States that have done little by way of regulating UAS have adopted a wait-and-see approach.[42] They first observe how regulations are applied elsewhere before they apply them in their respective jurisdictions.[43] While the wait-and-see approach is what these countries adopt at the onset of UAS regulation, they usually do this for the long-term as opposed to making it a precursor to immediate legal and policy development.

[38] Trible S "US open door to armed UAS exports" https://www.flightglobal.com/us-opens-door-to-armed-uas-exports/115939.article (Date of use: 16 July 2023).

[39] Trible https://www.flightglobal.com/us-opens-door-to-armed-uas-exports/115939.article (Date of use: 16 July 2023).

[40] https://www.nps.gov/articles/unmanned-aircraft-in-the-national-parks.htm (Date of use: July 2023).

[41] Jones (2017), p. 6.

[42] Jones (2017), p. 4.

[43] Ozerov A "Drones for Railway Infrastructure Monitoring" 2019-12-16 *International Union of Railways* https://www.unescap.org/sites/default/files/Item8_UIC_0.pdf (Date of use: 16 July 2023).

1.3 Contemporary Legal Gaps in UAS Operations

The motivation behind the writing of this book is the growing use of UAS technology without the necessary full integration into civil aviation by a unified international legal regulation. The void has caused diverse challenges, which are worsened by some States' failure to implement national policy and regulatory frameworks for UAS. States that have attempted to enact regulations are faced with safety, security and privacy challenges including difficulties in compliance and enforcement, which inevitably slow down the process of integrating UAS into civil aviation. UAS technological advancement and need for effective legal framework to respond to the influx into the airspace is a matter of urgent domestic and international legal concern.

It is anticipated that the UAS of the near future will be bigger in size, and with capacity for use in various sectors including carrying cargo and people, thus posing real safety challenges arising from possibility of accidents, increased avenues for terrorism and continued intrusion of privacy. Currently, the UAS-related safety, security and privacy concerns are facelifted and diversified in such a manner and form that are beyond contemplation of drafters of the Chicago Convention and State parties as at 1944. The possible future response to these concerns can first be deduced from the international legal framework for regulation of international civil aviation.

The international conventional framework, which is the basis of harmonization and coordination of integrating UAS into the civil airspace is difficult to implement partly because it relies heavily on soft law without which the conventional law is incomplete. Article 8 of the Chicago Convention refers to pilotless aircraft, which is the equivalent of UAS. The Article is rudimentary as it merely states that a pilotless aircraft cannot be used devoid of a pilot over and above the territory of a contracting party without special authorization from the host State. Further, it states that it is the duty of every State to provide security and safety within its borders. The Chicago Convention does not, however, define a pilotless aircraft or its classification. Such a definition is vital for purposes of designing a regulatory framework. Instead, the Convention only refers to conditions through which a pilotless aircraft is to be permitted into another country's airspace in a manner that is cognisant of security and safety considerations.[44]

In order to fill the existing *lacuna* in the hard law, ICAO has developed soft laws like UAS Circular No. 328 of 2011 as a guiding material to member States to provide for among others, the legal framework for regulation of UAS, its systems, and personnel.[45] It is noted that the framework developed under the Circular does not fully fill this void, but is more of a guide for State parties to the Chicago Convention. This and other ICAO-adopted instruments whose status in international law and binding force is considered in Chap. 3 herein are not themselves treaties.

---

[44] Chicago Convention, Article 8.

[45] ICAO Unmanned Aircraft Systems (UAS) Circular No 328 AN/190, Chapters 1–7.

There is a further *lacuna* in the substantive provisions. Despite its inherent challenges, the international framework focuses on safety and security of pilotless aircraft, but there is general tardiness regarding UAS-specific provisions providing assurances on the right to privacy. These challenges seem to continue to inhibit the ability of the civil aviation international law framework to respond to current and future safety, security and privacy concerns in use of UAS.

Following from the foregoing, challenges in the international frameworks have yielded a number of implementation challenges in domestic jurisdiction of State parties to the Chicago Convention. All frameworks in the US, South Africa and Kenya are faced with enforcement challenges. In Kenya, for example, the initial UAS Regulations gazetted on 6 October 2017, annulled in June 2018 and followed with a prohibition to fly Legal Notice No. 75 of 2019 is clear indication of backtracking in regulation of private, commercial and recreational use of UAS;[46] it is worth noting, however, the nullification was later remedied with gazettement of Kenya's UAS Regulations on 30 March 2020. For a number of years Kenya lacked UAS regulation, a period that saw the country lose critical opportunities to take risk-based approaches in regulation of UAS activities.[47]

Domestication of ICAO Standards was carried out at different times by various States. For example, the US enacted the FAA Modernization and Reform Act in 2012,[48] South Africa's Civil Aviation Act was enacted in 2009[49] and Kenya's Civil Aviation Act in 2013.[50] This shows the differential approach by State parties, which is based on among others, the laxity in adopting the SAPRs developed by ICAO. Regrettably, the challenges are lost opportunities for domestic regulation of UAS, which could otherwise be fast and flexible with regard to safety, security and privacy issues in use of UAS.

Some States like Kenya that have tried to embrace the integration and regulation of UAS are faced with the challenge of striking a balance between respect for human rights, including the right to privacy and public participation on the one hand, and the need to ensure safety, security and privacy, on the other. Other States like South Africa, despite making positive steps towards integration, are faced with execution challenges around timelines, annulment of regulations, limited approach in regulation by regulators, technicalities in passing laws, and conservative nature of regulatory authorities, thereby delaying the process of integrating UAS into civil

[46] Andae https://www.businessdailyafrica.com/corporate/tech/Kenya-flies-behind-African-peers-in-drones-adoption/4258474-5278452-fvbplqz/index.html (Date of use: 6 August 2023).

[47] See ICAO "Development of UAS Regulation" https://www.icao.int/safety/UA/UASToolkit/Pages/Narrative-Regulation.aspx (Date of use: 16 July 2023).

[48] FAA Modernization and Reform Act of 2012 Public Law No. 112-095.

[49] Civil Aviation Act 13 of 2009 (as amended in 2015).

[50] Civil Aviation Act No. 21 of 2013 (as amended in 2016).

aviation.[51] Further, existing regulatory framework is devoid of adequate provisions to address all challenges that come with ubiquity of UAS use and operations.

In addition, there is a problem concerning application of UAS for civilian purposes and whether they can be successfully flown without violating national or international aviation law.[52] This is compounded by the reality that without a uniform international legal framework for UAS, operators are subjected to numerous national and international regulations and standards. Even laws created by the international framework do not seem to fully mitigate issues arising therefrom.

Another challenge is that no specific study has been commissioned to analyse regulation of major UAS users considering the rapid growth of the aviation industry across the globe. This book provides analysis of the extent to which international law responds to integration of UAS into civil aviation and how the US, South Africa and Kenya have responded in their domestic legal frameworks, towards incorporating ICAO international standards on the regulation of UAS and their respective levels of success in this endeavour. It identifies the challenges associated with UAS operations and provides a roadmap for integration of UAS into civil aviation, with an opportunity for the two African States to draw lessons from the US, which has a longer history of UAS use. Evaluation is significant taking into cognizance the increased use of UAS, which seems to have become indispensable not only for military purposes, but also for civilian application.

To address the legal problem occasioned by the absence of a unified international UAS regulation, the book examines how international aviation law and domestic laws in the US, South Africa and Kenya have responded to challenges of safety, security and privacy in their pursuance of integration of UAS into civil aviation.

1.4 Conceptual Framework

In undertaking this book project, the author identifies certain concepts that cut across the book and whose terms are important to appreciate from the onset. Suffice to note that the approach is primarily informed by unity of the concepts of sovereignty of airspace and the doctrine of commingling.

[51] Ingham (2009), pp. 1–47. Also see Africa Goes Digital, training Africa's Pilots in homogenized regulatory environment (Africa Union and NEPAD) (Date of use 6 August 2023).

[52] Marshall (2009), p. 693.

1.4.1 *Sovereignty of Civil Airspace*

Sovereignty of States is the idea of exclusive control that a State has over its territory.[53] It also represents the independence of the State with regard to international relations.[54] The territory of the State includes land, airspace and territorial waters adjacent thereto. The *Black's Law Dictionary's* definition speaks more to the nature of this principle, whereby State sovereignty does not only represent a supreme power, but also an absolute authority above a property or State.[55] This means that aviation authorities have the power to regulate the airspace, including one that is used by the unmanned aircraft systems.[56]

State sovereignty as recognized under different international law instruments must be respected by other countries across the world.[57] Traditionally, governance of civil airspace has been dominated by a rule that States could not contend with anything less than complete sovereignty over their airspace, unless with exception of right of innocent passage.[58] The customary law rule has been that aircraft of one State have a right to fly over the high seas, but not over the territory or territorial sea of another State.[59] However, there are exceptions to this general rule in two principal instances. Firstly, it applies when a State whose territory is being overflown gives prior authorization, achieved either through bilateral or multilateral agreements among States. This exception is reaffirmed by the Chicago Convention of 1944, which provides that every State has complete and exclusive sovereignty over the airspace above its territory.[60] The second exception occurs in instances of innocent passage.[61]

1.4.2 *Commingling Concept*

In international aviation law, commingling is a regulatory concept that appreciates the need to allow operation and regulation of both UAS and manned aircraft within same airspace, instead of only allowing domination by manned aircraft. The concept has received overwhelming support from literary works of Bartsch, who notes that

---

53 Gevorgyan (2014), p. 432.

54 Gevorgyan (2014), p. 433.

55 See Black's Law Dictionary 6th ed.

56 Black's Law Dictionary 6th ed.

57 The Chicago Convention of 1944, Articles 1 and 2.

58 Dinu (1950), p. 43.

59 Dinu (1950), p. 43.

60 The Chicago Convention of 1944, Articles 1 and 6.

61 The Chicago Convention of 1944, Article 5 and UN Convention on the Law of the Sea of 1982, Article 19.

an attempt to regulate manned aircraft in isolation from UAS cannot be desirable.[62] Further, application of the concept has had a huge and long judicial history and has been affirmed as applicable to aviation rules by courts and authors. Generally, interpretations have been in favour of laws that regulate UAS operations. It has thus influenced the favour of most arguments for integration of UAS into civil airspace from a regulatory perspective. However, application of the principle has been controversial and not conclusive, as its premise seems to suggest.[63]

Amidst the challenge, there is no doubt that the concept still applies to motivate application of State laws to UAS operations. This was affirmed in the Australian case law of *Airlines* of *New South Wales Pty Ltd v New South Wales*[64] in which the High Court of Australia affirmed that Commonwealth law could extend to regulate interstate air navigation. The Court also noted that there was nothing that prevented Commonwealth laws from prescribing measures and mechanisms of UAS operations. The motivation of the regulation, the Court concluded, would be to ensure safety and efficiency.[65]

The commingling concept now applies to UAS operations in both the United States and Africa.[66] Considering this concept, therefore, defining an aircraft in terms of lateral size and shape for the purposes of regulation, is highly misplaced. In any event, the laws and courts do not intend to have manifestly unjust result of imbalanced regulation of manned aircraft alone in the airspace.[67]

1.5 Structure of the Book

The book is divided into eight chapters, each dealing with a specific and unique aspect of UAS integration into civilian aviation. Chapter 1 sets out the background and basis for concept. Chapter 2 discusses the background to the evolution of use and expansion in design and other specifications of UAS in order to create a general understanding of current safety, security and privacy challenges that necessitate a regulatory framework. Chapter 3 analyses how the international framework has responded to specific safety, security and privacy issues, together with associated challenges, and ends with a verdict on whether the framework is a perfect system of regulation.

Chapters 4, 5 and 6 focus on the historical, institutional, policy and legislative experience of the United States, South Africa and Kenya regarding their respective

---

[62] Bartsch (2012), p. 19.

[63] Bartsch (2012), p. 19 quotes the opinions of Learned Justices Evatt and McTierman JJ.

[64] HCA 3, (1965) 113 CLR 54.

[65] Mulero et al. (2014), p. 21.

[66] Mulero et al. (2014), pp. 21–23.

[67] See *Green v. Bock Laundry Machine Co., 490 US 504 (1989)* for more exposition on the principle against non-absurdity.

historical redress of the security, safety and privacy concerns of UAS use and operation. The analysis of the experience in Chap. 4 is deliberate, since it builds the background to certain deducible lessons applicable to South Africa and Kenya as analysed in Chaps. 5 and 6 of this book.

Chapter 7 provides a synthesis of the outcomes regarding the challenges of safety, security and privacy as well as lessons that can be learnt from the experiences of the United States, South Africa and Kenya. Lastly, Chap. 8 provides general conclusions regarding the effectiveness of the approaches taken by the respective States. It proffers recommendations for ICAO, South Africa and Kenya, the United States and regional economic communities particularly EAC and SADC concerning integration of UAS into civil aviation.

Considering this book is amongst the pioneer literature for African jurisdiction, civil aviation regulators, State agencies, universities, law firms, manufactures, importers, exporter and operators of UAS will find the book useful and helpful. For example, Africa is amongst emerging markets of UAS importation in the world, each exporter, manufacturer and users will find this book on the law of UAS expedient. Universities across the globe have limited literature on the African continent on UAS hence the book is of great benefit to civil aviation industry. The same applies to non-State actors and all interested parties. In addition, the book provides suggestions for areas of further research.

References

Books

Bartsch R (2012) International aviation law. Ashgate Publishing, London

De Garmo MT (2010) Issues concerning integration of unmanned aerial vehicles in civil airspace. The MITRE center for advanced aviation system development Mclean Virginia

Jones T (2017) Internationality commercial drones regulation and drones delivery services. RAND Corporation

Newcome L (2014) Unmanned aviation: a brief history of unmanned aerial vehicles. American Institute of Aeronautics and Astronautics

Nonami K et al (2010) Autonomous flying Robots, unmanned aerial vehicles and micro aerial vehicles. Springer, New York

Shima T, Rasmussen S (2009) UAV cooperative decision and control: challenges and practical approaches. Society of Industrial and Applied Mathematics Philadelphia

Thompson R (2015) Domestic drones and privacy: a primer. Congressional Research Service, Washington

Yenne B (2004) Attack of the drones: a history of unmanned aerial combat. Zenith Print

Journal Articles

Dinu MC (1950) State sovereignty in the navigable airspace. J Air Law Commun 17:43

Farber HB (2014) Eyes in the Sky on constitutional and regulatory approaches to domestic drone development. SLR Syracuse Law Rev 64:11

Gupta SG, Gonge M, Jawadhiya P (2013) Review of unmanned aircraft system. Int J Adv Res Comput Eng Technol, 1646

Ingham LA, Jones T, Maneschijn A (2006) Considerations for UAV design and operation in South African airspace. Aeronaut J, 695–699

Kerr SO (2004) The Fourth Amendment and new technologies: constitutional myths and the case for caution. Mich Law Rev, 86

Marshall D (2009) Unmanned aerial systems and international civil aviation organization regulations. North Dakota Law Rev 85:693

Mulero M et al (2014) Remotely piloted aircraft systems as a rhinoceros anti-poaching tool in Africa. PloS One, 21

Polkowska M (2012) Latest national regulations on unmanned aircraft systems in military and civil aviation in Poland. Eur Space Policy Inst Persp 60

Rawich TM (2009) Integration of unmanned aerial vehicles into the national airspace. North Dakota Law Rev 85:597–622

Stocker C et al (2017) Review of the current state of UAV regulations. Remote Sensing 9:459

Thesis and Dissertations

Ingham LA (2009) Consideration for a roadmap for the operation of UAV in South Africa Airspace. PhD Thesis Stellenbosch University

Workshops and Conference Papers

Gevorgyan K (2014) Concept of state sovereignty: modern attitudes. Proceedings of Yerevan State University 2014

Hayhurst KJ et al (2006) Unmanned aircraft hazards and their implications for regulation. In: Aviation History and Unmanned Flight. Twenty-Fifth Meeting of Digital Avionics Systems' Conference 15 October 2006

Nunes A, Laursen T (2004) Identifying the factors that led to the Ueberlingen mid-air collision: implications for overall system safety. Paper delivered to the 48th Annual Chapter Meeting of the Human Factors and Ergonomics Society, New Orleans 20 September 2004

Chapter 2
Abilities of UAS, Historical Expansion and Integration Challenges into Civil Aviation

2.1 Introduction

This chapter elucidates the functioning capabilities of unmanned aircraft system as appertains their use in war,[1] historical development, recognition in treaties and the practice of States. It examines the current and potential uses of UAS, emerging from their increase in the civil airspace.[2] There is analysis of their use in environmental and agricultural monitoring, surveillance, and security operations. An examination of their nexus with and impact on safety and security concerns is also made. Other concerns addressed include the matter of privacy, security of users and civilians in general. Beyond safety concerns, are other necessary concerns, such as the need to protect privacy and to ensure security of users and other civilians. Finally, there is discussion on efforts made to regulate the unmanned aircraft system, and the challenges in integrating UAS into civil aviation.

2.2 Design and Functioning Capabilities of UAS

The rules that apply to UAS are dependent on their design and size. Consequently, this book seeks to explore the dynamics of UAS from manufacture, operation, which includes height limitations, and impact on safety, security and privacy.

---

[1] Blom (2010), p. 65.

[2] Bart (2012), p. 7.

M. Wanyonyi Rodgers, *The Law Regulating Unmanned Aircraft Systems in the United States, South Africa and Kenya*,
https://doi.org/10.1007/978-3-031-49927-2_2

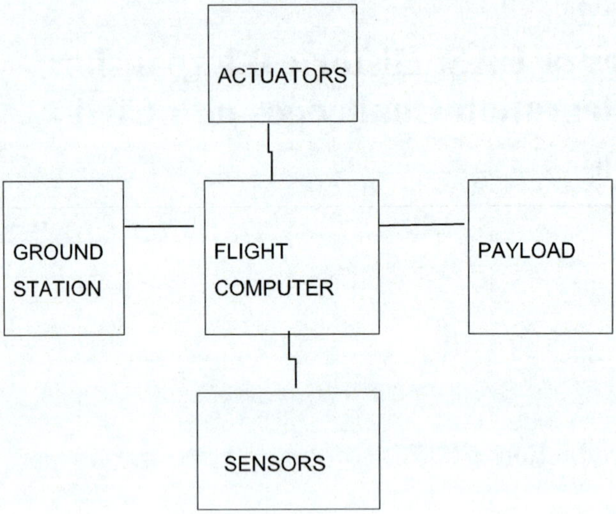

Fig. 2.1 UAS avionics

2.2.1 Elements of UAS

UAS comprise of the UA, ground control station, and the operator.[3] UA is an aircraft that is flown without a pilot, a pilot who is stationed on the ground or by a pre-programmed flight plan. It is a dynamic automation system capable of carrying lethal and non-lethal payloads (high and low resolution cameras/video), high reconnaissance, equipment, weapons and generally, any equipment required for the mission.[4]

2.2.2 Flight Computer/Aircraft Control System

Figure 2.1 shows the avionics of the UAS. Below it is a discussion of their operations.[5]

Flight Computer or **aircraft control system** is essentially used to fly the UAS.[6] It is either a two-way data link radio for remote control or an on-board computer with GPS navigation connected to the aircraft control system. Flight and operating system

[3]Gundlach (2012), p. 43.

[4]HaiYang and YangQuan (2010), p. 54.

[5]Ellen R et al. "An investigation into the next generation avionics architecture for the QUT UAV project" http://eprints.qut.edu.au (Date of use: 16 July 2023).

[6]Ellen et al. http://eprints.qut.edu.au (Date of use: 16 July2023).

control includes the control station, communication link, data terminal, launch and recovery systems, ground support equipment and air traffic control.[7]

Payload can either be high or low-resolution cameras/video cameras, day and night vision equipment, high power radar, electronic sights, relay systems, and warfare machinery (ESM, ECM and ECCM). UA requires high fuel consumption, which lowers the payload by between 10% and 20%.[8]

Sensors provide the basic functioning and capacity required to maintain motion in the absence of human input, radar, photo/video camera, and IR scanners. They have laser target designators to guide missiles and shells. Sensing payloads on UA include intelligence collection, reconnaissance and target acquisition, which provide support and weapon delivery given its capacity to detect and identify targets depending on constraints on rules of engagement and enhancing accuracy.[9]

Navigation sensors and microprocessors are critical elements in UAS for purposes of navigation. Processors allow and enable UAS to fly devoid of a human interface.[10] Aircraft on-board intelligence refers to the totality of information-gathering equipment placed in a UAS. The amount of intelligence put in a UA depends on the complexity of the task at hand and the oversight role of human beings. It is worth noting that these technologies are not well developed, hence their utility and reliability is limited.[11]

2.2.3 Control Types

The commonest forms of UAS control are ground control (remote piloting), semi-autonomous and autonomous forms or a combination of two or more of these.[12] These forms are briefly discussed below.

2.2.3.1 Ground Control (Remote Piloting)

UAS that is controlled from the ground is also known as a remotely piloted vehicle or RPV. It thrives on uninterrupted input from the operator. RPVs are sophisticated radio-controlled aircraft that use the same basic techniques covered in the preceding paragraphs. A few modern UASs are completely remotely controlled. Between the 1980s and 1990s, a rapid development of remote-controlled techniques and

[7] Bilbao (2008), p. 2.

[8] Austin et al. (2010), p. 6.

[9] Austin et al. (2010), p. 6.

[10] Nonami et al. (2010), p. 7.

[11] Nonami et al. (2010), p. 10.

[12] Nonami et al. (2010), p. 10.

programmes enabled establishment of guidance systems for UAS. Since the 1990s, however, the trend has been towards creation of more autonomy for UAS.[13]

2.2.3.2 Semi-Autonomous

This is a more widespread control system, which requires "ground input during critical portions of the flight such as take-off, landing, weapons employment and some evasive manoeuvres."[14] The system allows the operator to fully control the aircraft in pre-flight, take-off, landing and operations near the base. As soon as it gets airborne, the autopilot kicks in allowing the craft to fly along pre-programmed waypoints.[15]

2.2.3.3 Fully Autonomous

Human input in fully autonomous control systems is not needed as they consist of sophisticated autopilots, and are able to fly on programmed flight paths.[16] The operator's task is purely to monitor the system. In other words, an on-board computer controls the aircraft with minimal human intervention.[17]

2.2.3.4 Autonomous

The hallmark of UA is the autonomy of its operations, infrastructure and communication. Autonomy refers to the ability of an agent to carry out a mission without human involvement other than in an oversight capacity.[18] Decisions on-board UAS are made by an automated system or delegated to such system or subsystem.[19] To guarantee smooth flight, advanced control techniques such as neutral network, fuzzy logic, and sliding mode control are used.[20] Advances in wireless networks and micro-mechanical systems have enabled use of inexpensive micro-autopilots.[21]

---

[13] Nonami et al. (2010), p. 10.
[14] Nonami et al. (2010), p. 14.
[15] Nonami et al. (2010), p. 19.
[16] Nonami et al. (2010), p. 15.
[17] De Garmo (2010), p. 11.
[18] Fernández (2010), p. 67.
[19] https://www.caa.co.uk (Date of use: 23 July 2023).
[20] Gupta (2013), p. 1650.
[21] Fernández (2010), p. 67.

Table 2.1 Classification by performance specifications

Title	Weightiness range	Models
Super heavy weight	Above 2000 kg	Global Hawk
Heavy weight	Between 200 kg and 2000 kg	A160 Hummingbird
Medium weight	Between 50 kg and 200 kg	Raven
Light weight	Between 5 kg and 50 kg	Dragon Eye
Micro-weight	Below 5 kg	Silent Eyes

Table 2.2 Classification by endurance

Title	Durability	Range	Model
High endurance	Above 24 h	Between 1500 km and 2000 km	Predator B Global Hawk
Medium endurance	Between 5 h and 24 h	Between 100 km and 400 km	Shadow 600
Low endurance	Less than 5 h	Less than 100 km	Pointer

2.3 Classification of Civilian Unmanned Aircraft Systems

Arising from increased uses, varieties, sizes and functions of UAS, their classification is inevitable so as to enable lawmakers to come up with a regulatory framework. However, as Watts et al. aptly state, no universal classification exists due to the diversity in capability, size and operations of UAS.[22] Some States with regulatory frameworks have conveniently developed classification systems based on UAS size among other parameters.[23]

Some UAS are purely for the military, while others are for civilian use. Civil UAS are categorised according to the system payload as shown in Tables 2.1 and 2.2. Other parameters considered include endurance, radius of operational area, purpose and tasks performed, whether dirty, dull or dangerous. For military UAS, the classification is, as stated by Arjomandi, mostly based on altitude and wing loading capacity.[24] The section that follows is dedicated to an analysis of the criteria used in classifying UAS.

2.3.1 Classification by Performance Specifications

This entails the varying ranges of performance capabilities based on maximum weights of carried elements and fuel per UAS.[25] These range from the small ones

[22] Adam et al. (2012), pp. 1671–1692.

[23] Section 2.2.7 of ICAO Manual on Remotely Piloted Aircraft System of 2015.

[24] Arjomandi M "Classification of Unmanned Aerial Vehicles" http://www.academia.edu/2055673/ClassificationofUnmannedAerialVehicles2007 (Date of use: 10 August 2023).

[25] Jessica et al. (2008), p. 6555.

or micro UAS to the large ones with a wider reach, also known as global UAS. Five categories are recognized in this regard: super heavyweight, heavyweight, medium weight, light weight, and micro weight UAS.[26] The super heavyweight is capable of carrying a load of more than 2 tons. Examples are the X-45, Darkstar,[27] Predator B[28] and the Global Hawk.[29] Under heavyweight are UAS weighing between 200 kg and 2000 kg. They include the 60 Hummingbird and the Fire Scout. The medium weight category has UAS weighing between 50 kg and 200 kg. The lightweight comprises UAS of between 5 kg and 50 kg, for example, the Dragon Eye. The micro-weight UAS weigh less than 5 kg. An example is the Silent Eyes.

2.3.2 *Classification by Endurance*

Consideration under this classification is the ability of a UAS to attain and remain airborne.[30] The latter is critical as it determines a UAS' range of operations.[31] A high endurance UAS such as Global Hawk can be used within a range of between 1500 km and 2200 km. The medium range UAS are the most common, with an endurance of about 24 h and a range of 100–400 km. Examples of medium range UAS are the Shadow 600 or the Predator.[32] The low endurance UAS can remain airborne for 5 h or less.

This classification is important in determining the type of UAS to use for a specific mission.[33]

2.3.3 *Classification by Maximum Altitude*

Altitude is the vertical distance between a reference datum to the point or location of UAS.[34] UAS have a maximum operational altitude, which is the highest altitude within which a UAS operates optimally.[35] Flight ceiling is an important performance criterion in the context of UAS applications. Low-flying UAS are also called low

[26] UAS Manufactured by Teledyne Ryan.

[27] UAS Manufactured by Lockheed Martin.

[28] UAS Manufactured by General Atomic.

[29] UAS Manufactured by Northrop Grunman.

[30] Shawn and Renaud (2002), p. 668.

[31] Shawn and Renaud (2002), p. 668.

[32] The UAS was manufactured by General Atomic.

[33] Xiao-yd (2006), p. 4.

[34] Adam et al. (2012), p. 1614.

[35] De Garmo (2010), p. 11.

Table 2.3 Classification by altitude

Title	Maximum altitude	Models
Low altitude	Below 1000 m	Dragon Eye
Medium altitude	Between 1000 m and 10,000 m	Finder
High altitude	Above 10,000 m	Darkstar

altitude or micro-UAS.[36] Military UAS require low visibility to avoid detection by adversaries.[37] They are also preferred as they can operate at high altitude during reconnaissance and imaging.[38]

According to Watts et al., there are three categories of UAS under the parameter of maximum altitude.[39] Firstly, there is low altitude UAS, which has capacity to fly up to an altitude of 100 m. This type of UAS is purely experimental. Secondly, there is the medium altitude UAS that can fly up to a height of between 1000 m and 10,000 m. Thirdly, there is the high altitude UAS that can fly over 10,000 m. It is best suited for reconnaissance and imaging, according to Adam et al., UAS classification may be categorized as demonstrated in Table 2.3.[40]

2.3.4 *Classification by Endurance and Altitude*

This classification scheme combines the duo parameters of endurance and altitude. Under this classification are categories like Medium Altitude Long Endurance, High Altitude Long Endurance, Hypersonic, Orbital, and CIS Lunar Earth-Moon Transfer.[41]

Handheld UAS operates at an altitude of 2000 feet or 600 m, with a range of 2 km.[42] The close type flies up to 5000 feet or 1500 m and within a range of up to 10 km. The North Atlantic Treaty Organization (NATO) type UAS operates at an altitude of up to 10,000 feet or 3000 m, and within a range of 160 km. Medium Altitude Long Endurance UAS flies up to 30,000 feet or 9000 m and a range of over 200 km.[43] High Altitude Long Endurance UAS operates at altitude of over 30,000 feet with an indefinite range of distance.[44] Hypersonic types are high speed UAS, further classified into supersonic and hypersonic. Supersonic UAS have

---

[36] Thomas et al. (2016), p. 3292.

[37] Thomas et al. (2016), p. 3292.

[38] Thomas et al. (2016), p. 3292.

[39] Adam et al. (2012), p. 1614.

[40] Adam et al. (2012), p. 1614.

[41] Peterson (2006), pp. 522–551.

[42] De Garmo (2010), p. 11.

[43] De Garmo (2010), p. 11.

[44] De Garmo (2010), p. 11.

Table 2.4 Classification by range and altitude

Group	Range	Altitude
Handheld	2 km range	2000 ft (600 m)
CLOSE	Up to 10 km range	5000 ft (1500 m)
NATO type	About 160 km range	10,000 ft (3000 m)
Tactical	–	–
MALE	Over 200 km range	Up to 30,000 ft (9000 m)
HALE	Indefinite range	Over 30,000 ft
HYPERSONIC	Over 200 km	50,000 ft (15,200 m) or suborbital altitude
ORBITAL	Over Mach 25	Low earth orbit
CIS	Lunar Earth	Moon Transfer

speeds of between Mach 1 and 5, while Hypersonic UAS have speeds of over Mach 5.[45] Hypersonic UAS fly at heights of 50,000 feet or 15,200 m or suborbital altitude, with a range of over 200 km. Orbital UAS have a low earth orbit altitude with speeds of over Mach 25. Authors such as DeGarmo in the writings describe the range and altitude classification as shown in Table 2.4.[46]

2.3.5 *Classification by Wing Loading Capacity*

Wing loading capacity is the total area of an UAS divided by that of the wing, often measured in Ounce square foot.[47] UAS classification by wing loading capacity comprises three categories: low, medium and high. Wing loading capacity is calculated as follows:

$$\text{Total Wing Loading Capacity} = \text{UAV Total Weight (kg)}/\text{AV Total Wing Area}\ \left(\text{m}^2\right)$$

UAS with wing loading capacity of below 50 kg/m^2 are considered to be of low loading, while those with wing loading capacity of between 50 kg/m^2 and 100 kg/m^2 are considered to be of medium loading capacity. UAS with wing loading capacity of over 100 kg/m^2 are high loading capacity. The debate on wing loading capabilities has been discussed by different scholars such as Suraj et al., an approach of arrangement may be demonstrated in Table 2.5.[48]

---

45 Freeman (1956), pp. 366–387.

46 De Garmo (2010), p. 12.

47 J Thomas et al. (2006) (25th AIAA Aerodynamic Measurement Technology and Ground Testing Conference), p. 3307. An Ounce square foot is recorded as oz.ft2. For conversation purposes, 1 g.m2 = 0.379686 oz.ft2.

48 Suraj et al. (2013a, b), pp. 1652–1653.

Table 2.5 Classification by wing loading capacity

Designation	Wing loading in kg/m^2	Examples
Low loading capacity	Below 50 h	Predator B
Medium loading capacity	Between 50 h and 100 h	Silver Fox
High loading capacity	Above 100 h	Pointer

2.3.6 Classification of Military UAS

Military UAS is used to support operational, tactical and strategic operations of the military.[49] Use of military UAS dates back to the Second World War. In more recent times, use of UAS for military onslaught in Iraq reached 100,000 flight hours in 2005. A classification scheme that relates to the mission, size and capability of the military UAS come to the fore. This includes micro-aerial vehicles, local area support vehicles, tactical area support vehicles, and theatre area support vehicles.[50] This classification is dependent on the environment, which determines the level of autonomy and capacity of manoeuvrability required for purposes of accomplishing the mission at hand.[51]

2.3.7 Other Classifications

According to Arjomandi's panoptical views, there are other parameters for classification of UAS such as engine, which further yields further categories like Turbofans, two strike, Piston Rotary, Turboprop, Push and Pull, Electric and Propeller. These categories are distinct from the ones cited above.[52] Other parameters for classifications are based on power or thrust loading, which is defined by the amount of weight a UAS can lift.[53] This is different from the parameter of performance, which is the ratio between the thrust and its weight.

The import of the above classifications is that any effective UAS regulatory framework must focus on more than just omnibus prohibitions and prescriptions. Instead, it should be comprehensive enough as to cater for differences in among others weight load and performance capacities. It needn't be overemphasised that the use of UAS for strategic military operations raises security issues. Likewise, UAS that fly at high altitude have the potency to intrude into the privacy of the citizenry. How international law and some domestic regulations of the various classes of UAS is covered in subsequent chapters.

---

[49] Valavanism and Vachtsevanos (2015), p. 102.

[50] http://www.nasa.gov (Date of use: 9 August 2023).

[51] http://de.calameo.com (Date of use: 9 August 2023).

[52] http://de.calameo.com (Date of use: 9 August 2023).

[53] http://de.calameo.com (Date of use: 9 August 2023).

2.4 Brief History of UAS

The history of manned aircraft and UAS is important in understanding the invention and development of air transport. Since the invention of the first manned aircraft by the Wright Brothers in 1903, unprecedented leaps have been made in the aviation industry. The development of UAS use, which was originally preceded by scepticism, has surged especially after the impetus given by the nature of World War I, during and after the war into the Cold War era to date.

2.4.1 Early History of Manned Aircraft

The idea of flying has intrigued humankind since the beginning of civilization.[54] That humans could fly was first contemplated more than 2500 years ago in Greece and China.[55] Pythagoras and Archimedes conceptualized studies on autonomous mechanisms for various applications. Archytas from the city of Taranta created the earliest known and recorded flying machine or Tarentum in Southern Italy, known as Archytas or Tarentine,[56] and in 425 BC, became the first engineer to build a mechanical landing craft, which flew for about 200 m.[57]

During the same era, the Chinese documented the idea of a vertical flight aircraft. For many years, the Chinese had experimented with flying machines like hot air balloons, rockets and kites. In 1483, Leonardo da Vinci designed an aircraft capable of hovering, controlled by its aerial screw or gyroscope.[58] Later on, in 1508, he developed a mechanical bird that could flap its wings.[59] Over two centuries later, the first hot air balloon flew in 1782. The balloon was designed by the Montgolfier Brothers and was considered the first unmanned flight. Many more flying aircraft were developed in the period 1860 to 1909, initially focusing on vertical take-off and landing craft arising from limitations posed by the steam engine.

In the eighteenth century, there was general scepticism that human beings could fly through the air with equipment that was heavier than air. In 1895, Lord Kelvin commented that flight with machines that were heavier than the air was impossible. Thomas Edison, who held similar views, was convinced that possibilities of the airplane had been exhausted and that humanity ought to turn elsewhere in innovation.[60] Apart from the impossibility presented by authors of the eighteenth century, others such as Simon Newcomb, believed that the purported flights were not

---

[54] De Garmo (2010), p. 4.

[55] De Garmo (2010), p. 3.

[56] De Garmo (2010), p. 12.

[57] De Garmo (2010), p. 12.

[58] http://www.hiller.org/ (Date of use: 19 July 2023).

[59] De Garmo (2010), p. 12.

[60] De Garmo (2010), p. 1.

practical and, if anything, insignificant.[61] With this scepticism, it was apparent that the end of the eighteenth century was marked with uncertainty as to whether manned aircraft were needed in the airspace and whether the aviation industry meant anything to humanity.

The uncertainty was only tucked in the early days of the twentieth century. On 17 December 1903, the world witnessed a remarkable event, by way of the first manned aircraft flight by the Wright Brothers.[62] The flight, which took place at Kitty Hawk, North Carolina, set in motion mechanisms aimed at improving transportation, comfort, capability for pilots, as well as safety in the industry.[63] This was a historic moment because other than its pioneering role, it kick-started a long journey for the aviation industry culminating in the diverse entity it has become today.[64] It put to rest the issue of uncertainty, which was cultivated by the authors in the eighteenth century. Since then, the use of unmanned aircraft has reached unprecedented levels.

2.4.2 Development of UAS

Unlike the manned aircraft, the development of UAS has been largely associated with wars or military campaigns, testing and part of weaponry tools.[65] They have also been comparatively more spontaneous.[66] The first recorded use of UAS was in 1871, when the Austrian army dropped bombs in Venice, Italy, using unmanned balloons.[67] Current trends in UAS technologies, however, trace their origin to the First World War.[68] More development took place during the inter-war years between 1918 and 1939, the Second World War, the Korean War and the Vietnam War. There was further use of UAS in the Yom Kippur War of 1969, the Egypt-Israeli War of 1973, the first and second Persian Gulf Wars and the war against terror in Afghanistan.[69]

During the First World War, the focus of unmanned aircraft system technology was on manufacture of aerial torpedoes.[70] The Korean War involved experimentation in missions, sensors and munitions to enable strikes and reconnaissance for military commanders. Subsequently, in the 1950s, there was a shift towards

61 De Garmo (2010), p. 1.

62 Klaus (2013), p. 3761.

63 Wright (1916), pp. 100–106.

64 Wright (1916), p. 104.

65 Suraj et al. (2013a, b), pp. 1646–1658.

66 Suraj et al. (2013a, b), p. 1651.

67 Michaelides-Mateou et al. (2014), p. 113.

68 Keane and Carr (2013), pp. 558–571.

69 Cole (2012), pp. 558–571.

70 Cole (2012), p. 569.

development of cruise missile and UAS.[71] The use of UAS, however, highlighted two major weaknesses. First, the crew was unable to launch and recover the UAS as upon striking the target, it was destroyed instantaneously. The second challenge was difficulty of stabilizing the UAS while airborne.[72] These challenges necessitated further development of UAS to what is on offer today.

2.5 Current and Potential Use of Unmanned Aircraft System (UAS)

The history of UAS is replete with evidence of their use in warfare. Subsequent developments, from the 1910s to date, evidence an increase in deployment of UAS, not just for warfare, but also for varied military uses such as intelligence gathering, surveillance, reconnaissance, border patrol, counter-terrorism operations, and airstrikes.[73] Progressively, there has been an upsurge in the use of unmanned aircraft systems in civilian aviation for research, crowd control and homeland or internal security. Therefore, military use of UAS continues alongside the civilian use.

UAS have potential for use in missions that are not conducive or safe for human beings (pilots). Koldaev notes that the missions have certain chemical, biological, radiological and nuclear properties which present difficulties in their use.[74] He calls them "dull, dirty and difficult missions."[75] This book adopts Koldaev's distinction of missions by highlighting the peculiar safety, security and privacy issues that they bring forth. It is no doubt that the paradigm shift in use, operation, size and, consequently, mission have deepened concerns about safety, security, and privacy.

2.5.1 Dull Operations

Dull operations are those that would ideally be shunned by humans for being boring.[76] UAS are preferred for use in such operations because of their virtual ability to operate for long missions and to observe risk incidences to the tune of about

[71] Fahrney and RADM (1980), pp. 54–60. Cruise missile refers to a one-way lethal munitions designed to strike specific targets.

[72] Cole (2012), p. 564.

[73] Koldaev and Sokut (2005), pp. 100–104.

[74] Koldaev and Sokut (2005), p. 100.

[75] Koldaev and Sokut (2005), p. 100.

[76] Judson J "Future Unmanned aircraft to do the 'dull' and 'dangerous' work" 2018-3-26 *Defence News*. https://www.defensenews.com/digital-show-dailies/global-force-symposium/2018/03/26/future-unmanned-aircraft-to-do-the-dull-and-dangerous-work/ (Date of use: 22 August 2023).

30–40 h.[77] These tasks can be automated if need be, as they only require oversight rather than continuous and consistent human presence. The tasks comprise observations of patterns of life, surveillance of fixed locations, support of services over electronic warfare, relaying communication and aerial refuelling.[78] They could also raise other complex and sensitive tasks that are unlikely to be undertaken by a simple task platform.[79]

One of the most common dull operation is the internal security and border control. UAS can be used in civilian tasks like internal/homeland security, monitoring of the coastline and security provision in public gatherings. In the US, for example, after the terrorist attack of 11 September 2001, surveillance became a critical issue for UAS,[80] particularly for State institutions that require constant surveillance. Accordingly, the US patrol is operated under the Customs and Border Protection, along the border with Mexico and Canada.[81] The UAS is preferred as it can provide about 30 h monitoring, which would require the services of up to 10 manned helicopters.[82]

Also in the US, technology to secure and monitor coastlines has for long been applied to enhance border patrol. For example, the General Atomics MQ-9 Reaper is used along the Arizona-Mexico border to isolate not only persons entering the country illegally, but also those involved in smuggling.[83] rise in insecurity from terrorism as illustrated by the 9/11 debacle increased demand for UAS. In the US as earlier stated, the use of UAS for security purposes is restricted to customs and border surveillance on the US/Mexico and US/Canada borders. For customs and border protection, Predator has filled gaps in surveillance where the terrain is difficult.[84]

Sustained border coverage has significantly reduced risks of fatigue and harm to border agents.[85] Unmanned aircraft systems are equipped with infrared and high-resolution imaging equipment for monitoring drug smuggling along the Pacific Ocean, off the coast of El-Salvador. They are also deployed by law enforcement agencies for purposes of facial recognition forward-looking infrared imaging.[86]

---

77 Office of the Secretary of Defense "Unmanned Aerial Vehicles Roadmap 2002-2027" http://oai.dtic.mil/oai (Date of use: 18 August 2023).

78 Gupta (2013), p. 1646.

79 Gupta (2013), p. 1646.

80 Padgett T "Using Drones in the Drug War" *2012-6-8 Time* http://www.time.com (Date of use: 15 July 2023).

81 Haddal and Gertler (2010), p. 8.

82 Haddal and Gertler (2010), p. 8.

83 Customs and Border Protection Agency "US Customs and Border Protection UAS Overview" http://www.cbp.gov (Date of use: 4 August 2023).

84 Haddal and Gertler (2010), p. 88.

85 Haddal and Gertler (2010), p. 88.

86 Carr EB "Unmanned aerial vehicles: Examining the safety, security, privacy and regulatory issues of integration into U.S Airspace" https://www.e-education.psu.edu/geog892/sites/www.e-education.psu.edu.geog892/files/sp-Drones-long-paper.pdf (Date of use: 14 August 2023).

UAS help the police to respond to emergencies, conduct surveillance, search and rescue (especially in bad weather), as well as traffic monitoring, nuclear, biological and chemical sensing and tracking.[87]

On another front, unmanned aircraft systems technology is used in agriculture to monitor soil erosion, crop maturity, frost mitigation and application of fertilizers.[88] In Japan, for example, robotic helicopters attached to UAS and driven by the Fuji Heavy Industry are used to monitor more than 10% of the rice farms. Yamaha has also developed UAS for use in chemical spraying, with more than 8000 pilots in 2007.[89]

UAS are chosen for the above missions owing to their efficiency in image-taking. They have the capacity to fly pre-determined flight paths and take accurate pictures of target flight.[90] Accordingly, high-resolution vineyards and coffee field images that show crop maturity have been developed using UAS.[91] The efficiency results from UAS' use of technologies that include airborne platforms, thermal infrared imaging technology, and data telemetry. Others are development of algorithms that track tagged wild animals as well as monitor wildlife inventory.[92]

It is worth noting that the use of UAS is comparatively cheaper compared to technology in which humans are involved. There is evidence that UAS have helped farmers to detect crop growth and blight at a cost that is 25–50% less than that of fixed wing aircraft.[93] Consequently, farmers are able to save money, time and resources. This is a clear indication of UAS' potential in agriculture and wildlife conservation.

UAS is also used in scientific research, particularly where data is collected over long periods. Specific types of UAS fixed with advanced technological systems are preferred due to their high endurance capacity.[94] Compared to satellites, UAS have superior sensor capabilities suitable for collecting data.[95] That they are able to collect atmospheric data in air columns using inbuilt instruments means they are more efficient than satellite.[96] Consequently, humans have gained invaluable insights into atmospheric science for long was thought to be the preserve of science fiction. For this functionality to be fully realised, however, there is need to integrate UAS

[87] De Garmo (2010), p. 11.

[88] UAV Markets Space Consulting "UAV Agriculture and Wildlife Management" http://www.uavm.com (Date of use: 23 July 2023).

[89] Kenzo (2007), p. 124.

[90] Jensen et al. (2011), pp. 139–146.

[91] Johnson (2003), pp. 1–3.

[92] ResearchGate "UAV collaborative and UAV applications: fire management - project overview" http://www.uav-applications.org/projects (Date of use: 15 August 2023).

[93] Caumont A "Start-Up" 28-11-2016 *Washington Post* http://www.washingtonpost.com (Date of use: 23 August 2023).

[94] Hagenauer B "Ikhana UAV gives NASA new science and technology capabilities" *2007-3-29 NASA Press Release* http://www.nasa.gov (Date of use: 2 August 2023).

[95] Skrzypietz (2012), p. 18.

[96] Reuder (2009), p. 22.

into the existing civil aviation legal and policy frameworks. In the words of Ali Mazrui:

> Globalization is much more than the Information Superhighway and the new expansion of international markets. Globalization consists of all the forces, which are pushing the world towards becoming a global village. Globalization is the villagization of the globe.[97]

It is, therefore, undeniable that the UAS technology is here to stay, and States must adopt it in science for the benefit of humankind.

Dull missions may also take the form of environmental monitoring. UAS are pivotal in complementing existing satellite installations to increase capacity for monitoring climatic, and specifically, rainfall patterns.[98] They are equally useful in navigating hazardous environments such as volcanic activities.[99] Their capacity to monitor geophysical processes that relate to natural hazards like aerosols, gas levels in the clouds, changes in the ozone layer, pollution, quality of air, water vapour, composition of vegetation, and coral reefs, is unrivalled. UAS are also used to monitor emissions that pollute the ozone layer; oxygen and carbon dioxide levels in the clouds, soil moisture, extreme weather observation, and forecasting.[100]

2.5.2 *Dirty Missions*

A dirty mission is one that is chemically contaminated or has potential of radioactivity.[101] UAS use in dirty missions is preferred both in peace-time as well as in hostile environments that are unfavourable for manned aircraft. For example, after the dropping of an atomic bomb in Hiroshima and Nagasaki in Japan during the World War II, use of manned flights was virtually impossible due to the risk of exposure to radioactive materials. Admittedly, sampling and observation of chemical, biological, radiological and nuclear weapons is best suited for the unmanned aircraft system so long as it is fitted with appropriate sensors, with a choice of either small and portable systems for local tactical use, or large aircraft sized systems for global monitoring purposes.[102] In terms of civilian use, fire brigades apply UAS to locate fires in remote areas or those with huge smokes and flames. This allows for successful approach and containment.[103] There is possibility that the current contemporary exploration of space by satellite, may one day opt for the use of UAS in

[97] Ali Mazrui is academic professor, and political writer on African and Islamic studies and North-South Relations. 1933–2014.

[98] Efron (2015), p. 5.

[99] Gonzales and Harting (2014), p. 23.

[100] Gonzales and Harting (2014), p. 61.

[101] National Air and Space Museum "Drones Doing Dirt and Dangerous Jobs" https://airandspace.si.edu/stories/editorial/drones-doing-dirty-and-dangerous-jobs (Date of use: 22 August 2023).

[102] Gupta (2013), p. 1654.

[103] Cole (2012), p. 558.

navigating through different planets to mitigate the risk of exposing human life to danger.

2.5.3 Dangerous Missions

Dangerous missions are those that involve entrance into airspaces of conflict or spaces with contestations.[104] In military terms, a dangerous mission refers to one that may be used to suppress an enemy's air defense.[105] Since operations such as reconnaissance in enemy territory could expose manned aircraft to unnecessary risk, unmanned aircraft systems are preferred. Consequently, less expensive UAS are used to destroy enemy positions or force the enemy to expend a large number of missiles.[106] The potential for UAS to replace dangerous missions such as delivery of tactical supplies and identification of improvised explosive devices is unlimited owing to increase in areas that manned aircraft are unsuitable due to risk to human life.

2.6 Civilian Application of Unmanned Aircraft Systems (UAS)

Arising from the foregoing analysis, it is clear that UAS technology has consistently developed as a formidable component of civil aviation, offering innovative and exciting opportunities for day-to-day operations. It plays a critical role in management and prevention of disasters, fire-fighting[107] and real-time assessment of extent of damages.[108] For example, the technology was quite handy in collecting data after a devastating earthquake hit Haiti in 2010.[109] The gathered information, especially by aid of high-resolution photography, allowed for location of ideal areas for landing and take-off by response teams. A similar scenario was witnessed in Japan in 2011 when UAS known as High Altitude Long Endurance (HALE) was used to fly over

[104] Judson https://www.defensenews.com/digital-show-dailies/global-force-symposium/2018/03/26/future-unmanned-aircraft-to-do-the-dull-and-dangerous-work/ (Date of use: 22 July 2023).

[105] Judson https://www.defensenews.com/digital-show-dailies/global-force-symposium/2018/03/26/future-unmanned-aircraft-to-do-the-dull-and-dangerous-work/ (Date of use: 22 July 2023).

[106] O'Connell (2010), p. 1.

[107] Mika P (UAS Yearbook – UAS: The Global Perspective 2009/2010), p. 137.

[108] O'Connell (2010), p. 2.

[109] Petcoff RP "Global Hawk Collects Reconnaissance Data During Haiti Relief Efforts" *2010-1-15 US Air Force Press Release* https://www.af.mil/News/Article-Display/Article/118014/global-hawk-collects-reconnaissance-data-during-haiti-relief-efforts/ (Date of use: 4 August 2023).

the Fukushima Daichi Nuclear Plant to assess the extent of damage caused by a tsunami.[110]

UAS' emerging role in inspections and border controls, scientific research, environmental and agricultural monitoring cannot be gainsaid. In Kenya, attempts have been made to integrate UAS in tracking down stolen cattle, directing security personnel and surveillance to locate rustlers and their loot.[111]

It is no wonder, therefore, that UAS application is now an integral part of day-to-day life. They are used in information gathering, salvaging shipwrecks, crashed airplanes and their passengers.[112] Hence, if well utilised and regulated, UAS could play an even bigger role in bridging the information and technological gaps that were traditionally considered insurmountable.

The use and regulation of UAS is gaining global prominence as countries make advances in fields such as surveying and mapping.[113] Researchers in Kenya, among them Mbote and Muruingi, project potential use of UAS in the mapping and surveying of areas that are far removed from towns.[114] This is in addition to determining and surveying distribution of various species and habitats. UAS can be used to plan, fly, visualize, process, and deliver essential data for land mapping.[115] Advanced UAS make use of Global Positioning System that contains baselines and records kinematic observation with a high degree of accuracy in surveying and mapping. It needn't be overemphasised that UAS are also convenient for mapping due to their speed in data collection, collation and delivery.

According to Chad Bolebruch, UAS type mdLiDAR3000, for instance, is preferred as it can survey approximately four acres of land in just 18 min.[116] This is a speed that normal ground survey cannot match. As such, UAS offer opportunity for achievement of the much needed security in any country. Chad's position is affirmed by Bryan Phillip who observes, "UAS is a viable alternative to the traditional methods of land surveying owing to its capability and versatility."[117] In his book, he concludes that the flight time for UAS is comparatively shorter compared to traditional methods.[118]

---

[110] Petcoff https://www.af.mil/News/Article-Display/Article/118014/global-hawk-collects-reconnaissance-data-during-haiti-relief-efforts/ (Date of use: 4 August 2023).

[111] Odido and Madara (2013), p. 107.

[112] Odido and Madara (2013), p. 107.

[113] Odido and Madara (2013), p. 107.

[114] Kameri-Mbote and Muriungi (2017), pp. 159–169.

[115] Walter (2017), p. 5.

[116] https://www.microdrones.com/en/integratedsystems/mdlidar/mdlidar3000/?gclid=CjwKCAjwsMzzBRACEiwAx4lLG0I8cwrlVXYedXAB6U3PmzGwXLDhItULEHqj8uTMPcicAJTIuNwBgBoCxUIQAvD_BwE (Date of use: 19 August 2023).

[117] Phillip (2015), pp. 1–49.

[118] Phillip (2015), p. 41.

2.7 Challenges of Integrating UAS into Civil Aviation

The increase in civilian use and ownership of UAS calls for an urgent need to regulate their integration into civil aviation. Rawich argues that the ongoing development and use of UAS shows that the law regulating UAS always lags behind technology.[119] This is a pointer to the related struggles in integrating UAS into the national airspaces in different jurisdictions.

A recognition of the need to integrate UAS into civil aviation has gained momentum in the recent past. The ICAO Global Air Traffic Management Operational Concept, for instance, recognizes that UAS is an aircraft as per Article 8 of the Chicago Convention. This view was endorsed by the 35th Session of the ICAO Assembly of 28 September to 8 October 2004. Ordinarily, therefore, one would expect the manned and unmanned aircraft to be integrated into the civil airspace.[120]

There are certain concerns, however, that lead to segregation of the UAS in order to lessen imminent dangers. The use of UAS for surveying and mapping faces the challenge of high cost associated with hiring their service, with instances of bad weather and unclear visibility abounding.[121] This is in addition to the challenge of meeting the visual line of sight in expansive tracts of land.

Even more disturbing are safety, security, and privacy concerns, which though mild in the early use of UAS during the First and Second World Wars have since been emboldened.[122] As Yeonmin observes, the emboldening results from, among others, obvious growth in agitation amongst the citizenry, legislation, and judicial interpretation.[123] These agitations and developments are well demonstrated in analysis of the domestic UAS laws of the United States, South Africa, and Kenya in Chaps. 4, 5 and 6, respectively of this book. Despite these developments, prospects of growth in the use of UAS rates high owing to its ability to downsize risks and wade through missions that would otherwise be unfavourable to humans.[124]

2.7.1 Safety Challenges

Drawing from the history of the use of UAS, it is clear that the safety of manned and unmanned aircraft should be accorded equal attention. The laws on investigation of incidents should be similar to both types of aircraft.[125] However, owing to the

[119] Rawich (2009), p. 600.

[120] Marshall (2009), p. 105.

[121] Baseline Equipment Company "How to use GPS or Oland surveying" https://www.baselineequipment.com/gps-land-surveying-equipment (Date of use: 19 August 2023).

[122] Finn and Wright (2012), pp. 184–194.

[123] Cho (2014), pp. 38–56.

[124] Stansbury and Manan (2008), p. 8.

[125] Sharma (2016), p. 2.

differences in uses and design of the aircraft, the processes would ideally take different dimensions.[126] For instance, while investigation in manned aircraft would consider the embankment and disembankment of people, that of UAS would be effective if it considered the opening and shutting of the primary propulsion system.

The main UAS safety challenge concerns their design and in particular, sense and avoid. Instructively, safety management is defined under ICAO Annex 19 and UAS Circular 328–AN/190 under Clause 2.16, as being the state in which possibility of harm to persons or property damage is reduced and maintained at or below an acceptable level through a continuous process of hazard identification and safety risk management.

The design challenges arise from visual issues that are best explained via a comparative approach. Manned aircraft operate under a wide range of laws that guide air traffic control, including use and maintenance of visual ranges. UAS on its part faces numerous operational difficulties due to limited control and operational capacity.[127] Further, UAS has unique characteristics in terms of size and performance that require turbulence avoidance criteria. UAS are designed with capacities based on the weight. Some UAS have low loading capacity that can operate for more than 50 h, while others can operate within a range of 2 km under an altitude of 2000 ft (600 m).[128]

Some UAS have capability for indefinite range over 30,000 ft. Such variations offer challenges in cases where an operator is supposed to maintain visual sight of the UAS and yet it has ability to go beyond that range. This means the ground UAS operator could fail to avoid air collisions or not be in a position to control the safety of other air or ground operators.

UAS sense and avoid capability refers to an aircraft's capability to remain well clear from, and avoid collisions with, other airborne traffic.[129] In respect to manned aircraft, it is the pilot's ability to operate the instrument and to observe flight or visual flight rules required and to manoeuvre to avoid another aircraft and circumvent air accidents.[130] Sense and avoid provides functions of self-separation and collision avoidance to establish an analogous capability required by manned aircraft.[131]

Sense and avoid is a unique challenge for UAS. As for manned aircraft, it exists in civil aviation, based on a transponder concept known as global navigation satellite system.[132] This is a communication, navigation and surveillance system capable of calculating own position while transmitting the information, which is used in collision avoidance to other units within the vicinity.[133] The global navigation

[126] Sharma (2016), p. 2.

[127] Levush (2016), p. 86.

[128] Levush (2016), p. 86.

[129] Klaus (2013), p. 4.

[130] Klaus (2013), p. 6.

[131] Geyer et al. (2008), p. 9.

[132] GNSS "Transponder" http://www.lfv.se/ans/card (Date of use: 4 August 2023).

[133] GNSS http://www.lfv.se/ans/card (Date of use: 4 August 2023).

satellite system transponder is critical for separation and avoidance, pilot-in-command and autonomous operation.[134] The system is used by both civilian and military UAS, a development that is critical for full UAS successful integration into civilian use. Other operational requirements that UAS should meet in order to match the standards of manned aircraft include radar, visual sighting, separation standards and pilot behaviour.

Other operational requirements that UAS should meet in order to match the standards of manned aircraft are radar, visual sighting, separation standards and pilot behaviour. Crucially, these require massive improvement in order to harmonise integration of UAS into civil aviation.[135]

The importance of safety in airspace that is not segregated cannot be gainsaid. It, therefore, calls for effective collision avoidance as well as sense and avoid mechanisms.[136] Pilots in command are not only able to access information to facilitate collision avoidance, but also are accorded the technical assistance to enable them to detect and avoid collisions akin to what manned aircraft use in accordance with virtual flight rules.[137] This ultimately helps in ensuring safety for all concerned and in the case of failure, automatic systems should take over to ensure collision avoidance. UAS pilots-in-command are able to maintain meteorological conditions, detect conflicting traffic, while interacting with conflicting traffic in accordance with the right-of-way rules and ensure automatic collision avoidance in the event of loss of control data-link.[138] Despite the various challenges, the potential for civilian UAS use is on the rise as informed by the relative advantages UAS hold over manned aircraft. However, more needs to be done to improve the safety of the UAS, other aircraft and property on the ground.[139]

An area that urgently requires the law to quickly follow technology is adherence to Annex 2 of the Chicago Convention.[140] The Annex posits that all aircraft must bear nationality and registration marks of a contracting State. However, some contracting States lack specific regulations addressing unique characteristics of UAS, a persistent condition despite the fact that UAS by nature may fly across boundaries of different States. This is because the Chicago Convention was adopted with manned aircraft in mind, and did not envisage application of UAS in civil aviation.

---

[134] Klaus (2013), p. 6.

[135] Spriesterbach et al. (2013), pp. 572–583.

[136] Klaus (2013), p. 6.

[137] Klaus (2013), p. 6.

[138] EUROCONTROL "Specifications for the Use of Military Unmanned Aerial Vehicles as Operational Air Traffic Outside Segregated Airspace" https://www.eurocontrol.int/publication/eurocontrol-specifications-use-military-unmanned-aerial-vehicles-operational-air (Date of use: 30 August 2023).

[139] EUROCONTROL https://www.eurocontrol.int/publication/eurocontrol-specifications-use-military-unmanned-aerial-vehicles-operational-air (Date of use: 30 August 2023).

[140] Milde (2008), p. 69. Milde takes a position that the rules of air may not be legally bonding but have consequences which make them binding in practice.

Another area of concern is that development of UAS technologies was not made in contemplation of airworthiness standards. Consequently, material property, structure design standards, decision reliability standards, and other requirements should be evaluated in line with civil airworthiness standards for manned aircraft. As currently constituted, UAS operations are done according to performance characteristics totally at variance with manned aircraft. This is with respect to size, speed, or other flight capabilities.

Similarly, some UAS are incapable of providing the benefit of Sense and Avoid technology that remains an important defence against mid-air collisions.[141] Although the concept of 'Sense and Avoid' is not expressly provided for in ICAO regulations, it is noted that UAS should exercise vigilance in detecting circumstances that would lead to collisions because some of them lack automated collision avoidance systems.[142]

Owing to the design issues and characteristics, UAS pose a challenge to global regulators since international civil aviation law is based on concepts of safety and security in civil aviation that depend on a pilot operating an aircraft from within.[143] The way UAS are designed, removal of a pilot, as is the case, causes significant operational, technical, legal and operational challenges.[144] This calls for States to urgently introduce legislation that allow integration of unmanned aircraft into civil aviation. Majority of contracting State parties to the Chicago Convention of 1944 that are supposed to provide flight information lack policies and regulations that address challenges of UAS, such as safety of other airspace users.

2.7.2 Security Challenges

ICAO Annex 17 defines civil aviation security as a concept of safeguarding international civil aviation against acts of unlawful interference. There is also the danger of UAS falling into the hands of criminals such as terrorists, thus posing real vulnerability to national security.[145] Security and safety under ICAO are provided under Annexes 17 and 19 respectively. There is a close correlation between the two as they both concern damage and hazards. It has been touted by some authors that divorcing the two makes the airspace insecure. However, while safety is concerned with the design issues raised by the sense and avoid technology, security concerns

141 See Annex IV to the European Commission (EC) Regulation on Common Rules in the Field of Civil Aviation 216 of 2008, Articles 3(a) and (4).

142 https://www.icao.int/Meetings/anconf12/Document%20Archive/an02_cons%5B1%5D.pdf (Date of use: 6 August 2023).

143 Havel and Mulligan (2016), p. 107.

144 Gupta (2013), p. 1645.

145 Warwick G "Civil UAVs Need GPS anti-spoofing, but who pays. Aviation week" http://www.aviationweek.com (Date of use: 4 August 2023).

external acts caused by individuals, legal persons or other States as threat to the UAS or its operators.

Security threats attributable to the nature and use of UAS are in the realms of communication, imaging and monitoring. Ordinarily, proper security in the use of UAS is achieved when a pilot is able to ensure interconnection between unmanned aircraft and a control system. Unlike most aeroplanes with compartments for flight crew to monitor security, UAS are more exposed to sabotage and interference without the knowledge of the host State. Also, UAS are less restricted in their nature compared to manned aircraft. According to Kine, it is this restriction, together with limited inspection, coupled with its ubiquity that leaves it more exposed to possible cases of intrusion and interference. ICAO, which administers the Chicago Convention, recognizes these as serious integration challenges, hence development of the ICAO Circular on Unmanned Aircraft Systems in 2011 to address the matter.[146]

UAS employ diverse systems unlike manned aircraft that have determinable and controllable take-off and landing areas. Some take off in a vertical gradient like helicopters, others are hand-launched, while yet others are dispatched from remote stations such as high seas. Whereas this versatility enables them to be launched from almost any location, it creates a security concern as they could be used as conveyors of dangerous substances, including chemical and biological weapons. With increased technological advances, there is general reluctance in freely licensing these gadgets over security concerns.[147]

The expanded uses and operations of UAS have become a challenge to maintaining security generally. The challenge with regard to military use has all to do with maintenance of the air traffic control systems and exclusion of classified information. On civil use, the history and development in uses and expansion of classification with different weights and performance capabilities present security challenges of collision and, thus, potential air traffic accidents, some intentionally targeting manned aircraft.[148]

Owing to its nature and scope, UAS pose security challenges that border on policy, guidance and regulation to the citizenry, States and the international community. Effective regulation systems at regional, national or international levels must, therefore, ensure security of ground control stations and data link. From the foregoing, it is clear that security challenges principally arise from lack of command and control, and unmanned traffic control. Policies for integration of UAS should, therefore, address the two issues by detailing control of pilot stations, biometric access to aircraft, minimum-security standards, data and communication links.

---

[146] Kine (2008), p. 19.

[147] Milde (2008), p. 207.

[148] Milde (2008), p. 92.

2.7.2.1 Lack of Command and Control System

Command and Control System is a technological system used by security forces to monitor and control movement of manned aircraft. The system, which cuts across safety and security, has capacity to identify and destroy a manned aircraft while airborne in case they gain unauthorized access to another country. Most UAS lack capability of connectivity of the pilots in command,[149] which phenomenon brings to the fore security challenges to countries that have not erected such installations.

2.7.2.2 Lack of Unmanned Traffic Management

Unmanned traffic management (UTM) is a safety measure tool that cuts across security. An advanced traffic management ecosystem under development for autonomously controlled operations of UAS,[150] it is a system that can monitor increased activity based on digital sharing of each operator's scheduled flight details. Under the system, every aircraft user obtains airspace situational awareness unlike what happens in today's air traffic control.[151] UTM works as a networked collection of communication services based on common rules. Rather than relying on a centralized control, the frameworks around the world use the principle of distributed authority, which opens up the system to more service providers who can adapt as the market evolves. The system is useful for collision avoidance and additionally, plays a major role in providing security countermeasures.

UTM has capacity to detect UAS command and control centre for tracing those that enter other countries' territory.[152] Most States are vulnerable to external intrusion by UAS and interference as they lack UTM system installation. At the centre of regulation of aviation is the principle of State sovereignty, as affirmed in both the Chicago Convention, Article 1 and Article 2 of the United Nations Charter of 1945.

This challenge is paradoxical with regard to the use of UAS both as a tool and a threat. It adds a novel perspective to regulation, a delicate balancing act in regulatory framework for UAS. On the one hand, the regulation should not be too restrictive as to deny UAS use as a security tool while on the other, it must not be too liberal to turn UAS into a security threat.

[149] Franke et al. (2005), p. 1.

[150] Sándor (2019), pp. 96–105.

[151] Sándor (2019), p. 96.

[152] Prevot et al. (2016), p. 3292.

2.7.3 *Privacy Challenges in UAS Operations*

UAS have capacity to use Global Positioning System (GPS) technology to take aerial photos. This is in addition to their ability to fly above residential areas, which increases chances of taking photos containing confidential information without the targets' consent. The systems can be hacked in this era of increased cybercrime,[153] leading to leakage of information on location. The effects on privacy may be devastating when the photos or information find their way into phone-based or computer-based social applications.

Unlike manned aircraft that are not effective for dull operations, UAS are often preferred, potentially turning into privacy threats. They can also fly at comparatively lower levels compared to the manned aircraft. Accordingly, potential uses such as filming and delivery of goods could be turned into malicious uses that infringe on the right to privacy. A case in point is the admission by the FBI that it used UAS to follow up citizens' protests in Baltimore in 2018.[154] These 'eyes in the sky' have privacy implications owing to their intrusive nature. Historically, such intrusion began in the 1960s with the use of reconnaissance UAS.

Following the challenges posed by UAS on privacy, there has been a clamour for regulation with a view to meeting human rights standards under international law. The United Nations recognizes that member States must respect their citizens' right to privacy. For instance, the Universal Declaration of Human Rights[155] offers protection from arbitrary interference with individual's privacy, family, home or correspondence. This is further affirmed under Article 17 of the International Covenant on Civil and Political Rights (ICCPR).[156] Article 5 of the American Declaration on the Rights and Duties of Man, and Article 11 of the American Convention on Human Rights[157] recognize this right too. Article 11 of the Convention provides for the States' responsibility to protect the right of privacy in cases of surveillance.

Africa has such instruments as the African Charter on Human and Peoples Rights, 1981 and Article 4 of the Protocol to the African Charter on Human and Peoples' Rights on the Rights of Women, which guarantee the right to life through which privacy right is guaranteed.[158] Further, economic bodies like the Economic

---

[153] Zhi et al. (2020), pp. 95–101.

[154] INFOSEC "Beware of the drone! Privacy and security issues with drones" https://resources.infosecinstitute.com/privacy-and-security-issues-with-drones/#gref (Date of use: 23 July 2023).

[155] UN General Assembly Resolution 217 A (III) of 10 December 1948.

[156] UN General Resolution 2200A (XXI) of 16 December 1966 UNTS 171 (entered into force 23 March 1976).

[157] Rodriguez K, Hernandez V and Jara C "The Inter-American Legal Analysis: The 13 Principles and the Inter-American System for the Protection of Human Rights" https://necessaryandproportionate.org/americas-legal-analysis (Date of use: 22 August 2023).

[158] The Africa Union (AU) Protocol to the African Charter on Human and People's Rights on the Rights of Women of 21 July 2003 (entered into force 2005) (hereinafter referred to as the Maputo Protocol), Article 4(m).

Community of West African States (ECOWAS) and Southern African Development Community (SADC), have made significant steps in promoting protection of the privacy of the people.[159] They have also entered into agreements on privacy of data as well as adoption of model laws.[160] Specifically, SADC has come up with a model SADC Model Law on Data Protection,[161] while ECOWAS has the Supplementary Act, both of which protect the peoples' right to privacy.[162] Explicitly, Article 19 (1) of the Act provides that information, communication and technology systems should respect the privacy and liberties of citizens.[163] On its part, the East African Community (EAC) recognizes the fundamental and operational role the principle of human rights plays in its integration.[164] Respect to privacy is one such key right that is envisaged by the commitments.[165]

It is clear from the preceding discussion that the spirit of these international frameworks advocates the position that respect for personal data is vital for the protection of human life. The right to privacy is the foundation of other rights including the right of access to information, human dignity, and right to life. It is also related to the right to self-determination, which means the right to do what a person wants, including who to associate with. Important decisions are influenced by the protection of the right, and is interconnected with security and safety concerns. First, while the right to privacy is often claimed by citizens, security and safety are always the first line of defence for the State. In most instances, the former is sacrificed at the altar of the latter. It is no wonder, therefore, States have been reluctant to uphold privacy, especially when it compromises State security and safety.

2.7.4 Other Challenges Inhibiting Integrating UAS into Civil Airspace

There are other challenges that fall well outside the three categories as discussed above. First, the absence of consensus on regulatory framework from a global front is a major obstacle to achieving full integration of UAS into civil aviation across a

---

[159] Mabika V "Privacy and Personal Data Protection Guidelines for Africa" *2018-8 ITU* https://www.itu.int/en/ITUD/CapacityBuilding/Documents/IG_workshop_August2018Presentations/Session%207_Verengai%20Mabika.pdf (Date of use: 30 July 2023).

[160] Graham and Georges (2014), pp. 19–21.

[161] The SADC Model Law on Data Protection of 2010.

[162] https://www.statewatch.org/news/2013/mar/ecowas-dp-act.pdf (Date of use: 2 August 2023).

[163] ECOWAS Supplementary Act of 2007, Article 19(1).

[164] The Treaty for the Establishment of the East African Community of 1999 (entered into force 2000) (hereinafter referred to as the EAC Treaty 1999), Articles 6(d) and 7(2).

[165] *Media Council of Tanzania an Others v Attorney General of the Republic of Tanzania* App 5 EA 2019 (EACJ).

number of regions. ICAO, the UN's specialized agency for regulation of aviation in the world, only provides materials and circulars to guide States to enact their own domestic UAS regulations. However, there continues to be enforcement setbacks such as the inability to provide sanctions on member States, which are yet to implement the guidelines in enacting UAS regulations.[166]

Secondly, there is general lack of effective data collection and sharing among States concerning UAS operation. This makes it difficult for States to share the data collected and disseminated by UAS, a situation that is perhaps compounded by lack of consensus on policy formulation and co-operation among neighbouring States.

Thirdly, although ICAO requires States to establish agencies responsible for civil aviation with mandate on oversight, such civil aviation authorities lack sufficient manpower and mechanism to deter unauthorised or unlicensed operation of UAS.[167] In addition, aviation personnel are not everywhere to monitor and prosecute those found to be in violation of the State's aviation rules.

2.8 Conclusion

The development of UAS makes its integration into the civil airspace inevitable. There are potential applications in security and environmental surveillances, which further points to the extension of the need for its integration into civil aviation. UAS uses, whether traditional or modern, can be conveniently classified as recreational, dull, dirty and dangerous operations. These operations greatly distinguish UAS uses from those of manned aircraft. Manned aircraft have operations and uses that are less intrusive and have more elaborate laws governing specific aspects such as traffic control, visual sighting, take-off and landing management, as well as Sense and Avoid technologies.

Owing to the structural differences and versatility of UAS compared to manned aircraft, there is bound to be safety, security, and privacy challenges that arise from their use and ultimate integration into the national airspace. Little attention coupled with absence of standards for the training of air traffic controllers on UAS, ineffective policy for data collection, information sharing and poor oversight, raise safety and security concerns that slow down the process of integration.

Also worth noting is the possible push and pull between governments, the international community and civil societies in advocating for and balancing the safety, security and privacy concerns arising from the use of UAS. For example, the human rights approach taken in furtherance of privacy concerns must compete with sovereignty of States, which is a cardinal principle of international relations recognized in the United Nations Charter of 1945. The battle of wits can take an

[166] Marcontelli D and Douglas S. https://www.forbes.com/sites/oliverwyman/2018/09/10/why-the-use-of-drones-still-faces-big-regulatory-hurdles/#529c17ea1c0d (Date of use: 5 August 2023).

[167] Barnhart et al. (2012), pp. 135–155.

interesting turn in countries such as the US, South Africa and Kenya, where there is a guarantee of rights to security, safety and privacy in the national constitutions.

The following chapter is dedicated to providing an overview of the international civil aviation law and institutional framework, with focus on how the international law has provided redress of the identified safety, security and privacy challenges.

References

Books

Austin R, Wiley J, Chichester S (2010) Unmanned aircraft systems UAVs design, development. Wiley Publishe

Bart E (2012) Pilotless drones: background and considerations for congress regarding unmanned aircraft operations in the national airspace system CRS Reports for Congress

Blom JD (2010) Unmanned aerial systems: a historical perspective. Combat Studies Institute Press

Cole C (2012) Drone wars briefing. Drone Wars UK Oxford

De Garmo MT (2010) Issues concerning integration of unmanned aerial vehicles in civil airspace. The MITRE center for advanced aviation system development Mclean Virginia

Gonzales D, Harting S (2014) Designing unmanned systems with greater autonomy using a federated, partially open systems architecture approach. RAND Corporation, Santa Monica California

Gundlach J (2012) Designing unmanned aircraft systems: a comprehensive approach. American Institute of Aeronautics and Astronautics

Haddal CC, Gertler J (2010) Homeland security: unmanned aerial vehicles and border surveillance. Library of Congress Washington DC Congressional Research Service

Kine TS (2008) Enhancing combat survivability of existing unmanned aircraft systems. Naval Postgraduate School Monterey CA

Levush R (2016) Regulation of drones: comparative summary. The Law Library of Congress, Global Legal Research Center, Washington DC

Milde M (2008) International air law and ICAO. Eleven International Publishing

Nonami K et al (2010) Autonomous flying Robots, unmanned aerial vehicles and micro aerial vehicles. Springer, New York

O'Connell ME (2010) Drones under International Law. International Debate Series Whitney Harris World Law Institute

Suraj G et al (2013) Review of Unmanned Aircraft System (UAS), Vol. 2. International Journal of Advanced Research in Computer Engineering and Technology (IJARCET)

Valavanism KP, Vachtsevanos GJ (2015) Military and civilian unmanned aircraft: handbook of unmanned aerial vehicles. Springer, Dordrecht

Journal Articles

Adam W et al (2012) Unmanned aircraft systems in remote sensing and scientific research: classification and considerations of use. Remote Sensing, 1671–1692

Barnhart C et al (2012) Demand and capacity management in air transportation. EURO J Transp Logist, 135–155

Bilbao J (2008) How to design an unmanned aerial vehicle with great efficiency in the use of existing resources. Int J Comput, 442–451

Cho Y (2014) Lost in debate: the safety of domestic unmanned aircraft systems'. J Strategic Secur, 38–56

Finn RL, Wright D (2012) Unmanned aircraft systems: surveillance, ethics and privacy in civil applications. Comput Law Secur Rev, 184–194

Freeman NC (1956) On the theory of hypersonic flow past plane and axially symmetric bluff bodies. J Fluid Mech, 366–387

Geyer C, Singh C, Chamberlain L (2008) Avoiding collisions between aircraft: State of the art and requirements for UAVs operating in civilian airspace. Carnegie Mellon University, p 9

Graham G, Georges M (2014) African regional privacy instruments: Their effects on harmonization. Privacy Laws and Business International Report, 19–21

Gupta SG, Gonge M, Jawadhiya P (2013) Review of unmanned aircraft system. Int J Adv Res Comput Eng Technol, 1646

HaiYang C, YangQuan C (2010) Autopilots for small unmanned aerial vehicles: a survey. Int J Control Automat Syst, 36–44

Havel BF, Mulligan JQ (2016) Unmanned aircraft systems: a challenge to global regulators. DePaul Law Rev, 107

Jensen TA et al (2011) The use of an unmanned aerial vehicle as a remote sensing platform in agriculture. Aust J Multi-Discipl Eng, 139–146

Jessica H et al (2008) Flying qualities specifications and design standards for unmanned air vehicles. Atmospheric Flight Mechanics Conference and Exhibit, 6555

Kameri-Mbote P, Muriungi M (2017) Potential contribution of drones to reliability of Kenya's land information system. Afr J Inf Commun, 159–169

Keane JF, Carr SS (2013) A brief history of early unmanned aircraft. Johns Hopkins APL Technical Digest, 558–571

Kenzo N (2007) Prospect and recent research and development for civil use autonomous unmanned aircraft as UAV and MAV. J Syst Design Dyn, 120–128

Koldaev A, Sokut S (2005) Russia military conservatism in relation to industry. Syst Glob Persp, 100–104

Marshall D (2009) Unmanned aerial systems and international civil aviation organization regulations. North Dakota Law Rev 85:693

Michaelides-Mateou S et al (2014) Flying into the future with UAVs: the Jetstrea Flight. Annals Air Space Law, 113

Odido D, Madara S (2013) Emerging technologies: use of unmanned aerial systems in the realization of Vision 2030 goals in the counties. Int J Appl Sci Technol, 107

Peterson ME (2006) UAV and the current and future regulatory construct for integration into the national airspace system. J Air Law Commer, 522–551

Rawich TM (2009) Integration of unmanned aerial vehicles into the national airspace. North Dakota Law Rev 85:597–622

Sándor Z (2019) Challenges caused by the unmanned aerial vehicle in the air traffic management. Periodica Polytechnica Transportation Engineering, 96–105

Sharma RS (2016) Investigation into unmanned aircraft system incidents in the National Airspace System. Int J Aviat Aeronaut Aerosp, 2

Skrzypietz J (2012) Unmanned aircraft systems for civilian missions BIGS policy paper, 18

Spriesterbach T et al (2013) Unmanned aircraft system airspace integration in the national airspace using a ground-based sense and avoid system. Johns Hopkins APL Technical Digest, 572–583

Suraj GG, Ghonge MM, Jawandhiya M (2013) Review of unmanned aircraft system (UAS). Int J Adv Res Comput Eng Technol, 1646

Walter V (2017) Small unmanned aerial system mapping versus conventional methods. CTAWP, 5
Wright W (1916) The Wright Brothers' Aeroplane. Aeronaut J, 100–106
Xiao-yd HU (2006) Development of high-altitude long endurance UAV propulsion technology. Gas Turbine Exp Res, 4
Zhi Y et al (2020) Security and privacy issues of UAV: a survey. Mobile Netw Appl, 95–101

Thesis and Dissertations

Efron S (2015) The use of unmanned aerial systems for agriculture in Africa can it fly. PhD Dissertation Pardee Rand Graduate School
Fernández EG (2010) Management System for Unmanned Aircraft System. Masters thesis, Universitat Politècnica de Catalunya
Klaus RA (2013) Development of a Sense and Avoid System for Small Unmanned Aircraft Systems. MS Thesis Brigham Young University
Phillip FB (2015) Unmanned aerial systems for surveying and mapping: cost comparison of UAS versus traditional methods of data acquisition. Masters dissertation University of Southern California

Workshops and Conference Papers

Fahrney DS, RADM U (1980) The Birth of Guided Missiles. Paper presented at Conference of US Naval Institute December 1980
Franke et al (2005) Inverting the operator/vehicle ratio: approaches to next generation UAV command and control. Paper presented to the Confernece of AUVSI Unmanned Systems North America 2005
Johnson LS (2003) Collection of ultra-high spatial and spectral resolution image data over California vineyards with a small UAV. Paper presented to the International Symposium on Remote Sensing of the Environment. Honolulu 2003
Prevot et al (2016) UAS traffic management (UTM) concept of operations to safely enable low altitude flight operations. Paper presented to the 16th AIAA Confernece on Aviation Technology, Integration, and Operations Conference 2016
Reuder J (2009) UAS. In: Atmospheric research: reality visions challenges. Paper presented at the 17th UAVNet Workshop Brussels 12 October 2009
Shawn G, Renaud J (2002) Optimized unmanned aerial vehicle with wing morphing for extended range and endurance. Paper presented to Symposium on Multidisciplinary Analysis and Optimization 2002
UAS traffic management (UTM) concept of operations to safely enable low altitude flight operations (2016) Unmanned Aircraft Systems (UAS) Traffic Management (UTM). 16th AIAA Conference on Aviation Technology Integration and Operations Conference 3 June 2016

Chapter 3
International Air Law Response to Challenges in UAS Regulation

3.1 Introduction

This chapter addresses the regulatory framework in international air law for UAS, in particular how it addresses the challenges identified in the previous chapter of this book. Analysis is provided of the existing international legal and institutional frameworks applicable to civil aviation, particularly those regulating UAS. The prevailing legal framework consists mainly of treaty law, which include the Chicago Convention of 1944, and various decisions and instruments adopted by ICAO. These instruments include Annexes to the Chicago Convention developed as Standards and Recommendations Practices (SARPs). In general, international air law is defined as the rule that apply to both domestic and international aviation binding the States and international organizations to agreements in respect to their civil aviation. The rules oversee the multifaceted relationship between States, passengers, cargo, and service providers. In addition, the law equally oversees the impact of aviation on the environment and on individuals affected by aircraft operations including UAS.

Also covered are other sources of law including customary international law that complement the relevant international law as set out in the treaties. As a roadmap, the analysis of the framework is made with a view to describing, assessing and drawing conclusions on how the existing international legal structure and architecture has developed to address the threefold challenges of safety, security and privacy issues in the field of civil aviation.

M. Wanyonyi Rodgers, *The Law Regulating Unmanned Aircraft Systems in the United States, South Africa and Kenya*,
https://doi.org/10.1007/978-3-031-49927-2_3

3.2 Background to International Law and Rules Applicable to Civil Aviation Architecture

The legal framework and principal conventional law on regulation of UAS at an international plane is the Chicago Convention of 1944. The Convention lays down the core principles for regulation of international air transport and addresses the concerns of security through Annex 17 and safety Annex 19.[1] At the time of its adoption in 1944, the Chicago Convention envisaged the creation of a specialized institution, vested with support, advisory and organizational roles in achieving international cooperation.[2] The need for such a body immediately became paramount and led to the establishment of Provisional ICAO in 1945, succeeded by ICAO, effective from 4 April 1947.[3]

3.2.1 Overview of the Chicago Convention of 1944

Treaty law was the primary source of aviation law since the Paris Convention of 1919. The principal conventional law governing aviation today is the International Convention on Civil Aviation, also known as the Chicago Convention. Adopted in 1944, the Convention established the International Civil Aviation Organization (ICAO). The Convention was adopted in 1944 to replace the Paris Convention of 1919. ICAO plays a pivotal role as the conventional basis for dealing with aviation issues at regional, sub-regional, State and international levels.

From the commencement of the Convention, the principle of sovereignty under international law, safeguarding equality and mandate of States is a fundamental right and obligation of every State. By the time the Chicago Convention became operational in 1945, the new world order established under the United Nations had reaffirmed the right to sovereignty, equality and territorial integrity of States. The principle was maintained in the Chicago Convention as articulated under Article 1, which provides that:

> "Every State has complete and exclusive sovereignty over the airspace above its territory". Further, and in order to eliminate any ambiguity on definition of the State territory, Article 2 of the Convention defines the territory of each State to mean land areas and territorial waters adjacent thereto under the sovereignty suzerainty, protection or mandate of such State".

The relevant scope of the Chicago Convention is set out in Articles 3, 8, 9 and 12. That scope is twofold, the first being a transboundary nature that emanates from the

---

[1] The Convention on Civil Aviation of 7 December 1944 15 UNTS 295 (entered into force 4 April 1947) (hereinafter referred to as the Chicago Convention), Article 37 (a), (c), (e), (f) and (g).

[2] The Chicago Convention, Article 43 provides for creation of ICAO and its and organs while Article 44 outlines its objectives.

[3] https://www.icao.int/about icao/History/Pages/default.aspx (Date of use: 11 July 2023).

fact that aircraft move across boundaries of different States. Secondly, Article 3 is instructive that it applies only to civil and not State aircraft, which category includes the military aircraft. The excluded category of aircraft is regulated by the rules of international humanitarian law as well as respective domestic laws. The delimitation of State aircraft is necessary for avoidance of doubt since the Convention adopts a use-based approach in delimiting its scope of application to dedicated military rules. It is also possible that the distinction was made for convenience and to avoid complexity of laws due to the difference in functioning of the civil and military aircraft.

Regarding the civil aircraft, the Chicago Convention applies to both manned and unmanned aircraft. Similar to manned aircraft, UAS require special authorization to fly through the airspace of contracting States. The Convention is instructive at Article 8 that its substantive provisions apply to pilotless aircraft, which it refers to as 'aircraft capable of being flown without a pilot.' The Article repeats the spirit of the provisions of Article 15 of the Paris Convention. Specifically, Article 8 of the Chicago Convention reads as follows:

> No aircraft capable of being flown without a pilot aircraft shall be flown without a pilot over the territory of a contracting State without special authorization by that State and in accordance with the terms of such authorization. Each contracting State undertakes to ensure that the flight of such aircraft without a pilot in regions open to civil aircraft shall be so controlled as to obviate danger to civil aircraft.

Article 8 makes it clear that the original intention of the drafters was to create a special authorization requirement for pilotless aircraft to operate. It is envisaged that such authorization is provided in each State's rules and regulations. As such, it forms part of 'the rules and regulations relating to the flight and manoeuvre of aircraft' for every aircraft as envisaged under Article 12 of the Convention, which provides as follows:

> Each contracting State undertakes to adopt measures to ensure that every aircraft flying over or manoeuvring within its territory and that every aircraft carrying its nationality mark, wherever such aircraft may be, shall comply with the rules and regulations relating to the flight and manoeuvre of aircraft in force. Each contracting State undertakes to keep its own regulations in these respects uniform, to the greatest possible extent, with those established from time to time under this Convention. Over the high seas, the rules in force shall be those established under this Convention. Each contracting State undertakes to ensure the prosecution of all persons violating the regulations applicable.[4]

A reading of Articles 8 and 12 elucidates the two principal perspectives of the regulatory approaches and obligation of States under the Chicago Convention. First, it is unequivocal that the Convention applies to pilotless aircraft. For some time, it was not clear whether other provisions of the Chicago Convention applied to UAS. One could argue that this *lacuna* is cured by Chapter One of Annex 6 to the Convention regarding Operation of the Aircraft, which expands the definition of an aircraft to include any machine that can derive support in the atmosphere from the

[4]The Chicago Convention, Article 12.

reactions of the air other than reactions of the air against the earth's surface. ICAO, through the Eleventh Air Navigation Conference of 2003, has it settled that the Convention is applicable to the pilotless aircraft including include UAS.[5]

The second perspective is that the Convention grants wide discretion to States to make regulations regarding what, in their circumstances, would amount to a special authorization for flight and operation of pilotless aircraft. Despite such discretion, the contracting States are obligated to keep their own regulations in conformity with the rules established under the Chicago Convention to the greatest possible extent.

While there has been effective enforcement of rules and procedures by contracting States for manned aircraft due to coordinated communications to control towers, the same does not hold for unmanned aircraft systems as some of them are not identified by radar systems to allow for effective enforcement. This could perhaps be attributed to admittedly lack by the drafters of the Convention of contemplation of more technological developments in respect of UAS. It is commendable, however, that the member States to the Chicago Convention contemplated need for amendments of the Standards by ICAO from time to time and as may be necessary.[6] For effective implementation of the Chicago Convention, Article 37 states as follows:

> Each contracting State undertakes to collaborate in securing highest practicable degree of uniformity in regulations, standards, procedures, and organization in relation to aircraft, personnel, airways and auxiliary services in all matters in which such uniformity will facilitate and improve air navigation.[7]

Pursuant to Article 37, ICAO has developed 19 Annexes that contracting States are obligated to domesticate.[8] The Convention further recognizes that implementation must be through establishment of civil aviation authorities, which are mandated to provide legislative framework and oversight concerning airspace of their respective States.

Before delving into additional substantive and normative aspects of the framework, the chapter provides a descriptive analysis of the institutional framework underpinned by ICAO, also recognized under Section 38 of the Statute of the International Court of Justice to regulate the security and safety aspects of UAS. The section that follows addresses the structure, including the organs as well as the various decisions that ICAO makes, which contribute to the strengthening of the normative framework.

[5]https://www.icao.int/SAM/Documents/2003/ANCONF11SEM/ANConf11PREP_Ip03.pdf (Date of use: 24 August 2023).

[6]The Chicago Convention, Article 37.

[7]The Chicago Convention, Article 37.

[8]Annex 17 to the Convention on International Civil Aviation 9 ed, (2011) (hereinafter "ICAO Annex 17). The ICAO Annex 17.

3.3 Institutional Framework of ICAO

After a review of the Chicago Convention as the bearer of international law and rules applicable to civil aviation, this section focuses on the relevant institutional framework under ICAO. Created by the Chicago Convention, ICAO is the entity responsible for the regulation and administration of civil aviation matters across the globe.

3.3.1 ICAO Instruments and Legal Status

ICAO is ratified by 193 States that develop SARPs, which are documented as part of the Annexes to the Chicago Convention. Pursuant to Article 37 of the Convention, State parties undertake to collaborate to ensure they achieve the 'highest practicable degree' of uniformity in the SARPs. This degree may, *prima facie,* be understood to give a leeway for States to opt out of some of the Recommended Standards and Practices. Contextually, however, the same Standards apply to the binding rules of the air. While it is every State's obligation to comply, deviations under Article 38 are only possible if done in good faith and in accordance with the international rules of interpretation of treaties.[9] Further, the provision of Article 92 of the Chicago Convention unequivocally invites States to which it is open for ratification, to adhere to it. The two premises mean that the level of undertaking of States in respect to the Standards is not envisaged to be discretionary on the member States by virtue of the opt-out mechanisms provided for under Article 38 of the Chicago Convention alone. In any event, international law requires States to adhere to the treaty obligations in good faith owing to the operation of the principle of *pacta sunt servanda,* which guides States in the implementation of treaty obligations.[10]

Another key pointer to the binding nature of the Standards and Recommended Practices is the consensual nature of adoption and amendments to the Annexes to the Chicago Convention. The procedure of adoption and amendment of Annexes is an exemption to the general majority decision rule by the Council set out under Article 52 of the Convention. Article 90(a) prescribes a two-third majority of the Council to adopt or amend an Annex. Subsequently, a majority of the member States, acting in their individual capacities, have to approve the amendment or adoption.[11] Antwerpen affirms that the Standards and Recommended Practices are legally binding by virtue of principles and interpretation of international law.[12] According to Milde, the

[9]Vienna Convention on the Law of Treaties of 23 May 1969 UNTS 331 (entered into force 27 January 1980).

[10]Vienna Convention on the Law of Treaties 1969, preamble and Articles 2(1) (a) and 26.

[11]Chicago Convention, Article 90.

[12]Niels (2008), p. 32.

binding nature of the Standards and Recommended Practices can also be easily inferred by implication owing to their inescapable and inevitable effect.[13]

In addition, the formulation of all the Standards and Recommended Practices stipulated in the 19 Annexes shows that it is only in respect of the international standards that any State variance has to be reported under that Article, which may result in supplements to the Annexes.[14] This implies that the two major categories of instruments have different legal statuses or positions that elevate the legally binding status of the standards above those of the Recommended Practices and ICAO policies. Practically, the Standards have more elevated binding status since unlike the Recommended Practices, they attract the immediate and unconditional obligation to inform ICAO.[15]

ICAO also develops Manuals and Circulars, which are necessary for regulation of the various aspects of UAS. Adherence to the ICAO resolutions in the form of policies and manuals is yet to be expressly recognized as attracting compliance by State parties to the Convention. As such they are generally not binding, but are guidance materials only save for instances where they are adopted by States through other multilateral agreements.[16] This does not, however, mean that the same can be simply disregarded. Milde concurs with the notion that these ICAO resolutions cannot be ignored with impunity.[17] The author's compelling rationale is that ICAO resolutions are like the inevitable force of gravity, compliance with which is almost unavoidable in practice since there are enormous consequences attached to failure to do so.[18]

3.3.2 *ICAO: Main Functions and Organization*

ICAO is established under Article 43 of the Chicago Convention. It was originally conceived as a body with the capacity to enter into arrangements with any general organization. ICAO was made a specialised agency of the United Nations in 1947[19] pursuant to the Assembly's decision as per Article 64 of the Chicago Convention to get into international arrangements. As an independent and autonomous agency, ICAO has since played the pivotal role of providing guidance towards regulation of UAS at the international level. This includes propagation of international consensus on a number of issues relating to security, safety and privacy in UAS-related

[13] Milde (2008), p. 117.

[14] See the chart of flow of standard-making process at https://www.icao.int/about-icao/AirNavigationCommission/Documents (Date of use: 11 July 2023).

[15] See Niels (2008), p. 32 for more discussion on this.

[16] Niels (2008), p. 32.

[17] Milde (2008), p. 117.

[18] Milde (2008), p. 117.

[19] The ICAO Assembly Resolution A1-2 which authorized the relationship.

activities through development of SARPs, manuals, circulars and policies in civil aviation.

ICAO mainly focuses on ensuring aviation safety and security, and by extension privacy concerns for the orderly management of the international civil aviation sector, enhancement of efficiency, capacity and environmental protection, and building capacity of member States.[20] It works closely with member States to continually develop consensus on efficiencies in the management of civil aviation.

ICAO comprises of three principal organs, namely, the ICAO Assembly, ICAO Council and ICAO Secretariat. The ICAO Assembly is responsible for formulation of policies on standards and guidance to other bodies. It provides the avenue for creating consensus on policies to guide innovation in such areas as integration of UAS into civil aviation. The ICAO Council adopts the standards, recommended practices, and has investigative and dispute resolution powers. The ICAO Secretariat is headed by a Secretary General, and is responsible for the day-to-day running of the affairs of the organisation.

3.3.3 ICAO Structure and Organs

The 193 member States of ICAO give the organisation the backing it needs to fulfil its mandate.[21] As stated above, this is made operational through the three principal organs viz, the Assembly, the Council and the Secretariat.[22] The organization and functions of these organs are discussed below.

3.3.3.1 ICAO Assembly

It is the key policy-making organ, established under chapter VIII of the Chicago Convention.[23] It consists of all ICAO member States that are entitled to attend, for deliberations, ordinary meetings convened by the ICAO Council every three years or such extraordinary meetings as may be convened upon request by at least a fifth of member States.[24] The Assembly is responsible for formulation of policies on standards and guidance to the organs of ICAO. The Assembly also appoints the ICAO Council, considers and implements the decisions of the Council.[25] It has

[20] The Chicago Convention, Article 43 establishes ICAO and Article 43 provides the Objectives of ICAO.

[21] Chicago Convention, Article 47. See also Sochor (1991), p. 1.

[22] https://www.nationsencyclopedia.com/United-Nations-Related-Agencies/The-International-Civil-Aviation-Organization-ICAO-STRUCTURE.html (accessed on 11 July 2023).

[23] https://www.icao.int/Pages/default.aspx (Date of use: 12 July 2023).

[24] https://www.icao.int/abouticao/assembly/Pages/.(Date of use: 11 July 2023).

[25] See Chicago Convention, Article 49(a)-(k).

powers to delegate or revoke such delegation of powers to the Council.[26] Its mandate includes undertaking the functions under the Chicago Convention, which are not a reserve of the ICAO Council. Unless the Convention stipulates otherwise, the general rule is that majority of votes cast by delegates of each member State makes Assembly decisions.[27]

3.3.3.2 ICAO Council

The ICAO Council is a permanent body established under chapter IX of the Chicago Convention, comprising of members who are elected by the Assembly to serve for a three-year term.[28] Membership to the Council is geared towards representing the contribution of States in air transport and major geographical locations of the world.[29] The head of the Council is the President, who is elected from among the member States to serve a three-year renewable term.[30] The President is not a representative of the member States, but of the Council.[31]

The primary function of the ICAO Council is to adopt Standards and Recommended Practices as ratified by the Assembly.[32] It also has investigative and dispute resolution powers. The organisation plays a key role in implementing Standards and Recommended Practices via receipt of deviance notifications from international standards and procedures under Article 38 of the Chicago Convention.[33]

Standards that fall short of what is recommended are recorded as part of the supplements to the Annexes and have a binding effect on the member States that file them.

This 'difference system' *prima facie* is tantamount to a missed opportunity in realising uniformity of UAS regulation at the international stage since it allows for the application of two sets of rules to States towards complying with Article 37 of Chicago Convection. It must not be lost, however, that the system is capable of achieving harmonization of the UAS regulatory approaches in the long run as it recognizes the unique circumstances of individual States and allows them to strive towards the desired uniformity.[34]

[26] The Chicago Convention, Article 49(a)-(k).

[27] https://www.icao.int/Pages/default.aspx (Date of use: 12 July 2023).

[28] https://www.icao.int/Pages/default.aspx (Date of use: 12 July 2023). See also The Chicago Convention, Article 50(a).

[29] Chicago Convention, Article 50(b). The category of contribution has two sub-categories, which are contributors of chief importance and largest contributors in air transport.

[30] The Chicago Convention, Article 51.

[31] The Chicago Convention, Article 51(c).

[32] The Chicago Convention Article 37.

[33] The Chicago Convention, Article 38.

[34] Hsu (2016), pp. 231–234.

In carrying out the directives of the Assembly,[35] the Council is mandated to issue infraction notices to States that fail to comply with its determinations or recommendations. Where this persists, the Council reports the non-adherence to the ICAO Assembly.[36] Decisions of the Council are made by majority of votes cast by members unless the members are party to an issue under consideration.[37]

3.3.3.3 ICAO Secretariat

The ICAO Secretariat with its headquarters in Montreal, Canada, is headed by the Secretary General, who is appointed by the Council. The Council also makes provisions for other appointments of the Secretariat staff.[38] The Secretariat has regional offices in Nairobi, Paris, Dakar, Mexico, Lima and Bangkok that coordinate the day-to-day running of the organisation.[39] The Secretariat is run through the Air Navigation Bureau, Technical Cooperation Bureau, Bureau of Administration of Services, Legal Services and External Relations Bureau, all under the office of the Secretary General.[40] There are also Sections that deal with audits and programmes. The personnel appointed in the Office of the Secretary General boast an international legal character and conduct their activities independently.[41]

3.3.4 ICAO and UAS-Specific Instruments

ICAO has developed an array of instruments to regulate UAS. The instruments are contained in relevant Standards, Recommended Practices and ICAO Resolutions, which include ICAO policies, procedures, manuals, and circulars. It needn't be overemphasised that these are vital for the fulfilment of ICAO's mandate.[42] The SARPs developed by the ICAO Council are contained in 19 Annexes to the Chicago Convention. They serve to regulate safety and security in aviation.

Annexes on rules of the air, units of measurement, aircraft nationality and registration marks, and airworthiness are of international standards character. Others

[35] Chicago Convention, Article 54(d).

[36] The Chicago Convention, Article 54(j) and (k).

[37] The Chicago Convention, Articles 52 and 53. Instances of adoption and amendment of Annexes under Article 92 of the Convention is one such an exemption which requires two-thirds.

[38] The Chicago Convention, Article 54(h).

[39] https://www.nationsencyclopedia.com/United-Nations-Related-Agencies/The-International-Civil-Aviation-Organization-ICAO-STRUCTURE.html (Date of use: 11 July 2023). See also The Chicago Convention, Article 58.

[40] For full view of the structure of ICAO Secretariat, see https://www.icao.int/DownloadDocsFix/Organigramme_en.pdf (Date of use: 12 July 2023).

[41] The Chicago Convention, Article 59.

[42] Hsu (2016), p. 234.

that boast of international standards and recommended practices are Annexes on meteorological services, aeronautical charts and operation of aircraft. There are also Annexes on air traffic services, aerodromes, search and rescue, facilitation, environmental protection, security, aeronautical services, safest transportation and safety management. All these Annexes seek State collaboration in securing uniformity in regulations, standards and procedures in relation to aircraft, personnel and airways to improve air navigation.

The law mandates ICAO to issue instruments governing various UAS aspects in form of policies, procedures, manuals and circulars. The instruments, which provide guidance materials to States,[43] are mainly envisioned to harmonize concepts, terms and co-ordinate a regulatory evolution.[44] The circulars apprise States of the emerging ICAO perspective on the integration of UAS into non-segregated airspace and aerodromes, and aid in consideration of fundamental differences from manned aviation that such integration involves. They also encourage States to help with the development of ICAO policy on UAS by providing information on experiences associated with these aircraft.[45]

To date, ICAO has adopted UAS-related circulars and manuals that include Circular 330 AN/189 on Civil/Military Cooperation in Air Traffic Management of 2011, Manual on RPAs, Doc 10019 AN/507 of 2015, and Circular 328-AN/190 on Unmanned Aircraft Systems adopted in 2011.[46] The substance of the rules contained in these circulars and manuals are discussed in the section on international rules that follow hereunder. As Antwerpen observes, policies, manuals and circulars are complementary to the SARPs in the Annexes.[47]

Although ICAO has an elaborate mechanism for implementation of instruments through its various organs, Article 6 of the Convention would be invoked by some States that have little faith in the safety of the system. The ICAO Assembly has powers to disqualify a member State that does not comply with the Standards and Recommended Practices,[48] but this is yet to take effect.[49] Instead, the ICAO Council has put in place a reporting mechanism to monitor compliance at State level through legislation, and receive notifications of deviance.

In addition to reporting are research procedures, performance evaluation on safety and security audits. The audits usually take the form of Universal Safety Oversight Audit Programme (USOAP) and Universal Security Audit Programme (USAP).

---

[43]Niels (2008), p. 32.

[44]The Chicago Convention, Article 54 (I) of Chicago Convention one of the mandatory functions of the Council is to Adopt, in accordance with the provisions of Chapter VI of this Convention, International Standards and Recommended Practices; for convenience, designate them as Annexes to this Convention; and notify all contracting States of the action taken.

[45]Niels (2008), p. 32.

[46]Zafar et al. (2011), pp. 349–353.

[47]Zafar et al. (2011), p. 350.

[48]https://www.icao.int/abouticao/assembly/Pages/. (Date of use: 11 July 2023).

[49]https://www.icao.int/abouticao/assembly/Pages/. (Date of use: 11 July 2023).

They present opportunity for the organization to coordinate compliance by making practical recommendations to aviation authorities to adopt existing standards. The 'effective implementation' scores of every country are available online, move with capacity to catapult the rate of compliance.[50] It is obvious that with a high number of contracting States to the Chicago Convention, the ICAO audit team is overstretched. The strain in skill and human capital reduces the quality of audits as an oversight tool to promote safety, security and privacy assurance.

The implementation is replete with challenges as only a few member States report deviance from the Annexes and submit substantive comments in case of amendments.[51] Against this backdrop, in 2015, the ICAO Council adopted the strategic objective that no country should be left behind in implementation of the standards. This was dubbed the 'No Country Left Behind' (NCLB) campaign. The initiative sought to assist States to effectively implement ICAO Standards, Recommended Practices and Resolutions.[52]

3.3.5 ICAO and Partnerships Relevant for UAS Regulations

ICAO works in conjunction with other organisations in its quest to integrate the unmanned aircraft system into civil aviation and address the challenges on safety, security and privacy. These organisations include the World Meteorological Organization, World Tourism Organization, International Maritime Organization, and World Health Organization.[53]

ICAO also works with and gets support from regional bodies in its push for regulation of aviation safety, security and efficiency. For instance, ICAO recognizes that the European Civil Aviation Conference, an intergovernmental organization of 44 European States, augments its mission by creating a forum for understanding policy and harmonization of ICAO-adopted aviation Standards and Recommended Practices amongst member States.[54] The partnership in this regard is manifest in liaison with the European Organization for the Safety of Air Navigation and the Council of Europe.

In Africa, ICAO partners with the African Civil Aviation Commission (AFCAC), a specialised organ of the Organization of African Unity (OAU) responsible for civil

[50] https://www.icao.int/safety/pages/usoap-results.aspx (Date of use: 26 August 2023).

[51] Niels (2008), p. 33.

[52] https://www.icao.int/annual-report-2015/Pages/all-strategic-objectives-nclb-initiatives.aspx> (Date of use: 12 July 2023).

[53] https://www.icao.int/safety/RunwaySafety/GRSS2011/Pages/PartnersandSupporters.aspx (Date of use: 16 July 2023).

[54] https://www.icao.int/safety/RunwaySafety/GRSS2011/Pages/PartnersandSupporters.aspx> (accessed on 16 July 2023). See also https://www.ecac-ceac.org (Date of use: 15 September 2023) for more information on the operation of the European Civil Aviation Conference.

aviation matters in the continent.[55] AFCAC was formed at the Constitutive Conference convened by ICAO and the OAU in Addis Ababa, Ethiopia, in 1969.[56] Thereafter, AFCAC became the specialized agency of OAU/AU on 11 May 1978.[57] Article 2 of the AFCAC Constitution provides for its establishment as the specialized agency of the African Union (AU) responsible for civil aviation matters.

At yet another level, ICAO partners with individual States. For example, it works closely with FAA, the body responsible for regulation of civil aviation in the United States of America. It also works in cooperation with non-governmental organisations such as the International Air Transport Association (IATA).

Lastly, ICAO works through established regional offices. Relevant in the context of this book is the Eastern and South African Office located at Gigiri in Nairobi, Kenya. With regard to regional cooperation, ICAO has decreed the creation of Regional Aviation Safety Groups (RASGs) to serve as regional cooperative forums integrating global, regional, sub-regional, national and industry efforts in enhancing global aviation safety and security. RASGs develop and implement programmes that support regional performance frameworks for the management of safety on the basis of the Global Aviation Safety Plan. RASGs build on the work started by States and sub-regional organizations. ICAO encourages pooling of technical resources through Regional Safety Oversight Organisations (RSOOs) such as the East African Civil Aviation Safety and Security Oversight Agency (CASSOA) in a bid to develop safety oversight framework.

Despite these robust initiatives, there remain inadequate mechanisms by the regional bodies to provide avenues for partnerships with ICAO on UAS integration into civil aviation. This applies particularly among African States.[58] For instance, despite developing regulations, encouraging member States to domesticate the international framework for aviation regulation as well as regulation of audits on safety of aviation, the East African Community's Civil Aviation Safety and Security Oversight Agency (CASSOA) lack the requisite partnership arrangements with ICAO.[59] Lubner observes that partnerships are pivotal in strengthening regional aviation bodies, which is the binding force of member States in their effort to integrate UAS into civil aviation.[60]

The author concurs with Lubner's observation,[61] asserting that the US offers a most pragmatic example. The Organization of American States, the oldest regional organization, enjoys an entrenched partnership arrangement between ICAO and FAA. The success that FAA has made in the aviation sector is worth replication

---

[55] Abeyratne (1998), pp. 30–49.

[56] Abeyratne (1998), p. 43.

[57] Abeyratne (1998), p. 30.

[58] https://www.icao.int/safety/RunwaySafety/GRSS2011/Pages/PartnersandSupporters.aspx (Date of use: 16 July 2023).

[59] Abeyratne (1998), p. 30.

[60] Lubner et al. (2010), p. 80.

[61] Lubner et al. (2010), p. 80.

by sub-regional and continental entities as shall be seen in the chapter that follows. In any event, the EAC Treaty of 1999 contemplates adoption of common policies at the sub-regional level to achieve collaboration with ICAO.[62]

Such cooperation could offer an important avenue for ICAO to take advantage of the geographical proximity and interdependence of Regional Economic Communities (RECs). This is best exemplified by the partnership arrangements that the European Union civil aviation organisations have made with ICAO to harness compliance with safety requirements.[63] This is considering that Article 37 of the Chicago Convention relies heavily on the discretion of States for its implementation and the Annexes thereto. It is the author's take that owing to the transboundary nature of UAS, sub-regional economic blocs encourage members to comply with safety, security and privacy measures in support of integrating UAS into civil aviation.

Despite the noble idea of establishing AFCAC decades ago, little has been done to create unifying or binding regulations for UAS amongst African States. Attempts to address inherent challenges are met with obstacles that regional economic communities must overcome before they are ready to collaborate with ICAO.

The issue of capacity runs supreme. Even with the entry of South Sudan and DR Congo into the East African Community, CASSOA[64] is yet to create an office to specifically deal with UAS in the seven East African States. The entity also has a lean structure,[65] comprising of only 20 members of staff as at 2023. This is the number tasked with oversighting the whole of the East African region.[66] In addition, it is grossly underfunded, making it difficult to execute its other mandates like monitoring UAS entering the region, sharing data among member States and ensuring compliance with safety management systems as provided for under ICAO's Annex 19. The situation is no different in the South African region under SADC, where little effort has been made to establish a regional civil aviation agency such as the South African States Civil Aviation Safety and Security Oversight Agency (SASCASSOA). Only recently has SADC established an Interim SADC South African Safety Organization (iSASO) to deal specifically with civil aviation regulations in the sub-region. The organization is yet to be ratified by all the member States. It does appear that emphasis is on safety without much focus on how to address security and privacy challenges. While the step is commendable, the lack of a substantive body is a grave setback as regards cooperation with ICAO.[67] SADC member States consequently are denied opportunity to galvanize support, assist and encourage them to comply with ICAO Standards and Recommended Practices in the manner envisaged under Article 4(b) of the Constitution of AFCAC.

[62]EAC Treaty 1999, Article 92(3)(a).

[63]The Chicago Convention, Article 65.

[64]EAC Treaty 1999, Article 92.

[65]http://www.cassoa.org/cassoa/> (Date of use: 21 August 2023).

[66]http://www.cassoa.org/cassoa/> (Date of use: 21 August 2023).

[67]The Chicago Convention, Articles 65 and 77.

This sharply contrasts with the situation in the US, where the Federal Aviation Administration (FAA) is responsible for aviation matters.[68] The situation is similar in Europe where the European Aviation Safety Agency (EASA) is responsible for developing aviation regulations for EU member States.[69]

3.4 International Air Law Responses to Regulation of UAS Challenges

This section provides substantive elements of how existing international air law framework has provisions that regulate the safety, security and privacy issues arising from the use of UAS. It offers discussion of international rules including Conventions, Annexes and other instruments that address safety, security and privacy challenges as identified and expounded in Chap. 2 of this book.

3.4.1 International Response to Aviation Safety in UAS Regulation

Aviation safety is defined under ICAO Annex 19[70] Safety Management Manual Doc 9859, ICAO Annex 2 on Rules of the Air and Circular 328-AN/190[71] as the state in which the possibility of harm to persons or property damage is reduced to, and maintained at or below an acceptable level through a continuing process of hazard identification and safety risk management.[72] From the definition, it emerges that the obligation of ensuring the safety of UAS is a two-fold process. It involves identifying safety risk and managing the risk. The risk management aspects encapsulate reactive and proactive approaches to management of safety concerns.[73] As seen in Chap. 2, the challenge to safety arises from the lack of sense and avoid technology in some UAS, which inevitably increases the chances of collision. The international general rule stipulates that UAS use and operation must be safe and not compromise the lives of others.[74] Consequently, a mechanism to redress safety challenges was contemplated by the contracting parties through the establishment of frameworks for

---

[68] The Chicago Convention, Article 65 and 77.

[69] See Button et al. (2015), pp. 626–639.

[70] Annex 19 on Safety Management to the Chicago Convention (hereinafter referred to as ICAO Annex 19).

[71] ICAO Circular on Unmanned Aircraft Systems No. 328-AN/190 (hereinafter refered to as ICAO Circular No. 328-AN/190). See Section 2.16, 2.17, 2.18, 2.19, 2.20 and 2.21.

[72] See Safety Management Manual Doc 9859. Glossary and definition of terms at p vii.

[73] ICAO Annex 19, Paragraph 2.16.

[74] ICAO Circular 328-AN/190, Section 2.

aviation safety in the Chicago Convention.[75] The Convention thus established the ICAO, with mandate to regulate air safety, communication and technological aspects of international civil aviation, including aspects of UAS.[76] Article 8 of the Chicago Convention specifically provides the basis for regime of special authorization of aircraft. The objective of this authorization is to prevent safety concerns arising from accidents and collisions were the pilotless aircraft left to operate unregulated in the airspace.

Contracting parties to the Chicago Convention are obligated to allow flights of non-scheduled aircraft into their territories.[77] However, this obligation, which translates into a right on the operators of the aircraft, may be limited in case of movements where the States deem inaccessible. The limitation is at the discretion of the State, which can only be exercised on grounds of safety.

As per Article 9(a) of the Chicago Convention, public safety considerations inform the basis upon which countries may restrict or prohibit the flying of aircraft. However, State discretion has its limitations and cannot be exercised when it is unreasonable in terms of extent or rather prevent aviation. Other than prohibited areas, circumstances such as public safety and emergency, without express prohibitions communicated to ICAO, may warrant a limitation on the right for aviation provided there is no discrimination of the aircraft on nationality basis.[78]

Safety considerations are traced to the airports of member States, who are required to have navigation facilities and meteorological service for aviation safety.[79] States make similar considerations when imposing cargo restrictions as provided for under Article 35(b) of the Chicago Convention. To breathe more life into these provisions ICAO has mandate to ensure safe and orderly growth of international aviation,[80] and to promote safety of flight in international airspace.'[81] Further, ICAO adopts and amends SARPs from time to time. In particular, the Chicago Convention recognizes that the standard may deal with, among others:

> ...such other matters concerned with the safety, regularity, and efficiency of air navigation as may from time to time appear appropriate.[82]

It is clear, therefore, that the Chicago Convention's approach is establishment of broader frameworks for safety. The mechanism contemplated under Article 44(a) as read with 44(h) are dependent on ICAO's development of relevant SARPs. As regards the other restrictions and prohibitions of flights, the measures for their

[75] The Chicago Convention, Article 3 (d).
[76] The Chicago Convention, Article 44.
[77] The Chicago Convention, Article 5.
[78] The Chicago Convention, Article 9(b).
[79] The Chicago Convention, Article 15.
[80] The Chicago Convention, Article 44(a).
[81] The Chicago Convention, Article 44(h).
[82] The Chicago Convention, Article 37(k).

achievement are significantly dependent on discretionary regulations developed at State levels. An example is Article 9, which opens with the words,

> . . .each contracting State may, for reasons of military necessity or public safety, restrict or prohibit.[83]

The provisions of Article 15 of the Chicago Convention on requirement of facilities and meteorological services at airports for safety largely exclude UAS, are capable of launch from any location.

Other than the broader framework, the Convention recognizes and regulates two activities with a bearing on mitigating safety concerns for UAS use. The first of these activities is the certification of airworthiness envisaged under Article 31 of the Chicago Convention. Before registration for use in international navigation, a UAS should as a matter of principle be issued with a certificate of airworthiness[84] by the State in which it is registered.[85] A certificate of airworthiness is a measure of an aircraft's suitability for safe flight, only applicable to certified UAS. It is conferred on an aircraft by the aviation authority of a particular State, and remains valid subject to the aircraft's performance to the required standards. Until such a time that this requirement is harmonized, States continue to apply different criteria for certification.[86] It has not been effectively possible to offer all UAS with certificates of airworthiness due to rapid technological revolutions. More of these uncertified UAS are used in social gatherings to take photographs, a *lacuna* that is partly associated with absence of regulations or proper enforcement mechanisms.

The second activity for regulation of safety is pegged on licencing requirements, which are made under Article 32 of the Chicago Convention. The Article provides that:

> pilot of every aircraft and the other members of the operating crew of every aircraft engaged in international navigation shall be provided with certificates of competency and licenses issued or rendered valid by the State in which the aircraft is registered.[87]

Licensing is the authorization of defined events otherwise prohibited out of the hazards that would occur if poorly performed. Thus, licensing has safety of operation as one of its prime considerations when a decision to grant a licence is made by competent authorities. Applicants for a license must meet certain standards that are commensurate with complexity of the event to be performed.[88]

The practical activities of certification of airworthiness and licencing, without more, do not inspire full safety with regard to the sense and avoid technologies. From a plain reading of the provisions of Articles 31 and 32 of the Chicago Convention, the provisions focus on 'international aviation'. This technically leaves out of its

[83] The Chicago Convention, Article 9(a).

[84] The Chicago Convention, Article 31.

[85] The Chicago Convention, Article 31.

[86] ICAO Annex 8.

[87] The Chicago Convention, Article 32(a).

[88] The Chicago Convention, Article 32(a).

scope the concerns relating to safety of domestic uses of UAS. Article 32 in particular addresses the 'crew members' in licencing subjects despite that being uncommon for UAS.[89] Aviation safety demands that remote pilots and other UAS crew need to be trained in safety, and possess requisite qualifications, appropriate licenses or certificates of competence to provide a modicum of integrity in safety of the civil aviation system they eventually are part of. With little focus on the main conventional law, some States continue to operate without clear guidelines regarding pilots operating UAS.[90]

ICAO has developed two Annexes, Annex 2 on the Rules of the Air and a manual known as Safety Management Manual Doc 9859 providing guidance to States to develop their domestic legal framework. Also relevant to safety is the ICAO's UAS Circular No. 328 AN 190. The Circular is instrumental as it has rationalized the application of safety considerations to UAS among member States.[91]

Annex 19 was developed to address safety concerns. It consists of two programmes and systems, namely, State Safety Programme (SSP) and Safety Management System (SMS). These are divided as between operators of UAS and the State, and both aim at ensuring that the sky is safe to all users.

Through the State Safety Programme, ICAO sees to it that States set up regulations and activities for safety of the airspace.[92] The Programme recognizes the acceptable levels of safety in aviation practice. It is a system through which the civil aviation authorities, having regard to size and resource of the aviation system, regulate, monitor and administer safety.[93] The areas of regulation include oversight of safety, which comprises monitoring of safety elements and oversight in areas of significant safety concerns and high safety risks. Others are risk management, safety assurance and safety promotion. It, therefore, contemplates the conduct policy formulation based on safety information such as identification of hazards and safety arising from management, conduct of stakeholder awareness and internal audits.[94]

The Programme is crucial as it supports rule-making processes in the 193 ICAO member States on matters safety. It supports analysis of potential effects of UAS safety and third parties such as service providers regulated by civil aviation authorities.[95] This is in addition to determining the role of 'equivalent level safety' and 'acceptable means of compliance' in their possession. The SSP processes on safety assurance, risk management, and promotion are designed to proactively address hurdles that the use and operation of UAS pose while in the air. In other words, they

---

[89]Pepin (1957), p. 1.

[90]ICAO Annex 19, Paragraph 4.13.

[91]ICAO UAS Circular No. 328 AN 190. Section 2.16, 2.17, 2.18, 2.19, 2.20 and 2.21.

[92]ICAO Annex 19, Paragraph 2.19.

[93]ICAO Annex 19, Paragraph 2.19.

[94]https://www.iata.org/en/training/courses/state-safety-program/tcvg90/en/ (Date of use: 22 July 2023).

[95]https://www.iata.org/en/training/courses/state-safety-program/tcvg90/en/ (Date of use: 22 July 2023).

are part of countermeasures from a legal perspective that address challenges regarding UAS safety operations.

The Safety Management System on its part flows from the SSP of each State on the basis of which it instructs stakeholders to develop their respective SMS.[96] Service providers and operators under oversight of the State's implementation of ICAO Annex 19 that requires all contracting States to domesticate safety management measures within their jurisdiction establish the system, which targets a systematic approach to management safety through creating efficiency in organizational structures, accountability, policies and procedures.

As SSP and SMS are inseparable, pilots of UAS or manned aircraft are required to be knowledgeable about the rules of the air, flight performance, planning and loading, human performance, navigation, operation procedure and principles of flight.[97] They are given flight instruction, demonstrate skill and expertise, as well as be licensed. They also need to be proficient in the language of radiotelephony and meet the required medical fitness levels. For purposes of UAS, the former could be modified through integration of regulations to ensure that those who operate UAS meet the basic levels of space proficiency.

Further, SSP and SMS require States to establish bodies to oversight safety at the national level. Such authorities are specifically responsible for guaranteeing UAS safety for all when they are introduced into the civilian airspace.[98] SSP and SMS have influenced regulation of personal licencing in some ICAO member States, in effect helping to achieve integration of UAS into civilian application. This translates to personnel licensing harmonization in a single airspace across national and regional boundaries.[99]

UAS could experience challenges in meeting safety requirements such as introduction of technology for detection and avoidance, command and control, communication with ATC and prevention of unlawful interference.[100] The interference may occur because UAS have no pilot on board and there may be no capacity to communicate with ATC and seek clearance before landing at an airport. The Chicago Convention attempts to resolve this challenge by imposing UAS regulation and stipulation of conditions under which UAS can operate. The import of Article 8 of the Convention is to prohibit flying of pilotless aircraft over territories of other States without authorization.

[96] https://www.iata.org/en/training/courses/state-safety-program/tcvg90/en/ (Date of use: 22 July 2023).

[97] ICAO Annex 19, Paragraph 2.15.

[98] Provided in relevant ICAO Annex 6 on Operation of Aircraft to the Chicago Convention (hereinafter referred to as ICAO Annex 6); Annex 11 on Air Traffic Services to the Chicago Convention (hereinafter referred to as ICAO Annex 11" and Annex 14 on Aerodromes Design and Operations to the Chicago Convention (hereinafter referred to as the ICAO Annex 14).

[99] The Chicago Convention, Article 8 on pilotless aircraft.

[100] ICAO Annex 19, Paragraph 2.15.

Annex 2 on the Rules of the Air,[101] is instrumental in ensuring safety in civil aviation. The Rules stipulate the responsibilities of the pilot-in-command, that is, to ensure aircraft operation complies with the rules of the air, and prescribe punishment to those who violate them. The pilot-in-command of unmanned aircraft systems is the person controlling it while airborne and has final authority over it.[102] The rules apply whether the pilot is on board or at a remote location in the case of UAS. Further, it is the responsibility of a pilot operating a UAS to undertake a handing over process even where the aircraft is in flight.[103] Other responsibilities are avoidance of collisions and development of flight plans, provision of signals and obtaining of air traffic control clearances.[104]

There is a challenge as regards the implementation of ICAO Annex 2. Remote pilots could be long distances apart, yet they are expected to hand over to pilots in far-off places. Hand over by remote pilots is made more complex where they operate in different States or in the high seas.[105] It is also difficult, for example, to develop and submit a flight plan for use in filming. These are pointers to the fact that there are impediments to the full attainment of safety in licensing and regulation of UAS. Consequently, this could be a missed opportunity since rules of the air are, by nature, binding upon member States to the Chicago Convention.

Safety considerations underpin the power of States under international law, which according to Cooper, include jurisdiction over airspace and unilateral right to admit or deny entry, freedom over high seas, right of innocent passage, and nationality of aircraft.[106] This position in conventional, SARPs and the international customary law are supported by court opinions that consider safety as the basis for regulation of UAS. The *Libyan Arab Jamahiriya v United Kingdom*,[107] also known as the *Lockerbie case*, is instrumental in defining safety laws in the aviation sector. Though this case was applicable to manned aircraft, the principles developed by the court apply to UAS in the current framework under the Chicago Convention.[108] Perhaps the only limitation is that the effect of the binding nature of the judgments is limited to specific cases and respective parties.[109]

Safety concerns are also addressed through traffic clearances, which ensure flight completeness. As regards traffic management, it is clear that when the Chicago Convention was adopted, there was an agreement between parties that relates to

---

[101] Annex on the Rules of the Air to the Chicago Convention (hereinafter referred to as ICAO Annex 2).

[102] ICAO Annex 2, Paragraph 2.3.1.

[103] ICAO Annex 2, Paragraph 2.3.1.

[104] ICAO Annex 2, Paragraph 3.3–3.6.

[105] ICAO Annex 2, Paragraph 3.3–3.6.

[106] See Cooper (1967), p. 3.

[107] *Libyan Arab Jamahiriya v United Kingdom* 1992 88 (ICJ) Rep 3 [578].

[108] Bouve (1935), p. 299.

[109] The United Nations Charter of 26 June 1945 1 UNTS XVI (entered into force 24 October 1945) (hereinafter referred to as the UN Charter).

traffic management. The Agreement at Article 12 of the Convention partly states as follows:

> Each contracting State undertakes to adopt measures to ensure that every aircraft flying over or manoeuvring within its territory and that every aircraft carrying its nationality mark, wherever such aircraft may be, shall comply with the rules and regulations relating to the flight and manoeuvre of aircraft there in force.

Reference to 'aircraft carrying the nationality marks' in Article 12 of the Convention applies extraterritorially. This is a significant achievement in ensuring that foreign UAS do not cause mayhem or disruptions in the aviation airspaces of other countries. However, the actualisation of the provision is heavily dependent on development of laws at national levels, their harmonization and implementation through enforcement of criminal laws.[110]

The Chicago Convention requires aircraft engaged in international navigation to fulfil certain conditions that include carrying of documents aboard.[111] The documents are certificate of registration, certificate of airworthiness, appropriate licenses for each crew member, journey logbook, aircraft radio station license; if carrying passengers, a list of their names, places of embarkation and destination; and if it is for cargo, a manifest and detailed declarations of the cargo.[112] Other than for purposes of identification, certification and ownership, the documents are meant to ensure safety of the aircraft, its crew and property, and persons on the ground. The list of passengers allows for easier identification in the case of accident. Declaration of cargo ensures that only legal cargo is carried.[113]

The above regulatory approaches under Article 29 of the Chicago Convention are difficult to enforce when dealing with UAS as currently there are no cases of UAS carrying people. Carrying paper-based documents on board UAS is neither practical nor appropriate. Electronic or alternative versions of the documents ought to be considered.[114] It is commonplace that in the event of an accident, most aircraft are completely destroyed by fire. This calls for a regulatory framework that ensures advanced technology is fixed to UAS with back-up servers on the ground.

According to Pevot *et al*, international response to safety is faced with the challenges of unmanned traffic management. UAS require an advanced traffic management ecosystem under development for their autonomously controlled operations to ensure safety in entry into the airspace.[115] The system is one that that can monitor increased activity based on sharing of each operator's scheduled flight details in a digital form. Unfortunately, most UAS lack these systems.

That notwithstanding, the international response under Article 8 of the Chicago Convention contemplates UAS operation alongside the manned aircraft. As seen in

[110] The Chicago Convention 1944, Article 12.

[111] The Chicago Convention 1944, Article 29.

[112] The Chicago Convention 1944, Article 29.

[113] ICAO Annex 2, Paragraph, 2.1.1 also makes similar requirements.

[114] ICAO Annex 119, Paragraph 4.1.1.

[115] Prevot et al. (2016), p. 3292.

Chap. 2, this could be disruptive and pose security risks as UAS come in different shapes and operate in much lower altitudes than were originally designed for use by aircraft.

The rule of the air is to reduce the safety risks that could arise. Part 3.6 in particular deals with control of air traffic, and specifically provides as follows:

> An air traffic control clearance shall be obtained prior to operating a controlled flight, or a portion of a flight as a controlled flight. Such clearance shall be requested through the submission of a flight plan to an air traffic control unit.

The import of the word 'shall' is to make it mandatory for air traffic control clearance to be obtained when a person submits an air traffic control plan after submission of flight plans by civil aviation operators including UAS operators. Despite the provision, the requirements of ICAO Annex 2 direct towards two implementation challenges. Firstly, some of the requirements for flight plans and clearance to pilots in command could be impracticable for certain uses of UAS. Secondly, the idea of control as stipulated in the Chicago Convention and ICAO Annex 2 do not specifically provide for the command and control system. Accordingly, it depends on the State resources and design of the UAS to fully implement these provisions that are pivotal for safety in the airspace.

To further cure the challenges relating to unmanned traffic management in the ICAO Annex 2, ICAO developed Circular No. 328 AN 190. The Circular requires pilot-in-command to ensure operation of the aircraft complies with rules of the air and prescribes punishment to those who violate them. The pilot-in-command of unmanned aircraft systems is the person controlling it while airborne and has final authority over it.[116] This applies whether the pilot is on-board or at a remote location in the case of unmanned aircraft systems. Further, it is the responsibility of a pilot operating a UAS to undertake a handing over process even where the aircraft is in flight.[117] Other responsibilities are avoidance of collisions and development of flight plans, provision of signals, and obtaining of air traffic control clearances.[118]

ICAO has over the years developed a series of traffic rights known as Freedoms of the Air, which are the basis of the rights exchanged in air services negotiations.[119] This book contends, however, that this principle and its effect on UAS could present a contradiction. Although UAS could interact like manned aircraft, there are certain inconsistencies in the latter such as non-co-operation and non-compliance, which may complicate management of air traffic with current regulatory challenges.[120]

The above provisions speak to the general rules on safety. The UAS principle of responsibility and accountability anticipates that UAS missions will consistently

[116] ICAO Annex 2, Paragraph 2.3.1.

[117] ICAO Annex 2, Paragraph 2.3.1.

[118] ICAO Annex 2, Paragraph 3.3–3.6.

[119] Manual on the Regulation of International Air Transport (Doc 9626, Part 4).

[120] De Garmo (2010), p. 8.

require persons who are accountable, whether they are called commander or pilot.[121] From a legal perspective, action must be taken against persons or legal entities responsible for operations in case of foul play. The principle particularly appreciates that the UAS involves novel technologies, hence the need to create mechanisms to ensure responsibility and accountability in design, manufacture, maintenance and operations, equal to those of manned aircraft, even though the person in command is on the ground.[122]

3.4.2 International Response to Aviation Security in UAS Regulation

The overall international commitment to the field of aviation security is deducible from the preamble to the Chicago Convention as conceptualised and anchored under ICAO Annex 17, which defines security as the act of safeguarding international civil aviation against acts of unlawful interference.[123] As noted in Chap. 2, the security issues that concern the use of UAS arise from among other factors interference with State sovereignty, cyber-attacks and lack of command controls.

International air law has over time evolved to combat such acts in the aviation field, both for manned aircraft and the UAS. Traditionally, State security is assured through protection and affirming of territorial integrity and State sovereignty as principles of international relations.[124] This is based on the sovereign equality principle affirmed under Article 2(1) of the United Nations Charter of 1945. It is, therefore, the responsibility of each State to uphold security within her jurisdiction. So pivotal is the principle that State security, also termed as ‘public security,’ has been the basis of limitation of human rights and fundamental freedoms in the international bill of rights.[125]

With regard to specific aviation security, the Chicago Convention places security as the pivot upon which the regulation of civil aviation is based. This is evident from paragraph 1 of the preamble, which recognizes the power of international cooperation in the aviation field in developing friendliness. The paragraph has it that the abuse of the cooperation may be a threat to ‘general security’. The preamble to the Chicago Convention, therefore, contemplates a future where civil aviation can foster friendship and understanding among nations. At the same time, it appreciates threats to security and prohibits acts of unlawful interference against orderly civil aviation.[126] Thus, whereas it promotes the desire for peaceful co-existence among

[121] De Garmo (2010), p. 8.

[122] De Garmo (2010), p. 8.

[123] See ICAO Annex 17.

[124] Chicago Convention, Articles 1 and 2.

[125] See example acrimonious passage of the Kenya security amendment Act No. 19 of 2014.

[126] Chicago Convention, Article 4.

nations, it is also alive to the need for overall regulation for peaceful co-existence. In the ordinary sense, the general security referred to in the preamble is broader than the State sovereignty and public security concept in the United Nations Charter. This means that the Chicago Convention goes over and above the traditional view of State sovereignty and considers global security as a serious consideration in the regulation of aviation.

Other than the broad recognition, the Chicago Convention is specific on the activities that need to be taken to avoid the much-feared backlash in global security. Article 33 of the Convention provides as follows:

> Certificates of airworthiness and certificates of competency and licenses issued or rendered valid by the contracting State in which the aircraft is registered, shall be recognized as valid by the other contracting State, provided that the requirements under which such certificates or licenses were issued or rendered valid are equal to or above the minimum standards which may be established from time to time pursuant to this Convention.

On security, Article 33 establishes the basis for the licensing and certification of operations of the UAS in the airspace. The Article is the basis of recognition, and a further stipulation that such certificates must be of equal or above minimum standards in another State.[127] Article 17 of the Convention makes requirement for nationality marks of the State in which they are registered, and supplements the provision on certification and airworthiness. The Article States that "Aircraft have the nationality of the State in which they are registered."

Security issues can also be ensured through the utilization of partnerships and agreements between ICAO and other geographical security organizations.[128] Instructively, Article 64 of the Chicago Convention provides as follows:

> The Organization may with respect to air matters that are within its competence directly affecting the world security by vote of the assembly enter into appropriate arrangements with any general organization set up by nations of the world to preserve peace.

The provision enables ICAO to utilize the pre-existing security organization and thus save on financial and human capacity when dealing with security challenges. Additionally, dealing with regional organization may be much more efficient in terms of enforcement and ease of development of consensus on action based on a pre-existing agreement, which member States are obliged to adhere to by the principle of *pacta sunt servanda*.

Regarding further development of standards, procedures and regulation of security, the Chicago Convention contemplates airworthiness of aircraft, registration and identification as falling under the domain of ICAO for adoption and amendment of SARPs under Article 37(e) and (f) respectively. True to this higher calling, ICAO adopted ICAO Annex 17, which regulates the security concerns through security programming and requirement of nationality marks.[129] The nationality of an aircraft

[127] Chicago Convention, Article 33.

[128] Chicago Convention, Article 64.

[129] Chicago Convention, Art 17 & 20.

has not only become an important part of civil aviation and bilateral air transport agreements, but also the multilateral transit and transport agreements.[130] It is for this reason that substantial ownership and effective control requirements have effectively precluded adoption of the maritime law notion of "flags of convenience" into international aviation. Addressing the nationality of an aircraft is thus a key principle of the Chicago Convention.

ICAO Annex 17 also supplements the requirements of nationality marks in Article 17 of the Convention by its specifications for minimum-security standards for display of aircraft marks to indicate appropriate nationality and registration.[131] This makes it easier to trace unmanned aircraft systems in the air, especially in circumstances where they intrude into airspace territories of other States.

Whereas implementation of nationality requirements through identification marks and height requirements is easily achievable in manned aircraft, this is not necessarily the case for UAS. Some UAS are too small to affix identification marks and may need alternative modes of complying with the provisions of Article 17. The deficiency negatively impacts on the regulation of security of operation of unmanned aircraft. The situation is likely to persist until alternatives are sought and well defined.

ICAO has progressively diversified its role in assisting States, initiating policy initiatives and focusing on security audits. This is marked by development of Aviation Security Manual Doc 8973 (adopted in March 1974) and ICAO UAS Circular 328-AN/190. The focus on civil aviation under the Manual and not international aviation is a reflection of ICAO's desire to assist States at the domestic level to comply and take steps towards the implementation of security measures as a means of building the ultimate consensus at the international level.[132] Since then, there has been increased focus on audits, which has led to the development of Universal Security Audit Programmes (USAP) that are managed and coordinated by the Aviation Security section within ICAO.[133]

Under this guidance on the evolving nature of security, States have the responsibility of ensuring security of passengers, crew and ground personnel. This means that appropriate civil aviation authorities are mandated to develop National Civil Aviation Security Committees to oversee the establishment of programmes such as the National Civil Aviation Security Programme, National Civil Aviation Security Quality Control Programme and National Civil Aviation Security Training Programme.[134] Hence, individual member States are obligated to put in place such measures as to uphold security specifically in aerodromes.

[130] Chicago Convention, Art 66.

[131] Chicago Convention, Arts 17, 18 and 19 on Nationality of Aircraft, dual registration and National laws governing aircraft registration respectively.

[132] https://www.icao.int/Security/Pages/default.aspx?p=12 (Date of use: 22 July 2023).

[133] https://www.icao.int/Security/Pages/default.aspx?p=12 (Date of use: 22 July 2023).

[134] ICAO Annex 17 on Security to the Chicago Convention (hereinafter referred to as the ICAO Annex 17), Paragraph 2.1.2.

ICAO Circular 328-AN/190 was designed as a guidance document for member States to develop UAS regulations in conformity to security.[135] It is instructive that the Circular called on States to provide comments, particularly with respect to its application and usefulness.[136] The Circular represents an effort to proceed with development of fundamental international regulatory framework through SARPs, with supporting procedures for air navigation services and guidance material to underpin routine operation of UAS throughout the world in a safe, harmonized and seamless manner comparable to that of manned aircraft.

Other than the laws developed under the auspices of the ICAO, the idea of security is a key component of the explosive management framework through its International Explosives Technical Commission. The Commission is the custodian of the Technical Annex to the Convention on the Making of Plastic Explosives Convention of 1991.[137] Notably, this multilateral anti-terrorism treaty was developed for purposes of detection, prohibition, conveyance and prevention of manufacture and storage of unmarked plastic explosives. The Convention specifically targets the manufacture of aircraft and makes no serious distinctions between manned and unmanned aircraft in its application. The restriction under the Convention is limited to plastic explosives to individuals, who comprise a high number of users of UAS. ICAO has it that cyber-attacks on air navigation facilities could constitute an offence under the Beijing Convention for the Suppression of Unlawful Acts Relating to International Civil Aviation.[138] It illegalizes transport of Biological, Chemical, and Nuclear weapons and related materials, which UAS can easily transport, or hijackings and attacks on air navigation facilities by coercion or technological means.

Further, the law on security could also draw from the international custom of State sovereignty. In this respect, Article 1 of the Chicago Convention states as follows:

> The contracting States recognize that every State has complete and exclusive sovereignty over the airspace above its territory.

According to Brown *et al*, the principle of State sovereignty provides that every State has, to the exclusion of all others, independent and absolute right to permit or deny access into the area recognized as its territory, and similar right to control all activities within such territory.[139] Article 1 of the Chicago Convention is the basis for reaffirmation of the principle, which first featured under Article 1 of the Paris Convention of 1919. By doing so, the Chicago Convention codified the customary international law.

---

[135] ICAO Circular 328-AN/190, Paragraph 5.32.

[136] ICAO Circular 328-AN/190, Paragraph 5.32.

[137] https://www.icao.int/Security/Pages/default.aspx?p=12 (Date of use: 22 July 2023).

[138] Beijing Convention 2010.

[139] Brown et al. (1996), p. 88.

Based on an overview of the operation of the sovereignty principle and its embodiment in treaty law and international custom, it is evident that application of the principle majorly targets large aircraft systems. Though it applies to UAS, the limitation stands to be abused. Authorization is seen as a limitation of innocent passage that may be invoked by a State against an enemy, an instance that can limit achievement of the provisions of Article 8 that target the removal of all circumstances that obviate danger. The other challenge in the application of the principle is sovereignty itself. This arises from a common argument that the reasons States adopt national laws to complement ICAO Annexes and Circulars on security is to ensure efficient use of airspace; individual States have a responsibility to recognize each other's right to fly through the national air territory.

The other duty is to utilize certain areas of national land territories and territorial waters such as landing grounds and harbours. There is a school of thought that holds that airspace ought to be treated as belonging to humanity without exception and thus subject to international regulation.[140] It is submitted, therefore, that leaving these aspects of authorization to domestic regulation on prior authorization processes is self-defeatist and could amount to many UAS being discreetly gunned down by some States in the pretext of maintaining national security.

Other international customs relevant to aviation security in addition to State sovereignty are the right of innocent passage and its exemptions under international law of the sea. Under this law, it is the duty of the originating State to ensure aircraft exercising the right of transit or passage navigate or fly immediately through or over the passage of another State.[141] More so, the States given the right of way must refrain from activities other than those that are incidental to their normal modes of continuous and expeditious transit, unless rendered necessary by *force majeure* or necessity.[142]

Additionally, the general principles recognized by the developed nations also form a necessary regulatory framework for aviation security. Of particular interest is the principle of sovereignty of the airspace and its limitations. This principle is responsible for provision of specialized authorization to operate UAS in the territory of another State as required under Article 12 of the Chicago Convention. The Article, which is a restatement for Article 15 of the Paris Convention, limits the right of passage to the airspace above the open sea, a free airspace with principles ruling aviation in this space being similar to those applicable at sea level. The rule is based on the public law rule that prohibits a State from exercising power over another's territory.

The foregoing international legal framework is useful for the protection of UAS from illegal seizure. It is dependent on States to determine privileges to which such aircraft are entitled, and the States are reciprocally responsible for the international

[140] Pepin (1956), p. 70.

[141] Solomon (1966), p. 96.

[142] The Chicago Convention, Article 39(1).

good conduct in ensuring that the manned or unmanned aircraft are in good condition or not used to create insecurity.

The mode of implementing and monitoring international security mechanism may be inefficient in regulation of UAS for three principal reasons. Firstly, congruence of the security programmes with airport plans is impossible as most UAS can be launched from remote places. Secondly, the mechanism for protection under ICAO Annex 17 may be difficult to implement since ownership of UAS is increasingly becoming personal, more so as regards civil UAS to which the Chicago Convention applies. An expansive amendment to the Aviation Security Manual may be limited in application where UAS lack in-flight security personnel or passengers as envisaged by the manual.

The success of the regulatory mechanism is dependent on the presence and efficiency of control and command systems for UAS. To date, however, and as outlined in Chap. 2, there are outstanding challenges related to the control and command systems.[143] The Chicago Convention does not directly address the issue of command and control of the UAS, which partly explains why the UAS-specific Circular issued by ICAO recognizes the inevitability of these challenges.[144] The persistent challenges arising from lack of system cannot, however, be overlooked at the international level owing to security threats that emanate from exercise of freedom of overflight over high seas as provided for under Article 87(1) of the UN Convention on the Law of the Sea.[145]

Thirdly, security challenges could arise from the right of transit passage, which is recognized under Article 38, as read with Article 3 of the Law of the Sea Convention. The right allows exercise of the freedoms of navigation and overflight for purposes of continuous and expeditious transit through an international strait between one part of the high seas or an Exclusive Economic Zone. This could pose practical threats to State security as regard the use of UAS in the case of abuse.

3.4.3 International Response to Privacy Challenges in UAS Regulation

As explained in Chap. 2, the privacy concerns on use of UAS are real and practical. There is usually the potential privacy breach by way of secret photography by UAS, which make use of global positioning system (GPS) technology to take aerial photos owing to their ability to fly above residential areas.

At the enactment of the Chicago Convention, contracting parties were conscious of possible privacy concerns arising from UAS operations. Redress is given less prominence compared to aviation safety and security as there is not a single

143 Chapter 2, Sect. 2.7.2.1 of this book.

144 ICAO Circular Circular No. 328-AN/190, Paragraph 2.15.

145 Convention on the Law of the Sea Convention of 1982.

provision that expressly mandates State parties to develop regulation to reassure the privacy concerns in UAS use. Regulation of privacy can, however, be inferred by implication from the reading of some provisions of the Convention. Article 36 of the Convention provides on this issue, albeit from an approach of a right of the State. It provides as follows:

> Each contracting State may prohibit or regulate the use of photographic apparatus in aircraft over the territory.

Reference to possible State regulation of aerial photography in Article 36 of the Chicago Convention imputes the regulation of privacy. The import of Article 36 of the Convention is not to expressly prohibit the traditional photography by aircraft including UAS operating over territories of other States. The provision grants obligation on States to develop frameworks for putting the regulation into effect. This implies that prior to development of the contemplated regulation, the protection of privacy rights may not be fully assured without domestic regulations being adopted by States as per Article 36 of the Chicago Convention.

The approach on protection of privacy through regulation of traditional photography appears archaic and out of touch with the 21st Century challenges. The photography does not only target attack on other States, and there are information and communication technologies that can negatively affect the privacy rights not expressly recognized under Article 36 of the Chicago Convention. For example, it does not contemplate the challenge of cyber-attacks, which may target the systems of the very UAS, control towers or radars.

It is possible that ICAO has an avenue to overcome the challenges set out above through regulation of the provisional powers to develop standards and recommended practices and procedures, as well as its organizational objectives for promotion of all aspects of aviation under Article 37 of the Chicago Convention. However, a closer reading of the Article evidences what might just be another case of the non-dominant position of redress for privacy concerns under the Convention. The Article addresses the areas in respect of which ICAO can develop international standards and recommended practices. The topical standards and recommended practices for which Annexes can be adopted as listed at Article 37(a)-(k) do not *prima facie* expressly recognize privacy concerns in the use of UAS. The only possible means of developing regulations, standards and procedures on privacy is pursuant to the provision of Article 37 of the Chicago Convention that reads in part as follows:

> ...To this end the International Civil Aviation Organization shall adopt and amend from time to time, as may be necessary, international. Standards and recommended practices and procedures dealing with...and such other matters concerned with the safety, regularity, and efficiency of air navigation as may from time to time appear appropriate.

This means that when ICAO considers developing a standard or recommended practice, it can only do so in reliance to its miscellaneous power to do so on 'such other matters concerned with regularity, and efficiency of air navigation as may from time to time appear appropriate.' In so doing, ICAO can further justify a possible development of a privacy framework action as moulded on its objectives under

Article 44(i), which is to 'promote generally the development of all aspects of international civil aeronautics'.

ICAO is yet to develop an Annex to deal with the issue of privacy. Activities on regulation of privacy remain largely dormant at the international plane. The matter is left to be dealt with within the real State sovereignty. Even then, the audits that ICAO uses to ensure compliance at State level only target safety and security of aircraft operations and use, and not privacy compliance.

The scanty framework in the principal international Convention does not in any way mean that the victims of breach or threat to privacy are without distress. Actual or potential victims can seek redress in international human rights instruments such as the Universal Declaration of Human Rights (UDHR),[146] and the International Covenant on Civil and Political Rights (ICCPR).[147] Article 17(1) of the ICCPR provides as follows:

> No one shall be subjected to arbitrary or unlawful interference with his privacy, family, home or correspondence, nor to unlawful attacks on his honour and reputation.

The import of the above provision is that except as may otherwise be limited in accordance with the applicable laws or as derogated under Article 4 of the ICCPR,[148] States are under an obligation to among others respect, protect and fulfil the freedom from arbitrary or unlawful interference with a person's rights without distinction. This is a reaffirmation of the declaration at Article 12 of the Universal Declaration of Human Rights, 1948 that imposes similar prohibitions against interference.

Accordingly, reliance on international human rights treaties is pivotal in regulating activities of State aircraft, which are otherwise excluded from the application of the Chicago Convention by virtue of Article 3. The appurtenant challenge, however, is the fact that the international human rights discourse addresses States and not UAS operators. It is thus upon States to develop laws, policies and regulations aimed at protection of privacy. The challenges are laid bare in literature that shows that UN member States remain sceptical about low levels of adoption of the universal standards.[149] A common thread that runs across the development in the uses, sizes, functioning and history of UAS is the potential challenges associated with sovereignty, technological and technical underpinnings. This is evident from the lack of an international law convention or Annex on privacy matters relating to cybercrime, which have potential to infringe on privacy rights.

Following the scepticism, regulation of UAS differs from one jurisdiction to the next. The prospects of integrating UAS into civil aviation arise from the support extended by ICAO to member States in discharging their rights and obligations. Subsequently, some countries have taken or are taking steps to address the

[146] UN General Assembly, Universal Declaration on Human Rights 10 December 1948, 217 A (III).

[147] UN General Assembly, 16 December 1966 99 UNTS 171.

[148] See UN General Assembly, 16 December 1966 99 UNTS 171, Article 4(2) on the list of articles on non-derogable rights.

[149] Mark and Alison (2019), pp. 490–496.

challenges through their domestic legislation and regulations as conversed in Chaps. 4–6 in this book.

3.5 Conclusion

This Chapter reviews the regulatory framework in international air law for UAS and in particular, how the international framework addresses safety, security and privacy challenges identified in Chap. 2 of this book. It is established that the international civil aviation law framework under the Chicago Convention enjoys the support of 193 States, delineates mandatory application and interpretation of Article 8 to apply to UAS. Though the Convention's provisions were compellingly couched to give prominence to regulation of manned aircraft, they too can be extended seamlessly through the principles of fairness and transparency to apply to safety, security and privacy concerns of the UAS. Comparatively, however, mention of redress for privacy concerns is scanty and limited to traditional photography issues.

The deficiency notwithstanding, it is clear that the regulation of safety and security is widely addressed through ICAO's framework developed by way of adoption and amendment of SARPs pursuant to Article 37 of the Chicago Convention. Specifically, the ICAO framework targets both proactive and reactive regulation of the three aspects of UAS use. Despite the developments, certain practical challenges in development of higher standards of compliance for ICAO in requirement of autopilot software, management of air traffic, management and command control systems for UAS and the little attention given to the privacy concerns in the framework for regulation under the Chicago Convention, 1944 abound. Despite these challenges, the international human rights discourse has significantly shaped the redress for certain UAS concerns for privacy in order to fill the existing gap. In addition to the Chicago Convention, the full and effective redress of the safety, security and privacy challenges arising from UAS depends on further development of frameworks under ICAO, customary international law, and the international human rights discourse.

Chapters 4–6 review how specific States have responded to the absence of a unified international UAS regulation in dealing with identified challenges of safety, security and privacy in their national jurisdictions.

References

Books

Brown C et al (1996) State sovereignty as social construct. Cambridge University Press

De Garmo MT (2010) Issues concerning integration of unmanned aerial vehicles in civil airspace. The MITRE center for advanced aviation system development Mclean Virginia

Milde M (2008) International air law and ICAO. Eleven International Publishing

Journal Articles

Abeyratne R (1998) The future of African civil aviation. J Air Transp Worldwide, 30–49

Bouve C (1935) Regulation of international air navigation under the Paris Convention. J Air Law, 299

Button K et al (2015) African decolonisation and air transportation. J Transp Econ Policy, 626–639

Cooper JC (1967) Backgrounds of international air law. Yearb Air Space Law, 3

Hsu YM (2016) A new international legal order. Chinese (Taiwan) Yearb Int Law Affairs, 231–234

Mark E, Alison LY (2019) Privacy international in the Supreme Court: jurisdiction, the rule of law and parliamentary sovereignty. Cambridge Law J, 490–496

Niels V (2008) Cross-border provision of air navigation services with specific reference to Europe: safeguarding transparent lines of responsibility and liability. Kluwer Law Int, 32

Pepin E (1956) The legal status of the airspace in the light of progress in aviation and astronautics. McGill Law J, 70

Pepin E (1957) Development of the National Legislation on Aviation since the Chicago Convention. J Air Law Commun, 1–24

Sochor E (1991) Decision-making at ICAO: who governs the governing body? Polit Int Aviat, 1

Solomon S (1966) The right of innocent passage and the 1958 Geneva Conference on the Law of the Sea. Columbia J Transnatl Law, 96

Workshops and Conference Papers

Lubner B et al (2010) The Continuing Challenge of Aviation Safety in Africa. Paper presented to the 16th International Symposium on Aviation Psychology 2010

Prevot et al (2016) UAS traffic management (UTM) concept of operations to safely enable low altitude flight operations. Paper presented to the 16th AIAA Confernece on Aviation Technology, Integration, and Operations Conference 2016

Zafar MA et al (2011) Design and development of effective manual control system for unmanned air vehicle. Paper presented to the 3rd International Conference on Computer Research and Development 2011

Chapter 4
Legal, Policy and Institutional Framework for Regulation of UAS in the United States of America (USA)

4.1 Introduction

This Chapter examines the regulatory framework of Unmanned Aircraft Systems (UAS) in the United States of America. It analyses how the framework addresses safety, security, and privacy challenges inherent in the use of UAS. Specifically, it reviews the different safety, security, and privacy concerns arising from dirty, dull and dangerous missions of UAS in the US as earlier explained in Chaps. 1 and 2. Further analysis is made of how and to what extent the US jurisdiction has adopted the international legal framework detailed in Chap. 3, in order to address challenges associated with integration of UAS into civil aviation. There is also evaluation of the history of UAS regulation in the US, specific UAS guidelines, institutional and policy framework provided by the Federal Aviation Administration (FAA) as well as the role of courts in harnessing and addressing safety, security and privacy concerns.

4.2 History and Background of Regulation of Civil Aviation in the US

According to Carr, the US is one of the most developed States technologically and economically, coupled with advanced legislative framework for UAS.[1] As a result, UAS has become commonplace in the US airspace, and with development in technology, so has been the challenge of balancing demands of safety, security

[1] Carr EB https://www.e-education.psu.edu/geog892/sites/www.e-education.psu.edu.geog892/files/sp-Drones-long-paper.pdf (Date of use: 14 August 2023).

M. Wanyonyi Rodgers, *The Law Regulating Unmanned Aircraft Systems in the United States, South Africa and Kenya*,
https://doi.org/10.1007/978-3-031-49927-2_4

and privacy in Federal and State laws, regulations and economic interests.[2] Given her technological advancement, leadership, and many years' interaction with UAS, the US potentially provides experiences on integrating UAS into the civil airspace.

Regulation of the civil aviation industry in the US commenced in the early nineteenth Century, a feat that was beneficial to countries like South Africa and Kenya. As Heymann notes, the 11 September 2001 incident was a turning point in regulation of aircraft in the US.[3] The US undertook a massive security rearrangement to allow information sharing among agencies dealing with security, alignment of entities including customs, border control, immigration and aviation, which were placed under Homeland Security, to address uncoordinated security operations including aviation security. These policy changes ultimately led to the passage of the FAA Modernization and Reform Act[4] in 2012, marking the starting point in addressing challenges related to aircraft regulations for smooth integration into civilian aviation.

It is worth noting that even in the US where development and use of UAS is more advanced, the Federal Aviation Modernization and Reform Act was only enacted in 2012. The Act mandated the Federal Aviation Authority to develop and implement comprehensive procedures that would enable UAS integration into the national airspace system by September 2015.[5] Hitherto, FAA 2012, was developing polices, standards, advisory circulars, notices and orders designed to improve airspace safety, and this remains work in progress.[6] Despite the successes made, FAA 2012, faced the challenge presented by the dire need to create an environment that would spur technological innovation, while at the same time developing a regulatory framework that guaranteed safety for all aviation stakeholders. This was critical because, whereas the integration process was incomplete, operators of recreational UAS continued to use distinct rules for model aircraft in violation of the FAA Modernization and Reform Act, 2012.[7]

The evolution of legislative frameworks governing aviation in the United States marked a significant shift with the transition from the FAA Modernization and Reform Act of 2012 to the FAA Reauthorization Act of 2018. The former, enacted in 2012, laid the groundwork for enhancing the nation's aviation infrastructure,

[2] Carr EB https://www.e-education.psu.edu/geog892/sites/www.e-education.psu.edu.geog892/files/sp-Drones-long-paper.pdf (Date of use: 14 August 2023 2019).

[3] Heymann (2001), p. 441.

[4] FAA Modernization Reform Act of 2012 (Congress Public Law No.112-095) (hereinafter referred to as the FAA Modernization Reform Act).

[5] http://www.FAA.gov (Date of use: 4 July 2023).

[6] FAA "Advisory Circular on Reporting of Laser Illumination of Aircraft" https://www.Faa.gov (Date of use: 18 July 2023).

[7] The US Integration of civil UAS in National Airspace System Road Map of 2013. See also Secretary of Transportation "Unmanned Aircraft System (UAS) Compressive Plan: A Report on Nation's UAS Path Forward of September 2013" https://www.hsdl.org/?abstract&did=746317 (Date of use: 1 August 2023).

safety protocols, and regulatory processes. However, as the aviation landscape continued to evolve and new challenges emerged, the need for updated and refined legislation became apparent. This led to the passage of the FAA Reauthorization Act in 2018, which not only addressed the advancements in aviation technology and safety standards but also reflected a nuanced understanding of the dynamic aviation industry. The transition between these two acts underscores the proactive approach of policymakers in adapting to the changing needs of the aviation sector while ensuring its continued growth and resilience.

The US has a long history with UAS, which dates back to the period before the enactment of the Air Commerce Act.[8] In the pre-1926 regime, the aviation sector took a two-pronged dimension through the common law from State and local court decisions, as well as statutory law enacted at State level.[9] In the mid-1920s, it was deemed necessary that federal law would regulate the aviation industry through adoption of statutes and regulations at the federal level.[10] Prior to this development in 1934, the Department of Commerce renamed the Aeronautics Branch as the Bureau of Air Commerce with the objective of underlining the growing significance of aviation to the nation.[11] One of the tasks of the Bureau was to promulgate all-inclusive federal air commerce rules.[12]

The drafters of the initial federal law were of the view that the scope of rules should encompass all frontages of aviation, that is, the aircraft, the airmen involved in aircraft operation (the pilots and mechanics), and the rules of the air.[13] The experts modelled American federal law on the principles itemized in the draft description from the Aerial Navigation Convention.[14] The Bureau of Air Commerce recommended laws requiring that every aircraft shall be provided with: (a) a certificate of registration, (b) a certificate of airworthiness, (c) certificates and licenses of the commanding officer, pilots, crew and logbooks.

Arising from this development and the fact that aircraft could naturally navigate State and national boundaries, a uniform aviation law was ideal compared to a patchwork comforter of local laws.[15] Uniform regulation at the federal level was a logical preference due to the fundamental requisite to standardize aviation for military purposes.[16] Owing to the failure by the US Constitution to expressly define

[8] Air Commerce Act of 1926.

[9] Logan (2013), p. 510.

[10] Logan (2013), p. 510.

[11] https://www.FAA.gov (Date of use: 18 July 2023).

[12] https://www.FAA.gov (Date of use: 18 July 2023).

[13] The US Department of Commerce Information Bullet Number 7.

[14] The Convention Relating to the Regulation on Aerial Navigation of 13 October 1919 (entered into force 15 June 1929).

[15] Lee FP "The Air Commerce Act of 1926" 1926 *ABAJ* 371.

[16] Lee FP "Air Commerce" 376.

aerial jurisdiction, the government realized that there was an urgent need to legislate on it so as not to interfere with the inherent concept of federalism.[17]

In the aftermath of Congress' decision not to ratify the Treaty of Versailles, President Woodrow Wilson excluded production of the Aerial Navigation Convention to the Senate for debate.[18] In 1920, the American Bar Association adopted a resolution that aeronautics was within the admiralty jurisdiction of the United States and should be entertained accordingly.[19] Upon failure of this proposal and granted that there was precedence that transport by air was distinguishable from transport by sea, the American Bar Association sought other means to create federal jurisdiction over the skies. In 1922, the American Bar Association mooted an idea of endorsing a constitutional amendment.[20]

The amendment was deemed unrealistic and air law was divided along two paths—regulatory legislation that was nearly exclusively a federal responsibility, and non-regulatory legislation that is primarily a State responsibility.[21] For lack of a decisive federal action, the Uniform Law Commission, also known as the National Conference of Commissioners on Uniform State Laws,[22] undertook consideration of the necessities for durable State-level aviation law.[23] Set up in 1892, the Uniform Law Commission was tasked with providing States with non-partisan professional advice, with the Commission conceiving well-drafted legislation to bring clarity and stability to critical areas of State statutory law. This was a State-supported body that represented true worth for States providing services that most of them could not otherwise afford or duplicate.[24] To conform to values of federalism, each State willingly adopted a uniform State law for aeronautics which explicitly barred navigation of any aircraft otherwise than in conformity with the federal traffic rules.[25] The legislative step was thus a key assurance of safety and security concerns that would ordinarily arise from use of aircraft.

Beginning in 1926, the United States enjoyed a uniform aviation law system with federal laws such as the Air Commerce Act[26] being applicable to flying, commercial, non-commercial, intra-State and inter-State.[27] The objective of the Air Commerce Act was to establish federal regulations regarding aircraft, aviators, navigation facilities and establishment of aircraft regulations together with the Commerce

---

[17] Lee FP "Air Commerce" 375.

[18] Lee FP "Air Commerce" 372.

[19] https://legal.un.org/ilc/documentation/english/ASIL_1947_study.pdf (Date of use: 1 August 2023).

[20] https://www.americanbar.org/products/inv/book/184862428/ (Date of use: 23 August 2023).

[21] Lee FP "Air Commerce" 372.

[22] The Commission is also called National Conference of Commissioners on Uniform State Laws.

[23] MacCracken (1930), p. 418.

[24] http://www.uniformlaws.org (Date of use: 18 August 2023).

[25] http://www.uniformlaws.org (Date of use: 18 August 2023).

[26] Air Commerce Act of 1926.

[27] Lee FP "Air Commerce" 418.

Department's related rules. The uniform aviation law system was, however, donned with a serious setback since its formation fell within the era of *Lochner v New York*.[28] This was an era of Commerce Clause jurisprudence when the Supreme Court of the US made it a common practice to strike down economic regulations.[29] Despite this era coming to an end in 1937, judicial activism played a key role in the development of the uniform aviation law system. The courts did this through application of liberal interpretation of the constitutionality and applicability of the Air Commerce Act, with a view to harnessing its objective of ensuring aviation safety. In addition, cardinal to the judicial activism during the *Lochner* period was the expansion of otherwise narrow interpretation in order to protect personal liberty, which had a bearing on both security and protection of privacy rights.

Beginning with the Air Commerce Act, the federal government preserved the concept that the basic privilege to fly be limited only by the fitness of the aircraft and operating personnel in the interest of safety to those participating in aeronautics and to persons on the ground.[30] This is an indication that the adoption of the Air Commerce Act was underpinned with the overall intention of ensuring safety in all flights. The Act provided for the means of ensuring safety, which is by issuance of certificates of airworthiness and licenses to competent pilots and flights. It is, however, possible that the safety requirements could be potentially abused owing to the much discretion granted to States in granting the flights as privileges.[31]

After the passage of the Air Commerce Act of 1926, efforts were made to establish air procedures.[32] The Air Commerce Regulations of 1928 represent an inclusive set of rules developed shortly thereafter to ensure high-quality elementary engineering, manufacturing, repairs, and operation of aircraft.[33] All these requirements focused on safety of operation of UAS. Subsequently, the US Congress passed the Civil Aeronautics Act,[34] the Federal Aviation Act,[35] and the Department of Transportation Act.[36] The statutes organizationally streamlined the Bureau of Air Commerce into Civil Aeronautics, the Federal Aviation Agency, and eventually the Federal Aviation Administration (FAA). These federal provisions continued to apply with no discrimination between the commercial and non-commercial utility in

[28] See generally *Lochner v. New York* 1905 US 198 (SC) [45].

[29] For more information on how the period represented constitutional crisis, see Choudhry (2004), p. 2.

[30] Fang FD "Legal Basis of the Civil Air Regulations" *JALC* 9.

[31] Fang FD "Legal Basis" 9.

[32] Fang FD "Legal Basis" 12.

[33] Fang FD "Legal Basis" 12.

[34] Civil Aeronautics Act of 1938.

[35] Federal Aviation Act of 1958.

[36] Department of Transportation Act of 1966.

design of aircraft.[37] The efforts culminated in development of the Federal Aviation Modernization and Reform Act of 2012.

4.3 The Framework for US' Response to Regulation of UAS

The US embraced an international approach through which it was involved in discussions that culminated in the adoption of the Chicago Convention and the ICAO framework.[38] It did actively participate in the development of the framework that was attended by 54 of the 55 invited States. The Chicago Convention had 52 States append their signatures of approval as the conference came to an end on 7 December 1944.[39]

As a party to the Chicago Convention, the US is mandatorily obliged to follow the binding rule of the air contained in both Article 12 and Annex 2 on Rules of the Air. It also has an obligation to adhere to civil aviation security and safety as provided in ICAO Annexes 17 and 19 respectively.[40] In addition, the US is party to the Convention relating to Unification for Rules relating to International Carriage by Air, also the known as Warsaw Convention among other relevant treaties.[41]

At the domestic level, the US Constitution, which is the supreme law of the land addresses myriad matters that form the basis for the regulation of safety, security and privacy in UAS operation albeit at a high level. The US has a unique experience with UAS regulation since its constitutional structure as a federal State means that regulation and management of UAS is dealt with at four levels—two at the federal level and two at the State level.

Under 49 US Code § 106, the administrator is the head of FAA and has authority under the Act to make additional rules, regulations, circulars, and bulletins. This power is particularly recognized at Section 2(A) (iii) of the Code, which provides that:

> except as otherwise provided in paragraph (3), the administrator has power of promulgation of regulations, rules, orders, circulars, bulletins, and other official publications of the administration.

---

[37] See US Code of Federal Regulations, Title 14, § 23 on Airworthiness Standards: Normal, Utility, Acrobatic, and Commuter Category Airplanes and § The US Code of Federal Regulations, Title 14, § 25 on Airworthiness Standards: Transport Category Airplanes).

[38] https://www.icao.int/about-icao/History/Pages/default.aspx (Date of use: 28 August r 2023).

[39] https://www.icao.int/about-icao/History/Pages/default.aspx (Date of use: 28 August r 2023).

[40] https://www.icao.int/about-icao/History/Pages/default.aspx (Date of use: 28 August 2023 r). Specifically, the US Signed Chicago Convention on December 7, 1944 consented to be bound with the Convention on 9 August 1946 and the Convention was effective on 4 April 1947.

[41] As adherence of the US deposited at Warsaw July 31 July 1934 and entered into force 9 October 1934.

The import of the above provision is that the issuing of circulars towards operation of UAS is meant to be legally binding to operators unless there are contrary intentions or provisions for the same.

The FAA Reauthorization Act of 2018 holds significant relevance within the current framework guiding the United States' response to the regulation of Unmanned Aircraft Systems (UAS). This legislation represents a pivotal update to the regulatory landscape for UAS operations, building upon the foundation laid by its predecessor, the FAA Modernization and Reform Act of 2012. In this sub-section the FAA Reauthorization Act, 2018, serves as a critical focal point for discussing the legal mechanisms that have evolved to address the challenges posed by the rapid proliferation of UAS technologies.

The US Code of Regulations defines an aircraft as any contrivance invented, used, or designed to navigate or fly in the air.[42] Under the FAA Regulations, an aircraft is defined as a device that is used or intended to be used for flight in the air.[43] The FAA Reauthorization Act defines unmanned aircraft as follows:

> an aircraft that is operated without the possibility of direct human intervention from within or on the aircraft.[44]

The UAS fits into the above definitions by virtue of being a device that is used for flying in the air. The regulatory approach is even more definitive since the Act differentiates the small-unmanned aircraft and public unmanned aircraft systems depending on their weight and use.

The FAA Reauthorization Act 2018 acknowledges the transformative impact of UAS on various industries and sectors while recognizing the need to strike a balance between enabling innovation and ensuring safety and security. It signifies the U.-S. government's proactive approach in keeping pace with technological advancements, by providing updated guidelines and regulations tailored to the unique characteristics of UAS operations. The act reflects the increased importance of integrating UAS into the National Airspace System in a responsible and coordinated manner.

In 2014, the National Transportation Safety Board pronounced itself on a decision that brought UAS within the ambit of aircraft, affirming the already established definition.[45] It was a decision that affirmed the grip and jurisdiction of FAA over UAS.[46] The affirmation of the applicability of the definition is a boost to the pragmatic approach the US has taken in implementing the spirit of Article 15 of the Paris Convention as later contained in Article 8 of the Chicago Convention.

---

[42] US Code of Regulations, Title 49, § 40102(a) (6).

[43] US Code of Regulations, Title 14, § 1.1.

[44] The FAA Reauthorization Act 2018, Section 341(11).

[45] https://www.lmc.org/resources/drones-municipal-use-and-regulation/ (Date of use: 1 August 2023).

[46] https://www.lmc.org/resources/drones-municipal-use-and-regulation/ (Date of use: 1 August 2023).

The FAA Reauthorization Act of 2018 further solidified the regulatory framework for Unmanned Aircraft Systems (UAS) within the United States, in line with the pragmatic approach to aviation governance as influenced by international agreements like the Paris Convention and the Chicago Convention. The act, building upon its predecessor from 2012, reinforced the principles established by these international agreements and bolstered the Federal Aviation Administration's (FAA) authority over UAS operations. The act's provisions[47] can be seen as an affirmation of the National Transportation Safety Board's (NTSB) decision in 2014, which categorized UAS as aircraft and thus subjected them to the same regulatory oversight as traditional manned aircraft.

By explicitly addressing the regulatory status of UAS, the FAA Reauthorization Act 2018 reiterated the jurisdiction of the FAA over UAS operations. For instance, the Act provides for the strategy of responding to public safety threats and enforcement utility of UAS.[48] This legislative stance resonates with the NTSB's decision in 2014, underscoring the FAA's role in ensuring the safety, security, and efficient integration of UAS into the National Airspace System. The act's language and provisions likely extend to reaffirming the applicability of the previously established definition of UAS as aircraft, thus solidifying the FAA's grip over their regulation.

Furthermore, the alignment of the act with the principles of the Paris Convention and the Chicago Convention, emphasizes the United States' commitment to international norms and standards in aviation.[49] The act's provisions can be analysed to demonstrate how they uphold the spirit of Article 15 of the Paris Convention and Article 8 of the Chicago Convention, which pertain to the recognition of aircraft and the regulatory powers of the state of registry.

The Community-based Guidelines on Safety of Operations and Safety Code published by the Academy of Model Aeronautics are important in complementing the FAA efforts in regulation of safety issues regarding use and operation of UAS.

4.4 Overview of Federal Aviation Administration (FAA)

The overall mandate of integrating UAS into the US national airspace is bestowed upon the FAA, the national civil aviation authority under[50] the Federal Aviation Administration Act of 1958.[51] FAA is part of the US Department of Transportation Security Administration that established FAA.[52] Accordingly, the control of

---

[47] The FAA Reauthorization Act 2018, Section 341(11).

[48] *Ibid*, Section 366.

[49] Vajiram, Jayanthi, Negha Senthil, and Ritikaa Vn. (2023).

[50] The FAA Reauthorization Act 2018, Section 567.

[51] Federal Aviation Act of 1958 (Congress Public Law Number 85-726).

[52] https://www.faa.gov (Date of use: 27 August 2023).

activities and personnel of the FAA is done by the Secretary of Transportation pursuant to Section 106(f)(1) of Title 49 U.S Code.

FAA has the overall statutory mandate to ensure the safety and security of the national airspace.[53] It undertakes this solemn obligation through the regulation of all matters pertaining to aircraft, airmen, most categories of airline employees, commercial or common carrier operations, airports, and, more prominently, use of national airspace. The mandate extends to promotion of safe flight of civil aircraft in the airspace.

4.4.1 FAA Organs

FAA is headed by an Administrator and Deputy Administrator, who are citizens of the United States and appointees of the US President with experience in the field of civil aviation.[54] The officers are independent and carry out their duties in conjunction with the office of Secretary of Transportation to regulate and enforce aviation issues in the US.

The FAA Reauthorization Act, makes provisions for integration of civil unmanned aircraft systems into national airspace system.[55] This is in agreement with the provisions that had been made in the 2012 act establishing the UAS integration office.[56] The Office in turn established six UAS test sites, published the Integration of Civil UAS in the National Airspace System Roadmap, expanded use of small UAS in the implementation plan and the UAS comprehensive plan, and simplified the certificate of waiver or authorization process.

The UAS Integration Office was mandated to achieve integration of UAS by 2015. By December of that year, FAA announced that all UAS weighing more than 250 grams and flown for any purpose must be registered with it. Focus, however, was not on full integration, but rather on safe integration. The process was to be incremental, and not drastic, to give room for its effectiveness hence the development of the integration roadmap. This approach seems to be well thought out since it appreciates the unique circumstances of the UAS as opposed to taking an over-ambitious step of full integration.

The integration of UAS into the civil airspace as envisaged under Section 332 of the FAA Modernization and Reform Act aimed at uniting the following entities towards achieving integration: the UAS Integration Office, Department of Defense, National Aeronautics and Space Administration and the MITRE Corporation. The UAS Integration Office consistently works to collect safety data while the six test sites provide data collected during operations. The development of safety

[53] The US Code of Regulations, Title 49, §§ 40101(a) (1), 40103(b), 44701(a) (2012).

[54] The US Code of Regulations, Title 49, s 106.

[55] FAA Reauthorization Act, 2018, Sections 341–347.

[56] https://www.FAA.gov.UAS (Date of use: 1 July 2023).

management documents is aimed at facilitating understanding and mitigate hazards that could arise from integration.

While the UAS Integration Office was initially mandated to achieve integration of UAS by 2015 under the previous FAA Modernization and Reform Act of 2012, the subsequent 2018 Act, specifically in Sections 341-347, further solidifies the commitment to achieving this integration in a gradual and controlled manner. The provisions within Sections 341-347 of the new Act highlight the careful consideration given to the process of UAS integration. The focus on safe integration is reaffirmed, echoing the understanding that the unique characteristics and capabilities of UAS necessitate a cautious and stepwise approach.

The 2018 Act's provisions elaborate on mechanisms that support safe integration, such as the development of standards, protocols, and technologies to mitigate risks associated with UAS operations. Additionally, it introduces frameworks for collaboration between regulatory authorities, UAS manufacturers, operators, and other stakeholders to collectively ensure the safety and effectiveness of integration efforts.

The Office of the Rule-making is the other critical organ of the FAA, which is the repository for all published regulatory documents by FAA. The Office also provides the avenue for public participation in the rule-making processes undertaken by FAA.[57] Regarding the small UAS, there is in place a Small UAS Aviation Rulemaking Committee that was established to formulate rules aimed at facilitating integration of UAS into the national airspace, in a controlled manner.[58]

4.4.2 Rule-Making by FAA

Of all the regulatory tools adopted by FAA, the rule-making stands out. It has power to formulate proposals that are critical to integration of UAS into civilian airspace for effective management of airspace use, aviation experience, climate, geography and location of ground infrastructure, research needs, risk, and safety.[59] FAA's jurisdiction and rule-making powers are derived from Title 49 of the United States Code.[60] The FAA administrator is in particular, mandated to:

> ...the promulgation of regulations, rules, orders, circulars, bulletins, and other official publications of the Administration.

FAA embarked on creating policy statements, orders, notices, handbooks and manuals, and directives.[61] Through the Office of Rulemaking, FAA sought to

[57] https://www.faa.gov/regulations_policies/rulemaking/ (Date of use: 15 August 2023).

[58] https://www.faa.gov/regulations_policies/rulemaking/ (Date of use: 15 August 2023).

[59] Nevada Legislative Counsel Bureau "Research Brief on Unmanned Aircraft Vehicles" https://www.leg.state.nv.us/Division/Research/Publications/ResearchBriefs/UAS.pdf (Date of use: 1 August r 2023).

[60] US Code of Federal Regulations, Title 49, s 44702 (a) and s 40103 (b).

[61] https://www.faa.gov/regulations_policies/rulemaking/ (Date of use: 15 August 2023).

undertake other statutory roles to achieve a countrywide geographic and climatic diversity by developing regulatory and operational procedures and standards that would guide integration of UAS technology.[62] These procedures and standards include Advisory Circulars (AC) published by FAA as binding documents to provide guidance for conducting UAS operation in the US national airspace, since the US government has exclusive sovereignty over her airspace.[63]

FAA also develops aviation policies and regulations that form the basis for safety and security through guidance systems, personnel and skill development, operations, and procedures.[64] Courtesy of the regulations, all aircraft are required to meet the regulatory requirements for air navigation facilities, equipment and services, airports or landing areas, aeronautical charts, information and services, rules, and processes, technical data, workers, and materials.

Another tool is the development of advisory opinion and airworthiness directives by the FAA.[65] A technical standard could be created to address a problem emanating from the attention of FAA advisory circulars to advise the aviation committee on issues of regulation. Airworthiness Directives, on the other hand, are legally enforceable.[66]

The Circulars developed to give effect to the Federal Aviation Regulations are generally non-regulatory in nature and, therefore, non-binding in the strict sense; they only provide guidance and precautions on issues.[67] The decision of the court in the case of *FAA v. Raphael Pirker*,[68] demonstrates this position. This was a motion of appeal filed by the respondent (Pirker), a US citizen, challenging an earlier order for a civil penalty in the sum of $10,000 in favour of the FAA. The device in question was a commercial *Ritewing Zephyr* powered glider aircraft' in the vicinity of the University of Virginia. According to the FAA, the device was a UAS according to the US laws and regulations. That it fell under the purview of FAA regulations as it was operating for commercial purposes. However, the respondent contended that FAA, the complainant, did not have jurisdiction and regulatory authority over model aircraft operators hence the decision ought to have been dismissed. While agreeing with the respondent's motion, the Board cited among others, that model aircraft operation by the respondent was only subject to FAA voluntary compliance with Safety Guidelines in FAA Advisory Circular on Model

[62] https://www.faa.gov/regulations_policies/rulemaking/ (Date of use: 15 August 2023).

[63] US Code of Federal Regulations, Title 49, s 40103.

[64] US Integration of Civil Unmanned Aircraft Systems in the National Airspace System Roadmap of 2013.

[65] An example is The US Department of Transportation and Federation Aviation Administration Airworthiness Directive 2014.

[66] https://www.faa.gov/regulations_policies/airworthiness_directives/ (Date of use: 29 August 2023).

[67] https://www.faa.gov/regulations_policies/airworthiness_directives/ (Date of use: 29 August 2023).

[68] *FAA v Raphael Pirker* 2013 EA-5730 (NTBS).

Aircraft Operating Standards.[69] The Board also noted that at the time of the respondent's model aircraft operation, there was no enforceable FAA rule classifying model aircraft.

The above position does not in any way mean that the Advisory Circulars are to be ignored with impunity. The decision in the *Raphael Pirker case (supra)* is significant. It was made before both the FAA Modernization and Reform Act and FAA Reauthorization Act were enacted. Section 347 of the FAA Reauthorization Act provides that exemption of model UAS operators be determined by adherence to conditions attached to model UAS aircraft, the most important one being for recreational or purposes of hobby.[70] It would appear that if the *Raphael Pirker* case was decided after either 2012 or 2018, the respondent would have been found in violation of Section 336 of the 2012 Act or Section 347 of the 2018 Act. The exemption envisaged in the Act is, however, not absolute. For instance, when the model of UAS changes its use to commercial purposes, it shifts status to a civil UAS, and, therefore, requires a special authorization certificate in experimental category.[71]

In the same vein, the FAA issues advisory tools known as policy statements touching on UAS.[72] These policy statements have the full force of the law.[73] Of relevance to this book are statements on the UAS, particularly UAS statement 05-01[74] that seeks to clarify a statement that was carried in the Federal Register on 6 February 2007 titled, 'unmanned aircraft operations in the national airspace system'[75] and 'interim operational approach guidance 08-01.'[76]

FAA has also been able to utilize the use of notices in addition to policy statements. It has published road maps, wherein it consistently asserts its overall mandate to regulate national airspace and aviation in general. There is diverse opinion that there is little difference between published road maps[77] and policy statements. A road map is more practical and has timelines in the redress of UAS security and safety concerns. From the wording alone, a road map is more coordinated, distinguishable, and, therefore, important in the regulation of aviation. It provides, *inter alia,* broad timelines, tasks and considerations needed to enable UAS integration into the national aviation system for the planning purposes of the expanded UAS community. The road map has built a basis for the national aviation

---

[69]FAA Advisory Circular on Model Aircraft Operating Standards No. 91-57.

[70]Henshon (2014), p. 26.

[71]The Code of Federal Regulations, Title 14, s21.175(b).

[72]The Code of Federal Regulations, Title 14, s 21.175(b).

[73]Gonczy ST *Federal Aviation Administration (FAA) airworthiness certification for ceramic matrix composite components in civil aircraft systems* (MATEC Web of Conferences 2015) 2.

[74]https://www.faa.gov/documentLibrary/media/Notice/N_JO_7210.889_Unmanned_Aircraft_Operations_in_the_NAS.pdf (Date of use: 1 August 2023).

[75]https://www.faa.gov/documentLibrary/media/Notice/N_JO_7210.889_Unmanned_Aircraft_Operations_in_the_NAS.pdf (Date of use: 1 August 2023).

[76]FAA, Aviation Safety Unmanned Aircraft Program Office Interim Operational Approval Guidance No 08-01 of 2008.

[77]The US Integration of Civil UAS in the NAS Roadmap of 2013.

airspace transition from UAS accommodation to UAS integration. It also provides a strategy to align proposed agency actions with the Congressional mandate in the FAA Reauthorization Act of 2018. The road map too has a unique provision that tasks FAA to consider incorporating lessons and related findings in successive periodicals to include further refined goals, metrics, and target dates to address the ever-changing UAS technological landscape.[78]

After 2007, the FAA published various notices such as the 'inspection and maintenance programme requirements for airworthiness certification of unmanned aircraft operating under 55 pounds,[79] aviation-related videos or other electronic media on the internet;[80] and sporting event temporary flight restrictions'.[81] Other notices are on 'education, compliance and enforcement of unauthorized UAS operators,[82] at least seven orders,[83] two additional advisory circulars,[84] three guidance documents[85] four legal interpretations[86] and one special rules on interpretation.'[87]

4.4.3 Partnerships by ICAO

Under Section 567 of the FAA Reauthorization Act of 2018, the Administrator of the Federal Aviation Administration is mandated to enter into partnerships on regulation of civil aviation with regard to Nextgen technologies. FAA recognizes its partnership with ICAO. In particular, FAA is an active participant of the ICAO Dangerous Goods Panel meetings. It also participates in the revision and updating of the Technical Instructions for the Safe Transport of Dangerous Goods. The latter expressly admits that FAA is a pivotal partner in the area of regulation of civil aviation.[88] It trains small and middle-sized enterprises, and makes contribution towards the success of the ICAO's Safety Oversight System Project. It also contributes towards the success of the ICAO's programme for regional technical

---

[78] Integration of Civil UAS in the NAS Roadmap, Section 2.2.1.

[79] http://www.faa.gov Notice/N_8900.291.pdf (accessed 3 July 2023).

[80] http://www.faa.gov Notice/N_8900.291.pdf (accessed 3 July 2023).

[81] US Department of Transport "Federal Aviation Administration FDC. NOTAM 4/3621, Sporting Event Temp. Flight Restriction" https://www.faa.gov/uas/regulations (Date of use: 2 July 2023).

[82] http://www.faa.gov (Date of use: 4 July 2023).

[83] http://www.faa.gov (Date of use: 4 July 2023).

[84] US Department of Transport "Identification and Registration Marking" http://www.Faa.gov (Date of use: 2 July August).

[85] https://www.FAA.gov/uas/regulations policies (Date of use: 2 July 2023).

[86] https://www.FAA.gov/ (Date of use: 2 July 2023).

[87] https://www.FAA.gov/uas (Date of use: 2 July 2023).

[88] https://www.icao.int/safety/RunwaySafety/GRSS2011/Pages/PartnersandSupporters.aspx (Date of use: 15 August 2023).

cooperation, called the Multi-regional Civil Aviation Assistance Program.[89] The partnership, among others, supports the collaborative approach that the FAA takes towards its integration efforts in respect of the UAS into the national aviation system.[90]

4.5 US' Domestic Response to Safety, Security and Privacy Concerns of UAS

This sections explores the substantive issues and responses to challenges experienced in operation of UAS, namely: safety, security and privacy as were identified in Chap. 2 of this book.

4.5.1 The US Response to Safety Concerns of UAS

As seen in Chap. 2 of this book, aviation safety is one of the challenges to integration of UAS into civil aviation. The US recognizes that safety issues in the use of UAS abound. Statistics by the US Accountability Office indicate that since 2014, over 6000 cases of unsafe use of UAS have been recorded.[91] It is against this backdrop that the US leverages on its active participation in and membership of ICAO to ensure compliance with safety requirements under the Chicago Convention and ICAO Annex 19.[92]

The following section details how the US legal framework responds to these live safety challenges associated with the operation of UAS. The principal framework is provided under the FAA Modernization and Reform Act and the US Code of Federal Regulation. The framework is complemented by the FAA Advisory Circulars. The application of the framework to the UAS was affirmed by court in *Philadelphia Indemnity Insurance Co v Hollycal Production Inc et al*[93] where the Supreme Court noted the fact that a drone is unmanned does not make it less of an aircraft that is

[89] https://www.icao.int/WACAF/Documents/APIRG/APIRG%2022/WPs%20-%20FINAL%20ENG/WP%2051%20-%20%20U.S%20UAS%20Integration%20Update%20-%20FAA.pdf (Date of use: 15 August 2023).

[90] ICAO "Update on US. Unmanned aircraft systems integration activities" (Paper presented to the Twenty-Second Meeting of the AFI Planning and Implementation Regional Group 29 July-2 August 2019 Accra) 3.

[91] US Government Accountability Office "Unmanned Aircraft Systems" https://www.gao.gov/key_issues/unmanned_aerial_systems/issue_summary (Date of use: 9 August 2023).

[92] See Chap. 3, Sect. 3.4.1 on exposition of the specific safety requirements.

[93] *Philadelphia Indemnity Insurance Co v Hollycal Production Inc et al* 18-768 SA (2018) 7 (SC) [4].

subject of regulation.[94] The import of this judgment for the purpose of safety is that safety precaution applicable to manned aircraft should be applicable to UAS as well.

Section 181 of the FAA Reauthorization Act is instructive of general safety considerations regarding the integration of UAS into the national civil aviation airspace of the US. The section provides as follows:

> The Administrator of the Federal Aviation Administration shall exercise leadership in the creation of Federal and international policies, regulations, and standards relating to the certification and safe and efficient operation of civil supersonic aircraft.[95]

The import of this rule is that the general safety consideration must be made in a prospective manner considering the level of development in technology regarding the use and operation of UAS at any given time. Part 5 of the Code of Federal Regulations is more elaborate on how the safety goals can be achieved. The Code creates mandatory obligations for development of safety management system as being prerequisite for grant of operator certificates. Part 5.51 provides in this regard as follows:

> A certificate holder must apply safety risk management to the following: (a) Implementation of new systems. (b) Revision of existing systems. (c) Development of operational procedures. (d) Identification of hazards or ineffective risk controls through the safety assurance processes in subpart D of this part.

The formulation of rule 5.51 is couched in mandatory terms. The avenue for the use of the system is expansive and futuristic since it is not allowed for revision in event of change in circumstances. Further, the FAA has made strides, through rule-making, to further this general assurance of aviation safety in the area of the mandates of the service providers. It has done so through issuance of Advisory Circulars. These Advisory Circulars generally provide guidance materials but are not strictly binding on the public.[96] For the purposes of standardization and complementariness of the principal statute, it is a compelling communication of the best practices of operations.[97]

According to FAA Advisory Circular on Safety Management Systems (SMS) for Aviation Service Providers,[98] air carriers are obligated to apply SMS founded on

---

[94] *Philadelphia Indemnity Insurance Co v Hollycal Production Inc et al* 18-768 SA (2018) 7 (SC) [4].

[95] FAA Reauthorization Act 2018, Section 181.

[96] https://www.faa.gov/regulations_policies/advisory_circulars/index.cfm/go/document.information/documentID/74299 (Date of use: 22 July 2023). See paragraph 3 on explanation of AC systems.

[97] https://www.thebalancecareers.com/what-s-an-advisory-circular-and-why-should-youcare282774#:~:text=Advisory%20circulars%20can%20be%20directional,Standardization%20is%20one%20common%20reason (Date of use: 22 July 2023).

[98] FAA Advisory Circular on Safety Management Systems for Aviation Service Providers No. 120-92B.

Part 5 of the Code of Federal Regulations.[99] This Advisory Circular offers an account of governing requirements, guidance, and approaches of developing and executing Safety Management Systems. Chapter 3 of the Circular provides the minimum contents of the management systems to conclude regulatory requirements, summary of process, setting out of safety objectives and scalability. Part 3.3 mandates the service providers to develop a safety policy that provides, for among others, accountability and authority responsible for safety risks. Under this part, FAA requires aviation organizations to adopt policies that reflect the safety culture, open reporting, vigilance, information sharing and risk reduction. Also relevant are the requirements under Part 3.4 of the Circular, which impose an obligation on service providers to develop a system for safety risk management including the maintenance of the risk register to be used in monitoring aviation safety risks.

The passage of the Advisory Circular reflects the adoption of safety risk management, assurance goals and domestication of international guidance material developed by ICAO as set out in Chapter 2 of ICAO Circular No. 328-AN/190. The safety provisions are elaborate and easy to understand. They take a step by step approach to highlight the would-be contents of a safety policy in a more robust manner than is provided for in Section 2.19 of the ICAO Circular No. 328-AN/190.

The framework in the Circular recognizes that the recreational UAS can enjoy statutory exemption from the safety management systems, a requirement that could pose safety challenges. In this respect, the FAA Advisory Circular on Model Aircraft Operation[100] that was cancelled in 2015 represented FAA's efforts to adopt provisions of ICAO Circular No. 328-AN/190. This Circular, which is discussed in Chap. 3 of this book, addresses safety concerns through regulation of operations, personnel licencing, provision of rules of the air, certification and surveillance, among others.[101] The FAA Advisory Circular, now amended and replaced with Advisory Circular on Exemption for Limited Recreational Operations for Unmanned Aircraft,[102] offers a non-binding guidance to operators of UAS used for recreational purposes. The Circular pronounces its aim of ensuring safety of operators by offering them interim safety guidance.[103] Paragraph 7(1) of the Circular states in part that:

> FAA assumes owners and operators of unmanned aircraft are generally concerned about safety and willing to exercise good judgment when flying their aircraft. However, basic aeronautical knowledge and awareness of responsibilities in shared airspace are not common knowledge.

---

[99] The circular (AC) offers material for title 14 of the Code of Federal Regulations (14 CFR) part 121 carriers.

[100] FAA Advisory Circular on Model Aircraft Operating 91-57.

[101] See Chap. 3, Sect. 3.4.1 of this book.

[102] The FAA Advisory Circular now amended and replaced with Advisory Circular on Exemption for Limited Recreational Operations for Unmanned Aircraft No. 91-57B of 2019 (hereinafter referred to as the AC 91-57B).

[103] The AC 91-57B, Section 1 and The Code of Federal Regulations, Title 49, s 44809.

The import of the regulation is to recognize that even the recreational flyers of UAS must be conscious of the safety concerns arising from their operation. The guidance further includes the need to fly strictly for recreation, following safety guidelines, keeping UAS in line of sight, providing a way to manned aircraft and avoiding controlled airspace.[104] The Circular supports ICAO's initiatives and the US legal framework as described in Section 44809 of Title 14 to the Code of Federal Regulation providing exception for limited recreational operations of UAS.

The model UAS flyers and recreational flyers subject to the FAA Advisory Circular on Exemption for Limited Recreational Operations for Unmanned Aircraft[105] are subject to a complementary regulatory framework created under the Safety Code.[106] The Safety Code as established by the Academy of Model Aeronautics is relevant with regard to setting up of actual safety standards that must be met for flyers who are members of the Academy.[107] The first paragraph of the Code is an affirmation by members not to 'fly a model aircraft in a careless or reckless manner.' Also, an operator of a small UAS is required to maintain and inspect it before each flight to guarantee safety of the operation.[108]

The FAA Advisory Circular on Aviation Safety Action Programme[109] also establishes rules for reporting of safety information by employees. The rules are applicable to UAS regulation just like for manned aircraft, repairers and controlling pilots or persons who launch them. These categories of persons, including operators of chase aircraft, are well placed to undertake the reporting obligation. The information obtained is an integral part of the risk and safety management, as well as a preventive measure against accidents as envisaged by Chapter 2 of the ICAO Circular No. 328-AN/190. While the Circular anticipates a high rate of compliance as the programme is voluntary between carriers and UAS operators, the voluntariness could also pose be challenging should carriers opt not to negotiate or agree on it. As a result, there is bound to be an increase in UAS that are launched from any place and in the event of investigations, the tasks provided under Section 6(4) of the Circular could overstretch FAA.

Other safety standards relate to the visual line of sight requirements. As was provided under section 333(b) of the FAA Modernization and Reform Act, 2012 that made provisions for rules governing UAS sets, among others, the following as a parameter for assessment of UAS:

[104] Advisory Circular 91-57B, Section 7.1.3. See also FAA AC 91-57B, Sections 7.1.4–7.1.8.

[105] FAA Advisory Circular on Exemption for Limited Recreational Operations for Unmanned Aircraft No. 91-57B of 2019.

[106] The Academy of Model Aeronautics Safety Code of 2018.

[107] Academy of Model Aeronautics (AMA) is a nationwide organization representing model aircraft enthusiasts with its headquarters in Muncie and that was established in 1936.

[108] The Code of Federal Regulation, Title 14, Section 107.15 (a) & (b).

[109] FAA Advisory Circular on Aviation Safety Action Programme (ASAP) No. 120-66B. It replaced ASAP AC NO. 120-66 and 120-66A.

> . . .operation within visual line of sight do not create a hazard to users of the national airspace system or the public or pose a threat to national security.

The provision of the Act, however, had a *lacuna* for its non-definition of the visual line of sight. Part 107.31 of the US Code of Federal Regulations fills this *lacuna* by recognizing and defining a visual line of sight as capability of vision that is unaided by any device other than corrective lenses, the remote pilot in command, the visual observer (if one is used); the person manipulating the small unmanned aircraft system must be able to see the unmanned aircraft all through the flight.

With regard to the model UAS, the Safety Code of 2018 as established by the Academy of Model Aeronautics makes provision for model aircraft to operate within the line of sight of the operator as already indicated above under the previous 2012 act. Associated requirements are operation five miles away from the airport, remaining clear of people or stadiums and 400 feet above the ground. The last parameter is repeated as a requirement for model aircraft available in Section 349 of the FAA Reauthorization Act, 2012. The members of the Academy of Model Aeronautics expressly and in personal terms affirm in the Code that:

> I will not operate any model aircraft while I am under the influence of alcohol or any drug that could adversely affect my ability to safely control the model.[110]

All these safety conditions aim at achieving safety and are in tandem with Part 2.21 of the UAS Circular No. 328 by ICAO, which requires safety rule-making, policy development and oversight. While the requirement for non-operation 400 feet above the sea level appears justified for safety reasons, it is deemed insufficient as it does not address the issue of visibility. Regarding the same, the FAA Advisory Circular on Surface Movement Guidance and Control System only addresses safety issues at airports and is, therefore, inapplicable to UAS. It means that the need to maintain a visual line of sight, though well intentioned, may continue to inhibit full integration efforts since the technologies may be a recipe for segregation.[111] For the requirement of visual line of sight by FAA Reauthorization Act to be met, an accompanying "chase" aircraft must maintain visual contact with the UAS. Though this is a plausible idea, it does not seem to make practical sense given that UAS can be launched from anywhere and not strictly at designated airports as is the case with manned aircraft.

The other standards relate to the sense and avoid technology. An analysis of the international framework on the provision of sense and avoid facilities in paragraph 5.2 of the ICAO Circular No. 328-AN/190 shows that sense and avoid is not limited to other aircraft. The rules envisage collision avoidance from other things and hazards. Fulfilling the requirement for UAS against other hazards including bird

[110]The Academy of Model Aeronautics Safety Code of 2018, Paragraph 3.

[111]ICAO Circular No 328328-AN/190, Paragraph 3.15.

strikes or attacks by eagles on hunting missions might be an uphill task given the deficiency in the regulatory framework and systems capability.[112]

The provisions of Section 349 of the FAA Reauthorization Act, 2018 are instructive. They require model aircraft to fly safely and ensure no interference with manned aircraft. Subsection 349(4) and (5) of the Act provides the following as parameters for recognition and regulation of model aircraft:

> the aircraft is operated in a manner that does not interfere with and gives way to any manned aircraft; and (5) when flown within 5 miles of an airport, the operator of the aircraft provides the airport operator and the airport air traffic control tower (when an air traffic facility is located at the airport) with prior notice of the operation (model aircraft operators flying from a permanent location within 5 miles of an airport should establish a mutually-agreed upon operating procedure with the airport operator and the airport air traffic control tower (when an air traffic facility is located at the airport.

The Safety Code established by the Academy of Model Aeronautics is also relevant in its requirement that all Academy of Model Aeronautics must 'not interfere with and will yield the right of way to all human-carrying aircraft using AMA's See and Avoid Guidance and a spotter when appropriate'. Since failure to give way to manned aircraft is actionable under the FAA Modernization and Reform Act, the salient provisions set out above are authoritative representation of the requirements by ICAO Circular No 328-AN/190. These requirements resonate with the spirit of paragraphs 2.9 and 2.15 of the ICAO Circular No 328-AN/190 that calls for development of regulatory framework that require UAS to have systems and facilities that ensure detection and avoidance of collisions.

Certification of small UAS weighing below 55 pounds: a proprietor is allowed to apply for a Certificate of Waiver, which allows the UAS to deviate from certain operating rules if the FAA is satisfied that the proposed operation is permissible under the rule. The exclusion of small UAS regarding the model aircraft, however, obviously seems to be limiting on mandate of FAA, at least from the plain reading of the Act. This resonates with the FAA's argument that if the exclusion clause were broadly applied, it would diminish or limit its statutory mandate of ensuring safety and security in the aviation sector. However, when looked at in the bigger picture, model operators are excluded from the reach of FAA to the extent that they remain within narrow limits of hobby users, the careless and reckless ones would pose grave danger to all airspace users, as well as those on the ground.[113] The exclusion of the small UAS, therefore, is justified.

There is a real technological challenge as consensus is yet to be reached by the FAA on standards of technology to enable UAS to detect and avoid other aircraft and

[112]The rationale is that the framework on recognition of hazards that are contained in Advisory Circulars on Hazardous Mountain Winds and Their Visual Indicators, Generic Glideslope Indicators, Maintenance of Airport Visual Facilities, Visual Flight Rules and Runway Visual Range all target manned aircrafts and not UAS.

[113]FAA Interpretation of the Special Rule for Model Aircraft Federal Register of 2014.

maintain a link between airports and the UAS.[114] Also, though UAS pilots require constant link to ground aircraft control crew, the UAS in the US lack technology to prevent 'lost link.' As a result, disruptions created between the ground operator and the UAS are serious safety concerns. Not even the learned judges in the case laws referred to in this book Chapter were able to agree on matters regarding UAS' emerging technologies, which need to be accepted and addressed as globalization takes centre stage.[115]

Another notable regulatory issue with safety underpinnings is airworthiness in civil aviation. An aircraft is said to be airworthy only when its conditioning and design support safe operation. The challenges in this area as appertains to UAS have all to do with design, which often compromises efficiency of safety regulation during operation. Consequently, ICAO developed ICAO Annex 8 on Airworthiness of Aircraft that, among others, requires maintenance of safety and survival equipment to support the system software.

Airworthiness issues are dealt with under Sections 348 of the FAA Reauthorization Act. The regulatory framework under this principal legislation is complemented by the Circular on Propeller Instructions for Continued Airworthiness, and Circular on Instruction for Continued Airworthiness Academy of Model Aeronautics' Safety Code.

The FAA Reauthorization Act makes provision for regulation of design and production of aircraft through a certification system provided in Section 242. The certification under the authority of the Administrator targets to certify compliance with minimum requirements for aircraft, aircraft engines, propellers, and appliances with the requirements and minimum standards prescribed in Section 44701(a) of the FAA Act.

The FAA Act is also committal on providing further design specifications for the model aircraft. As per Section 333(3) of the Act, a model aircraft is limited to not more than 55 pounds unless otherwise certified through a design, construction, inspection, flight test, and operational safety programme administered by a community-based organization. Model aircraft flying within the provisions of the FAA Act are complemented by Safety Code, 2018 as established by the Academy of Model Aeronautics. There is further commitment to 'only fly models weighing more than 55 pounds, including fuel, if certified through AMA's Large Model Airplane Program.'[116]

The FAA Circular on Propeller Instructions for Continued Airworthiness[117] provides that any operation within controlled airspace would require permission of an

[114] US Department of Transportation https://www.oig.dot.gov/sites/default/files/FAA%20Oversight%20of%20Unmanned%20Aircraft%20Systems%5E6-26-14.pdf (Date of use: 2 August 2023).

[115] See divergence of opinion of judges in *Dow Chemicals v the United States* 1986 476 US 227 (SC).

[116] The Academy of Model Aeronautics Safety Code of 2018, Paragraph 7.

[117] FAA Advisory Circular on Propeller Instructions for Continued Airworthiness No 35.4-1 (hereinafter referred to as the FAA AC No. 33.4-1). In addition, Civil UAS are currently

air traffic controller. But due to lack of training, air traffic controllers lack the tools that allow them to safely manage the airspace, just as they do with manned aircraft. This has potential negative consequences as air traffic controllers are forced to segregate UAS from manned aircraft for lack of sufficient information particularly on speed, capacity and rates of climb on the UAS.[118] The situation may be worsened by the fact that air traffic controllers lack training on how to address this lost link.[119]

Part 5 of the Circular on Instruction for Continued Airworthiness[120] provides for the general provision that requires holders of approvals for aircraft designs to furnish their instructions on continued airworthiness to the aircraft owner when it is delivered or when the certificate of airworthiness is issued. The import of this obligation is to ensure that airworthiness is not only ensured through design approvals at manufacture and design stages, but also continued during the subsequent period of use by aircraft operators.

In addition, the Circular[121] limits the applicants' discretion for the certification processes. It creates a layer of approval of the certification programmes by the FAA in respect of the applications for design approvals and type certification. FAA issues special airworthiness certificates to community operators on a case-by-case basis for experimental or certain restricted categories. These are issued to UAS manufacturers and researchers. The basis of this issuance is to enable research and development, flight-testing, crew training, market surveys, product demonstration as well as other commercial applications under the purview of Section 333 exemptions.

Other than certification requirements, the US also utilizes the licensing and authorization mechanism as a means for enforcement of safety of UAS. Part 11 of Title 14 of the Code of Federal Regulations and FAA Reauthorization Act provides for authorization and certification of flying. Under these provisions, the FAA authorizes non-hobby or recreational UAS operations.[122] In the US, UAS flights

---

accommodated with experimental certificates under FAA Order on Airworthiness and Certification of Unmanned Aircraft Systems and Optionally Piloted Aircraft No 8130.34D.

[118] FAA Order on Unmanned Aircraft Operations in the National Airspace System (NAS) No N JO 7210.846.

[119] The Air Traffic Safety Action Program is a voluntary safety reporting program for air traffic personnel that enable them to report air traffic safety events and retain confidentiality.

[120] FAA AC No. 33.4-1. Also see The US Code of Federal Regulations, Title 14 on Airworthiness standards for existing aircraft are codified with processes described for FAA type certification in FAA Order 8110.4 and airworthiness certification in FAA Order 8130.2. The FAA has the authority and regulations in place to tailor the design standards to specific UAS applications, and plans to use this authority until further experience is obtained in addressing the design issues that are unique to UAS. Generally, the FAA cannot issue an exemption from specific statutory mandates such as requiring airworthiness certificates. The statutory provision in 49 U.S.C. 44807, sets aside that prohibition. This allows the FAA to grant relief to a petitioner from the requirement to hold an airworthiness certificate for the UAS when certain criteria are met.

[121] FAA AC No. 33.4-1.

[122] FAA Advisory Circular on Certification process for Agricultural Aircraft Operators Document Information No 137-1B (hereinafter referred to as the FAA AC 137-1B), Section 1.9 exemption to The US Federal Code of Federal Regulations, Title 14, Part 137.

are supposed to be operated by authorized aircraft (certified or exempted), validly registered, with a certified pilot, in addition to FAA authorization (Certificate of Waiver or Authorization).[123] These terms are envisaged by Article 8 of the Chicago Convention to be within the jurisdiction of the sovereign. The first category of operators of UAS comprise the Government and public bodies.[124] The FAA allows such operators to be granted authority to operate aircraft as long as a Certificate of Authorization is issued to them.[125]

Under the provisions of Section 341 of the FAA Reauthorization Act, operations by petition are guaranteed upon satisfaction by FAA that the flight will be safe,[126] including weighing less than 55 pounds, flying below 200 feet above the ground, and straying clear of airports, in compliance with the Certificate of Authorization. Other commercial UAS operating under the proposed rules are allowed to fly if they operate between sunrise and sunset, when visibility is clear or within 3 miles.[127] Under the proposals, UAS are allowed to fly below 500 feet above the ground at a maximum speed of 100 km per hour.

Public aviation operators are required to be licensed pilots. Those who make applications for public UAS are taken through a process of review to ensure the intended operations are in the interest of the public, they are safe, and do not endanger the safety of other traffic or persons on the ground. Issuance of a Certificate of Authorization is limited to 60 business days. Though Article 3 of the Chicago Convention limits its operation to State aircraft, the functional definition appears to be pegged on ownership and not use. This approach enables the regulation of public UAS operators even in cases where public operators lease them from private individuals.

The framework adopts slightly different rules regarding authorization of commercial UAS,[128] where individuals are issued with a short-term certificate placed under experimental category in Title 14 of the Code of Federal Regulations.[129] Under these provisions, it is the experimental category requirements that tick the safety issues. This category is important because one of the key parameters for passing it is safety before the individuals can obtain a Special Authorization Certificate to operate the second category. It also appears to be the difference with the UAS public operator's authorization that only requires pilots to be licenced without imputing the categories. The difference is underlined by a presumption that safety issues are more prevalent in civil and commercial uses as opposed to public uses. Though the presumption is debatable, it is worth noting that the experimental

[123] Carr (2014), p. 29.
[124] Carr (2014), p. 30.
[125] Carr (2014), p. 29.
[126] US Department of Transportation http://www.transportation.gov (Date of use: 30 July2023).
[127] US Department of Transportation http://www.transportation.gov (Date of use: 30 July2023).
[128] US Department of Transportation http://www.transportation.gov (Date of use: 30 July 2023).
[129] The US Code of Federal Regulations, Title 14, s 21.175(b).

airworthiness certificate means that the UAS should not be used to carry passengers, cargo, or even for hire, according to FAA Order 8130.34B.

Under these provisions, the regulations governing commercial authorization of UAS fall into three categories, namely: those solely operated for recreational purposes; small UAS weighing less than 55 pounds and used for purposes other than recreation; and UAS weighing over 55 pounds, and which require an exemption under Section 333 of the FAA Modernization and Reform Act. The authorization draws from the provisions of Article 8 of the Chicago Convention, which places the special authorization mandate on sovereign States.

The framework adopts unique rules for authorization of model aircraft for purely recreational or hobby utilities.[130] Though these aircraft essentially do not require FAA authorization, they must comply with strict rules pursuant to FAA Advisory Circular 91-57. They are required to operate in a manner that is safe and within the confines of the law as stipulated in Section 336 of the FAA Modernization and Reform Act. The provision also requires the model UAS to be capable of being sustained in the atmosphere and to ensure that they are strictly flown for hobby or recreational purposes in accordance with society safety rules, and in compliance with giving way to manned aircraft.

The framework for regulation under the FAA Reauthorization Act, 2018 is complemented by FAA Advisory Circular on Reporting Laser Illumination of Aircraft, FAA Orders[131] that makes provisions for prohibition of directing a laser pointer at an aircraft by unauthorized individuals. The FAA Advisory Circular on Reporting Laser Illumination of Aircraft requires reporting of incidents of unauthorized illumination with details of colour, altitude, among others. The crew are also required to mitigate the incidents through reporting, filling FAA Laser Beam Exposure Questionnaire and deviating from flight paths with prior clearance. The framework is also the basis of initiatives to ensure both safety and security of aircraft.

The framework for regulation of safety is further boosted by the provisions of Community-based Guidelines on Safety of Operations and Safety Code published by the Academy of Model Aeronautics. The Code stipulates guidelines on safety in flights including those of UAS.[132] The FAA appears cognizant of the non-binding nature of the guidelines, and as such uses them as a basis for collaboration with some community-based organizations for recreational purposes and recognizes them as having the force of law within that domain, purpose and area.[133] The guidelines

[130] Carr (2014), p. 17.

[131] FAA Order on Air Traffic Control No JO 7110.65 and FAA Order on Facility operation and Administration No JO 7210.3.

[132] FAA Advisory Circular on Exemption for Limited Recreational Operations of Unmanned Aircrafts No 91-57B, Section 7 (2) and (3).

[133] FAA Advisory Circular on Exemption for Limited Recreational Operations of Unmanned Aircrafts No 91-57B, Section 1. It provides that "purpose of this advisory circular (AC) provides interim safety guidance to individuals operating unmanned aircraft, for recreational purposes under the statutory exception for limited recreational operations of unmanned aircraft (Title 49 of the United States Code (49 U.S.C.) s 44809). The Circular restates the statutory conditions to operate

enable development of rules at the community level for model UAS owners weighing less than 55 pounds to support the FAA framework.[134] Larger or heavier UAS are also covered so long as their design, construction, inspection, flight-testing and operational safety programs are administered under the rubric of community-based organizations.[135]

The guidelines play an important role in creating the distinction between aircraft models based on use and capability. It shouldn't be lost that the distinguishing feature of a model aircraft is not its size, but use and capabilities. The Safety Code, published by the Academy of Model Aeronautics, bolsters the effectiveness of public and community involvement through community-based organisations. The Code requires creation of awareness, education and participation of the public in safety matters as a means of addressing the safety challenges associated with UAS operation.

From the foregoing discussion, it suffices to conclude that FAA has made legislative steps towards an effective and express regulatory framework and standardization for safe operation in areas of certification, standards of air traffic procedures for safe management of UAS with manned aircraft, and air traffic control-training programme for UAS. Despite these achievements, authors such as Jiang *et al* observe that the one challenge that stands out in respect of all the promising efforts is the fact that the format of reporting to UAS regional inspectors on authorization and overseeing operations is not clear.[136] Hence, FAA's effectiveness in managing oversight is wanting and unless it addresses such hurdles, integration of UAS into civil aviation will continue to be slow and marked with low safety standards.[137]

4.5.2 The US Response to Security Concerns of UAS

The security challenges of UAS at the international plane are regarded to arise from their possible use in activities that cause unlawful interference, including spying and attacks to aviation infrastructure that threaten the territorial integrity and sovereignty of another State.[138] While the challenge is real owing to development in UAS

under the exception and provides additional guidance on adhering to those conditions. Per 49 U.S.C. s 44809, recreational flyers may only operate under the statutory exception if they adhere to all of the conditions listed in the statute.

[134] FAA Advisory Circular on Exemption for Limited Recreational Operations of Unmanned Aircrafts No 91-57B, Section 7.1.1, 7.1.2 and 7.1.2.1.

[135] FAA Advisory Circular on Exemption for Limited Recreational Operations of Unmanned Aircrafts No 91-57B, Section 7.1.1, 7.1.2 and 7.1.2.1.

[136] Jiang et al. (2016), pp. 123–135.

[137] https://www.oig.dot.gov/sites/default/files/FAA%20Oversight%20of%20Unmanned%20Aircraft%20Systems%5E6-26-14.pdf (Date of use: 2 August 2023).

[138] See Chapter 2, Part 7.2 of this book for more exposition.

technology and uses, the traditional means of achieving security in aviation through arming of pilots, use of sniffer dogs, data management and storage are largely inapplicable to most UAS. This explains why the analysis in Chap. 2 of this book rationalizes the need for UAS specific security measures and regulations.[139]

It was against the backdrop of such challenges that the Chicago Convention made robust albeit general provisions to ensure aviation security. In recognition of its dynamism, the Convention donated powers to the ICAO to develop standards relating to security, which ICAO did through promulgation of the general standards through ICAO Annex 17 and Aviation Security Manual Doc (8973). Additionally, ICAO No. 328328-AN/190 makes specific provision on security applications and surveillance of UAS.

This section explores how the US domestic framework responds to these security challenges. The US regulatory framework requires UAS to comply with general security requirements prescribed by the FAA.[140] The framework is provided under Title 49 of the US Code of Federal Regulations, FAA Modernization and Reform Act as complemented by the FAA Advisory Circulars, Orders and Guidance Materials.

Under Title 49 of the US Code, FAA has the overall responsibility of protecting aircraft in the airspace. Section 40103(a) of the Code states that the US has the exclusive sovereignty of its territorial airspace.

The provision affirms the spirit of Article 1 of the Chicago Convention, and is the basis for control and exclusion of UAS activities that can cause unlawful interference. To assure UAS security surveillance by FAA officers, Section 40108 of the Code provides for the power of the FAA Administrator to operate schools for training officers and staff.[141]

The FAA Reauthorization Act provides security as key to regulation of UAS. Within the context of UAS operations, security concerns encompass a wide range of potential risks, including unauthorized access, interference with critical infrastructure, potential use in malicious activities, and threats to national security. The act recognizes that as UAS technology becomes more accessible and capable, there is an increasing need to ensure that UAS operations are conducted in a manner that does not compromise safety or security. The act recognizes that in making an assessment, the Secretary of Transportation must consider if the UAS poses a threat to national security. Section 333 of the same act goes further to list the factors that form the basis for assessment such as operation's capability, and proximity to airports or populated areas. It is only after the UAS is adjudged not to pose national threat that certificate of operation can be issued, unless otherwise excluded from the process of application for reasons of statutory waiver or recreational nature of the operation. As seen earlier in this section, the framework of the FAA Modernization and Reform Act on

---

[139] See Chapter 2, Part 7.2 of this book.

[140] Carr (2014), p. 20.

[141] The US Code of Federal Regulations, Title 409, Section 40108(a).

certification and authorization on safety is crosscutting and aids in planning and design of aviation security.

The FAA Modernization and Reform Act, 2012 recognizes the role played by the United States Department of Homeland Security, a move that boosts support to deal with evolving security measures occasioned by rise in international terrorism. The Department comes in handy by providing screening of devices and enforcement of security protocols.[142] It has put in place heightened surveillance to ensure creation of a baseline for aviation security.

The FAA Advisory Circular on Foreign Air Carrier Security, 1982 complements the framework under the FAA Modernization and Reform Act, 2012. The Circular stipulates conditions to be met by foreign carriers in the US.[143] The provisions require submission of Security Program that apply to operations of aircraft. The Circular also prohibits dangerous and deadly weapons aboard aircraft. Part 6 of the Circular provides as follows:

> Although foreign air carriers are not required to submit their security programs, the Administrator for approval, each such carrier is required to submit, upon his request and in accordance with applicable law, information in with respect to the security program applicable to its operations and the implementation thereof...[144]

Although the provision does not make it necessary for submission of a security programme, the Administrator may require that it be provided whenever he imputes an obligation of the carriers to maintain the programmes. Further, as the scope is such that the requirement applies to all foreign carriers with requisite permit, no distinction is made between State or civil, manned or unmanned aircraft. The provision on screening majorly applies to manned aircraft for the reason that they land at designated airports where passengers, cargo and baggage are screened at the terminals. This is unlike UAS, which land in remote places with no screening facilities unless they are scheduled to specifically land at airports.[145] UAS Circular's requirements act as response mechanism for bomb and piracy threats arising from aircraft through security inspections, countermeasures such as bomb disposal facilities, sniffer dogs, expert search are challenging and not easily available in all places where UAS operate, launched or land.

The FAA Guidance on Recommended Trainings and Advisory Circular on Foreign Air Carrier Security complements the FAA Advisory Circular on Foreign Air Carrier Security.[146] This Guidance material addresses the security concerns by stipulating the requirement of training for members of the crew who operate aircraft

---

[142] Homeland Security "Remarks for the Council for New American Security" https://www.dhs.gov/news/2017/06/28/remarks-council-new-american-security-conference (Date of use: 6 August 2023).

[143] FAA Advisory Circular on Foreign Air Carrier Security No.129-3.

[144] FAA Advisory Circular on Foreign Air Carrier Security No.129-3, Part 6.

[145] FAA Advisory Circular on Foreign Air Carrier Security No 129-3, Section 8 on screening of passengers and property.

[146] FAA Advisory Circular on Foreign Air Carrier Security No 129-3, Section 8.

in areas such as anti-hijack. The FAA Guide further harnesses the training requirement for private flyers.[147] The integration of the trainings is achieved through the Circular on Pilots Schools, Certification and Compliance. The Act requires maintenance of training records of students, and harmonization of the syllabus. Since training is a preventative approach to security threats, the Guidance material serves to complement the basic security knowledge imparted in schools. The uniformity in training is laudable for it makes compliance with security regulations much easier.[148]

The FAA passed the Small UAS Regulations, 2016 under which certified operators of small UAS are required to undergo refresher courses that entail passing recurrent knowledge exams after every 24 months.[149] Operators with visible physical and mental handicap likely to affect safety or security are not allowed to operate UAS, although a medical certificate is not a mandatory requirement. Under the Regulations, should one choose to use operator or observers, they are restricted to flying or observing one UAS at a time.[150]

Security assurance is also enhanced through the development of the National Strategy for Aviation Security in December 2018 after revision of the 2007 version.[151] The Strategy provides development of, and the need to keep up with the UAS technologies as the key motivating factor for its development.[152] The material documents two main strategies: one, the protection of the vital United States National Interest, which covers the protection of the homeland, American people, American way of life as well as its prosperity. Two, the achievement of the desired End-State, which is a secure aviation ecosystem through proper coordination and integration planning.[153]

The assurance recognizes the need to protect US' global interest in aviation ecosystem by detecting deterrence and prevention of terrorist, criminal and hostile acts, whether by physical, spectrum or cyber means.[154] This means that the strategy guides stakeholders to combat acts of illegal interference. It seeks to maximize aviation ecosystem security and implement an efficient, balanced and safe movement of cargo and people. Other aims of the security assurance are to enhance resilience, mitigate damage and expedite recovery from attack on the aviation ecosystem; and to effectively engage sector partners to ensure there is active engagement by agencies, the private sector and international stakeholders in matters of safety and security.

It, therefore, needn't be overemphasised that the regulation of UAS through the frameworks for approval, security programmes and trainings plays a key role in

---

[147] FAA Advisory Circular on Federal Aviation Administration No 150/5000-16.

[148] The US Code of Federal Regulations, Title 61.

[149] The US Code of Federal Regulations, Title 14, Part 107.

[150] The US Code of Federal Regulations, Title 14, Part 107.

[151] The National Strategy for Aviation Security of 2018.

[152] The National Strategy for Aviation Security of 2018, Page 1.

[153] The National Strategy for Aviation Security, 2018, Page 2.

[154] The National Strategy for Aviation Security, 2018, Pages 7–10.

ensuring their security in the US. These arrangements are in tandem with ICAO Annex 17 and ICAO Guidance Security Manual by focusing on security mitigation. Despite US' robust systems, its response to aviation security has on occasion been stretched and found wanting, especially following terrorist attacks such as the 11 September 2001 incident. Ron identifies inability by institutions to develop machinery necessary to deal with new technological development in the aviation sector as the hallmark of such attacks.[155]

4.5.3 The US Response to Privacy Concerns of UAS

A key privacy challenge as regards UAS use is its potential to cause or be used as a tool of aerial photography, subsequently causing intrusion to privacy.[156] This arises from UAS' ability to overfly over people and private property. The international law response heavily depends on human discourse through enforcement of relevant State obligation to respect, protect and fulfil the rights under international instruments, among them the ICCPR.[157]

The US is no stranger to privacy concerns relating to UAS. Law enforcement agencies like the FBI spy on members of the public, and the process violate the right to protection from unreasonable search and seizures. Other concerns arise from potential and actual threats or breaches to the right to privacy of persons who are likely to be affected by such searches and seizures. Violation of privacy is also perpetrated by neighbours and civilians who capture videos or steal photos owing to increased use of UAS for civilian purposes in the US.

To avert the challenge, the US Constitution sets the stage for the general protection of privacy rights. The Fourth Amendment to the Constitution provides as follows:

> The right of the people to be secure in their persons, houses, papers, and effects, against unreasonable searches and seizures, shall not be violated, and no Warrants shall issue, but upon probable cause, supported by Oath or affirmation, and particularly describing the place to be searched, and the persons or things...

The import of the Constitutional provision is not only to recognize the right to privacy, but also to create the mandatory due processes to be followed before the right to privacy is limited through legal means and in deserving cases only. The provision also seeks to prohibit acts with the effect of interfering with the security of privacy.

Under Title 49 of the US Code of Regulations, the Secretary of Transportation has powers to make Regulations to prevent unwarranted invasion of personal

[155] Ron (2011), p. 1.

[156] See Chap. 2, Sect. 2.7.3 of this book for more exposition on this. Cavoukian (2012), p. 2.

[157] See Chap. 2, Sect. 2.7.

privacy during security operations by use of an aircraft.[158] Concerns for privacy were for long couched around regulation of passenger records obtained through means such as screening, with a view to protecting the passengers on board an aircraft. They, therefore, had little relevance to the privacy concerns of UAS use.

Privacy protection underpinnings are provided under the FAA Modernization Reform Act, 2012. Title III, Part B, which addresses the provisions on privacy protection, has no express provision on assurance against privacy invasion.[159] The rules may only be implied from a not so farfetched provision such as Section 336 of the FAA Modernization and Reform Act. Section 336(a) provides that:

> Notwithstanding any other provision of law relating to the incorporation of unmanned aircraft systems into Federal Aviation Administration plans and policies, including this subtitle, the Administrator of the Federal Aviation Administration may not promulgate any rule or regulation regarding a model aircraft, or an aircraft being developed as a model aircraft, if the aircraft is flown strictly for hobby or recreational use;

The requirement for strict adherence to purpose of flight can be interpreted to mean restriction to intrusive surveillance. Therefore, even if the application by implication were possible, it suffers the limitation of being applicable to model aircraft alone. The upshot of the foregoing is that the US principal framework under the law in Title 49 of the US Code as amended by the FAA Modernization and Reform Act, 2012 has not sufficiently addressed the challenge of privacy restrictions related to use of UAS. This challenge of inadequacy is akin to what is contained in the Chicago Convention, which only applies to privacy assurance in the most marginal form.

The Academy of Model Aeronautics Safety Code of 2018 attempts to cure the regulatory inadequacy set out above by providing guidance on how members of the Academy can ensure protection of the privacy of others during operation of model aircraft. Under Paragraph 4 of the Code, the members affirm to avoid flying directly over unprotected people, moving vehicles, and occupied structures. It goes on to state the following:

> I will not fly a powered model outdoors closer than 25 feet to any individual, except for myself or my helper(s) located at the flight line, unless I am taking off and landing, or as otherwise provided in AMA's Competition Regulation.[160]

Though the complementary regulation under the Safety Code, 2018 is express, it has no binding effect. It is a representation of the recognition of the need for regulation of UAS privacy concerns.

Lack of binding aviation-specific instruments at the federal level may be attributed to the existence of divided opinion among law enforcers and the public on extent of regulation of privacy.[161] This is elucidated by the sharp distinction in opinion and approaches by parties to a case in which the Electronic Privacy

[158] The US Code of Federal Regulations, Title 49, s 40119 (b)(A).

[159] Ison (2014), p. 24.

[160] The Academy of Model Aeronautics Safety Code of 2018, Paragraph 8.

[161] National Research Council (2007), p. 150.

Information Center filed a brief for *amicus* stating that intrusion of the privacy of iPhone users was necessary to prevent crime.[162] On its part, Apple contested the order by court stating that forming a software to access a locked iPhone was unlawful and unconstitutional, and would in itself be undermining the security of the people, and hence create a bad precedent for the American people.[163]

Some States in the US have taken measures to address uses of UAS with impact on privacy.[164] Georgia and Louisiana, for example, have laws that prohibit people from peeping into others' private activities or lives through windows or doors for purposes of spying upon or invading their privacy. The Official Code of Georgia[165] provides that a person violates privacy rules when they go about undertaking surveillance upon the premises of another.[166] The Code applies to regulation of UAS deployment in surveillance.

The State of Virginia has a statute that criminalizes creation of photos and video images of non-consenting persons with reasonable expectation of privacy.[167] Mississippi State also has a statute that criminalizes photographing, taping or filming a person against his or her expectation of privacy.[168] These laws are part of the framework for regulation of UAS use and operation. They spell express prohibition of acts that limit enjoyment of the right to privacy and set the standard that a person is worthy of protection if he has a reasonable expectation of privacy.

In the light of the constitutional protection, State-level laws are important as they entail unique directions taken by States in creating a delicate balance between protection of privacy and enhancement of security from crime and social violence. They also spell out the particularity of operations and exemptions. The challenge they pose is the possibility of multiplicity of laws and resultant potential for conflict that makes difficult the goal of harmonisation and integration of UAS into the national system.

With regard to the implementation of the existing legal framework, US federal and State courts have made remarkable judicial steps towards recognition of the protection of privacy rights. These steps are indicative of prospects of overcoming

---

[162]Electronic Privacy Information Center "Apple v. FBI" https://epic.org/amicus/crypto/apple/ (Date of use: 23 August 2023).

[163]Electronic Privacy Information Center https://epic.org/amicus/crypto/apple/ (Date of use: 23 August 2023).

[164]US Integration of Civil Unmanned Aircraft Systems in the National Airspace System Roadmap of 2013 is a guide outlining FAA's plans for integrating UAS into the NAS over a 5-year period.

[165]Official Code of Georgia of 2017, Section 16-11-60.

[166]Official Code of Georgia of 2017, Section 16-11-60.

[167]Virginia Criminal Law Statute, Section 6 where it is a cause of action for criminal trespass. This could be relevant if the perpetrator trespassed or installed technology in the victim's home or workplace that was tantamount to trespass in procuring images. See also The Code of Virginia § 18.2-386.1.

[168]Mississippi Criminal Code of 2013, Section 97-29-63. The Code makes provisions on photographing or filming another without permission where there is expectation of privacy; when victim is adult; when victim is a child under the age of 16 year.

the practical challenges arising from scanty federal provisions on privacy protection in respect of UAS in the US.

In the State of Georgia, the Court addressed itself to privacy concerns in the case of *Smith v State.*[169] In this case, the Court of Appeal of Georgia found Donald Smith guilty of being a peeping tom. Under the Georgian Code, a peeping tom was a person who invaded the privacy of others by peeping through a door or window. The facts of the case were that police officers were dispatched to an apartment complex in response to a suspicious call. They found Smith standing in a secluded dark patio some three feet from the window to an apartment, looking at two people he did not know. He was arrested and tried with compelling witness accounts of similar conduct in the past. The *Smith* case may have no direct link to UAS, but is relevant to violation of privacy by advanced technology of UAS. For if the use of the naked eyes by a peeping tom is tantamount to a breach of privacy, it follows that in the era of technological advancement, the UAS that has eyes from the sky should, due to the use of progressive technology, infringe on the right to privacy. Thus given the sophistication of today's UAS, it could as well be the peeping tom or the tool used by peeping toms. The principle is relevant regarding violation of people's privacy from a vantage point with aid of innovative equipment like the UAS.

At the federal level, the US Supreme Court has addressed specific concerns regarding the right to privacy.[170] From its decisions, an emerging trend has been laid out in determining whether UAS observations and impact on privacy are constitutional or not. Case law suggests that the court considers a number of factors in determining whether the use of a UAS raises constitutional questions. These include whether UAS is in manageable airspace; whether there is undue disturbance on the ground below in terms of noise or wind; whether imaging systems used on the UAS can be taken from inside the home; whether violation was excessive; and whether the plaintiff has reasonable expectation of privacy.[171]

4.5.3.1 *Dow Chemical, Ciraolo, and Riley 476 US 227, 229 (1986)*

Dow Chemical v the United States[172] concerned the action by the Environmental Protection Agency (EPA) to observe a chemical plant from the sky. When Dow Chemical denied EPA access to inspect the plant, the agency hired a commercial photographer to take pictures from above but within lawfully navigable airspace[173] as there was vegetation barrier on the ground. The surveillance took place within the concealment of structures until a chemical plant was eventually discovered.[174] When

[169] *Smith v State* 1999 238 US 605 (Ga. App) [2].

[170] Parker (2017), p. 84.

[171] *Smith v State* 1999 238 US 605 (Ga. App) [2].

[172] *Dow Chemicals v the United States* 1986 476 US 227 (SC).

[173] *Dow Chemicals v the United States* 1986 476 US 227 (SC).

[174] *Dow Chemicals v the United States* 1986 476 US 227 (SC) [239].

the matter went to court, the Supreme Court held that shooting photos above the ground of a developed vegetal convoluted from navigable airspace was not a search forbidden by the Fourth Amendment.[175]

The Supreme Court deliberated on the superiority of features exposed in the photos,[176] the technology used, and the area under survey. It recognised some hypothetical limits by stating that, "Surveillance of private property by using vastly sophisticated reconnaissance kit, not commonly obtainable to the public, such as satellite technology, might be constitutionally prohibited by absence of a warrant".[177]

In the verdict, majority opinion held the view that ordinary photography was not a Fourth Amendment search because it was not complemented by a physical trespass and the equipment used was not the most sophisticated form of technology available to the Government. This reasoning has been criticised for its capacity to abandon the Katz principles, which originated from the Supreme Court ruling in the case of *Katz v United States.*[178] The ruling redefined what constitutes search and seizure with regard to the protection of the Fourth Amendment of the US Constitution. The decision in the *Dow* case was premised on the technique of search rather than the latitude of the right being safeguarded. This formed the basis of Justice Powell's dissension, contending that its justification would lead to the wearing away of the right to privacy.[179] The authority in the dissension shows that use of physical trespass would not be mandatory when determining if objects, including UAS, have committed breach of privacy rights. That UAS utilize complex technology means the sophistication concept contained in the majority opinion is justification for regulation against privacy breaches.

4.5.3.2 *Electronic Privacy Information Centre (EPIC) v. FAA*

Electronic Privacy Information Centre (EPIC) v FAA[180] arose from FAA's rule promulgated under the FAA Modernization and Reform Act, in which Congress directed FAA to consider whether certain UAS could be safely integrated into the national airspace and to establish prerequisites for their safe operation. EPIC, who petitioned the FAA to create privacy safeguards prior to deployment of commercial UAS in the US in 2014, opposed the directive. In response, FAA argued that UAS privacy implications did not raise instant safety concerns. It continued to state that privacy concerns were part of the project contrary to EPIC's position on the matter.

[175] *Dow Chemicals v the United States* 1986 476 US 227 (SC) [239].

[176] *Dow Chemicals v the United States* 1986 476 US 227 (SC) [238]. The mere fact that human vision is enhanced does not give rise to constitutional problems.

[177] *Dow Chemicals v the United States* 1986 476 US 227 (SC) [238].

[178] *Katz v United States* 1967 389 US 347 (SC).

[179] *Dow Chemicals v the United States* 1986 476 US 227 (SC) [238]. 107.

[180] *Electronic Privacy Information Centre (EPIC) v FAA* 2018 No 16-1297 US (D.C Cir.).

In 2015 the FAA declared rulemaking on commercial UAS, stating that privacy issues were beyond the scope of the rulemaking. EPIC appealed and challenged FAA's failure to embrace privacy in the small UAS rulemaking.

The D.C Circuit dismissed EPIC's petition on a technicality appertaining to the drafting of the affidavits and failure to establish a standing on the matter. Unfettered, the FAA finalized the Small Drone Rulemaking in 2016, which prompted EPIC to file another suit challenging FAA's failure to address privacy in the Small Drone Rulemaking.[181] It suffices to state that the court lost an opportunity to pronounce itself on the place of privacy in regulation of UAS. Technically, the court lost a good opportunity to pronounce itself on the place of privacy on regulation of UAS. That notwithstanding, the court has at its disposal Article 36 of the Chicago Convention in its endeavour to protect the right of privacy of citizens.

4.5.3.3 *Carpenter v the United States*

The *Carpenter v the United States*[182] was an appeal from the Sixth Circuit Court. It related to the cell-site location information, which is generated automatically or intentionally by phone users. The police used data from the cell phone of an accused confessor to obtain additional information on the call logs of members of an organized robbery gang. The provisions of the Stored Communication Act sanctioned such usage. The Act protects private content and related information, while providing for exception where there are reasonable grounds to believe that the material is the subject of criminal investigations. This position was affirmed in previously decided cases in which the police did not require a warrant to obtain information where a third party was involved. They instead requested for information from the telecommunication company on the site locations of the persons.

The issue for determination was whether the police required the telecommunication companies to generate a warrant to access geological information of cell phone users. This could be resolved with a determination of a sub-issue on whether as per Section 2703(d) of the FAA Modernization and Reform Act, orders are searches within the meaning of the Fourth Amendment to the US Constitution. The trial magistrates ruled that the search was not unconstitutional, a determination that was affirmed on appeal where the Sixth Circuit Court stated that cell-site location information was business data not within the Fourth Amendment definition of search. The appellant was dissatisfied with the finding and appealed to the Supreme Court, seeking an order of *certiorari*.

The FAA Reauthorization Act emphasizes the necessity for courts to interpret Fourth Amendment principles within the context of evolving technological landscapes. This encourages a nuanced approach where the unique nature of digital data, including cell-site location information, is taken into account. The act also

[181] https://epic.org/privacy/litigation/apa/faa/drones/ (Date of use: 2 August 2023).

[182] *Carpenter v the United States 2018 No. 16-402, 585 US (SC).*

encourages lawmakers and legal practitioners to explore how existing legal frameworks, like Section 2703(d) of the FAA Modernization and Reform Act, align with contemporary notions of privacy and constitutional protections.

Majority of the learned Judges considered the origin and importance of the Fourth Amendment and noted that the influence of new technology on privacy rights through intrusive monitoring had redefined obtaining data on site-location. For instance, phone details are today so detailed that conveying them amounts to significant features of Global Positioning System (GPS)-like intrusion to the human anatomy since it keeps tabs on a person's every movement. These issues were seemingly beyond the decisions in *the United States v Mille*[183] and *Smith v. Maryland.*[184]

The underlying principles in a case are relevant to the regulation and integration of UAS into civil aviation owing to the use of modern technology. It is instructive to note that the court distinguished the current matter from previous cases involving articles in cars and banknotes, as well as traditional history of writs and subpoenas. The dissenting opinion was majorly based on classification of the cell-site location information as a business record by the dissenting justices and affirmation of the traditional third-party principle. The judges were apprehensive that the approach by the majority would water down surveillance as a governmental administrative tool.

The Supreme Court was non-committal on time but it held that a seven-day intrusion was enough to be intrusive and thus fall within the ambit of the Fourth Amendment Search. It held that a warrant was required to obtain Section 2703 (d) orders unless in deserving emergency cases, and consequently issued a request for certiorari. It is possible that even at the time that the courts cited the *Smith* case, there was an emerging opinion that aggregation of information, which is more intrusive, infringes on the privacy guarantees under the Fourth Amendment to the US Constitution. This could be the thread of reasoning that inspired the Supreme Court in its decision of five to four, a clear indication that matters of digital privacy are heavily contested. It is debatable whether this applies also to specific issues in the regulation of privacy, given Roberts, CJ's decision that the court was not disturbing the previous case laws or even disrupting surveillance by the State. It is apparent, however, that the middle ground taken by the majority was based on the need to build consensus on somewhat divisive opinions.

The restriction in UAS usage is an indicator that the regulatory framework in the US is still in its infancy.[185] The existing rules allow FAA to make informed assessment of technical development of UAS to facilitate the emergence of regulatory frameworks that ensure a secure national airspace system.[186] The FAA is alive to the state of manufacture and maintenance of UAS that are not at par with manned

[183] *United States v Miller* 1939 307 US 174 (SC).

[184] *Smith v Maryland* 1979 442 US 735 (SC).

[185] FAA Strategic Plan for the Financial Year 2019-2022.

[186] The US Integration of Civil Unmanned Aircraft Systems in the National Airspace System Roadmap of 2013, Section 3.

aircraft. Without proper monitoring, they are a security and safety risk. Most UAS pilots are neither trained nor certified, and are unfamiliar with rules of the air that guarantee the safety and security of all users of the national airspace system.[187]

4.6 Other Cross-cutting Challenges in Integration of UAS into Civil Aviation

4.6.1 Challenges of Enforcement of Safety and Security Regulations

The FAA has the mandate to promote voluntary compliance with its regulations by educating individuals on safe operation under existing laws.[188] In enforcing compliance, it uses a number of tools such as cautionary warnings, letters of correction and civil penalties.[189] The FAA is empowered to take enforcement measures against any unauthorized UAS user who endangers the safety of the National Airspace System (NAS).[190] The State and local rule enforcement agencies play the critical roles of detecting, deterring, investigating and, as appropriate, enforcing conduct that amounts to unauthorized use of UAS operations.[191]

The FAA aviation safety inspectors are foot soldiers who make follow-up on unauthorized UAS operations.[192] According to Byrnes and Kalas, the inspectors are hampered by lack of capacity in terms of numbers, underfunding and inability to cover very long distances.[193] FAA's activities could very well fall within the ambit of criminal law enforcement, in which case the FAA needs to be cautious to avoid mixing issues.[194] It should serve public interest through co-ordination, mutual understanding, and co-operation among government agencies that operate under the umbrella of law enforcement.

It is apparent many violations of the FAA's regulations could be addressed administratively given that even FAA itself is in agreement with the fact that some

[187] The US Integration of Civil Unmanned Aircraft Systems in the National Airspace System Roadmap of 2013, Section 3.

[188] Cracknell (2017), pp. 8–10.

[189] Cracknell (2017), p. 9.

[190] Cracknell (2017), p. 8.

[191] By applying any laws falling within the enforcement authority of the law enforcement agency in question.

[192] Fallon and Richard (1990), p. 389.

[193] Byrnes PT and Kalas MJ "FAA Admits UAS are a Severely Underfunded Mandate" https://www.jdsupra.com/legalnews/faa-admits-unmanned-aircraft-systems-i-37914/ (Date of use: 2 August 2023).

[194] Byrnes PT and Kalas MJ https://www.jdsupra.com/legalnews/faa-admits-unmanned-aircraft-systems-i-37914/ (Date of use: 2 August 2023).

federal criminal statutes are violated by UAS operators.[195] Like all criminal and civil actions, success in enforcement is reliant on appreciation of the facts and event. So long as that the FAA is thin on the ground, development of an accurate factual report that is contemporaneous with the event is impossible under the current set-up. Remedy lies in using law enforcement officers, who despite not being aviation experts, can offer invaluable aid to the FAA through identification of witnesses, interviewing and documentation. The information given to safety inspectors can then be used to, among others, contact witnesses as part of the investigations carried out by the FAA.

Apart from the FAA, there are other law enforcement agencies that are equally equipped to identify suspected UAS operators, participants and support personnel.[196] Their involvement is rationalized by their potential to view and record locations, and take pictures at close range. The pictures are helpful in describing such phenomena like lighting, weather patterns, damages; and identifying sensitive locations, events or activities that help the FAA to protect restricted airspaces. It is no secret that local area enforcement officers have been deployed alongside the FAA regional officers in the US. By virtue of their proximity to an event, such officers notify one of the FAA Regional Operation Centres to facilitate initiation of investigations.[197]

Local enforcement officers also help in identifying and preserving public or private security systems that provide photographic evidence of UAS activity, including video and still pictures. These systems do not store data permanently and may need to be reset automatically to erase such captured data. Law enforcement can interfere with resetting and in the process preserve the data, which is then presented as evidence. The fact that these items are within reach of law enforcement, officers' toolbox is a positive sign, but it does not tell the whole story. Whereas the FAA has enforcement mandate, its executional capacity is limited. This is partly due to reliance on other government agencies in evidence gathering. The same also happens when unauthorized UAS activity occurs in remote places where evidence is hard to get.

4.6.2 General Design Challenges

It was seen in Chap. 2 of this book that UAS design is both a safety and security challenge. In the US, design approval holders, modifiers and civil aviation authorities have a duty to regulate chemical oxygen installations. Provisions of Section 25.795 of the Code of Federal Regulations and the Advisory Circular on the Chemical Oxygen Generator require aircraft's chemical oxygen generators to be

[195] The US Code of Federal Regulations, Title 49, Section 4471.

[196] Cracknell (2017), p. 10.

[197] FAA Modernization Reform Act, 2012.

tamper proof. Aircraft, including UAS, are required to install tamper-evident features for ease of detecting tampering and as a security counter measure.[198]

The cross-cutting safety and security challenges mirror the provisions of Part 5.33 of the ICAO UAS Circular that requires UAS design to be tamper proof. A multi-agency approach comprising of the FBI, Department of Homeland Security, and Transportation Security Administration is required for effective implementation of the regulations. Dependence on these government agencies, however, may prove to be a challenge when the UAS in question is publicly operated. Also, though the requirements on chemical oxygen generation may be considered at the design and manufacture stages, the implementation, which requires human intervention, may be challenging as most UAS are pilotless.

4.6.3 Other Challenges of Integration of UAS Into Civil Aviation

Integration of UAS into civil aviation has made marked progress in the US. The passage of the FAA Reauthorization Act in 2018 gave impetus to the process by granting the FAA broad mandate to publish a 5-year roadmap, establish six test ranges and to integrate UAS into the national airspace system by September 2015. It is worth noting that this goal was not met as planned. The FAA was also required to mitigate safety research to facilitate the integration process, and eventually address challenges of UAS requirements as contained in the Act.

The FAA has encountered technological, regulatory and management hurdles in its endeavour to integrate UAS into civil aviation in a safe and secure manner.[199] One such regulatory barrier relates to inefficiencies in framework for data collection, analysis and sharing. It has been reported that the FAA does not even access data held by the Department of Defense due to concerns of its sensitivity.[200] The FAA lacks elaborate procedures to ensure that all UAS incidents are not only reported, but tracked and processed for data sharing with the US Department of Defence, which is the largest user of UAS.

---

[198] FAA Advisory Circular on the Chemical Oxygen Generator provides guidance for an acceptable means of showing compliance with the requirements of The Code of Federal Regulations, Title 14, Section 25.795(d). Particularly, Section 25.795(d) requires each chemical oxygen generator or its installation to be designed so it meets one of several criteria. The means of compliance described in this document provides guidance to supplement the engineering and operational judgment that must form the basis of any compliance findings relative to a COG installed on an airplane.

[199] US Department of Transportation https://www.oig.dot.gov/sites/default/files/FAA%20Oversight%20of%20Unmanned%20Aircraft%20Systems%5E6-26-14.pdf (Date of use: 2 August 2023).

[200] https://www.govinfo.gov/content/pkg/GAOREPORTS-GAO-02-77/html/GAOREPORTS-GAO-02-77.html (Date of the use: 1 August 2023).

There is also delay in schedule of integration, which as stated above was put as September 2015. The implications of the delay are unresolved safety, security and privacy issues. Whereas the FAA Act contains seventeen UAS-related provisions, only nine of them have been fully satisfied. These broadly relate to UAS Test Sites, publication of a UAS Roadmap, submission of a comprehensive UAS plan, simplified certificate of authorization process and the Arctic Plan.[201] As regards the other eight provisions, the FAA encountered delays on the issue of a final rule on "Small UAS" that was scheduled for August 2014, and safe integration of civil UAS into the National Airspace System (NAS) whose deadline was September 2015.

Finally, there is the challenge of conflict between State and local laws. State, local and municipal jurisdictions inevitably have diverse requirements on standards for UAS such as overflights. This calls for the different levels to work together, including in other aspects like limitations of UAS on flight altitude, flight paths, operational bans, and regulation of navigable airspace.[202] Federal courts have been instrumental in regulating areas with glaring gaps.[203] For instance, the court had opportunity to intervene in the case of *Montalvo v. Spirit Airlines.*[204] In the case, the 9th Circuit Court cited *City of Burbank v Lockheed Air Terminal Inc*[205] with approval and held that due to "the interdependence of these factors" what Congress enacted in respect of these was "a uniform and exclusive system of federal regulation."[206]

In addition to judicial intervention, consultation is critical in harmonizing equipment and training in support of UAS aviation safety such as geo-fencing.[207] State and police power in land use, zoning, privacy, trespass, law enforcement, and operations remain constant, and thus not subject to federal regulation.[208] The FAA has identified certain common laws that are permissible at both State and local levels with respect to police obligation to obtain a warrant prior to using a UAS for surveillance. The common laws specify that UAS may not be used for voyeurism,

---

[201] https://uas.noaa.gov/Portals/5/Docs/Library/FAA-sUAS-Arctic-Implementation-Plan-2012.pdf (Date of use: 28 August 2023).

[202] Federal Aviation Administration "Office of the Chief Counsel, State and Local Regulation of Unmanned Aircraft Systems: UAS Fact Sheet" https://www.faa.gov/news/updates/?newsId=84369 (Date of use: 2 August 2023).

[203] See the cases of *City of Burbank v Lockheed Air Terminal* 411 US 624 (1973), *Skysign International Inc. v City and County of Honolulu* 2002 276 F.3d 1109 US (9th Cir.) [1117], *American Airlines v Town of Hempstead* 1968 398 F.2d US 369 (2d Cir.) and *American Airlines v City of Audubon Park* 1969 407 F.2d US 1306 (6th Cir.)

[204] *Montalvo v. Spirit Airlines* 2007 508 F.3d 464 US 471 (9th Cir.) [471].

[205] *City of Burbank v Lockheed Air Terminal Inc* 1973 411 US 624 (SC) [638-39].

[206] *City of Burbank v Lockheed Air Terminal Inc* 1973 411 US 624 (SC) [638-39].

[207] *Med-Trans Corp. v Benton* 2008 581 F. Supp. 2d US 721 (EDNC) [740]; *Air Evac EMS, Inc. v Robinson, 486* 2007 F. Supp. 2d US 713, 722 (MD. Tenn.) [713].

[208] *Skysign International Inc. v City and County of Honolulu* 2002 276 F.3d 1109 US (9th Cir.) [1115].

hunting or fishing, interfere with or harass an individual who is hunting or fishing and attaching firearms or similar weapons to UAS.[209]

4.7 Conclusion

The fact that the US has a unique and long interaction with UAS cannot be gainsaid. After the enactment of the Air Commerce Act of 1926, the US first commitment to UAS regulation at the international level was demonstrated in 1944 when it galvanized support for adoption of the Chicago Convention. Since then, the US has taken a stranglehold in the development of the regulation, institutional frameworks and providing integration of UAS into civil aviation. Series of legal enactments and deliberate amendments to cover the UAS framework have consistently reshaped its framework's ability to respond to safety, security and privacy concerns in the use of UAS. Also instrumental is the active role played by the FAA whose regulatory framework, including advisory opinions and circulars, have incrementally improved the depth and width of UAS regulation. The FAA's provisions on airworthiness, visual line of sight, safety standards and safety management systems have enabled effective safety and security systems in UAS regulation. The security programmes and trainings under its framework largely mirror the ICAO-based framework. UAS regulation in the US is further, strengthened by involvement of stakeholders through community-based organizations. Self-regulation is a lesson that African countries can learn in their pursuance of integration of UAS into civil aviation.

Though in place, safety, security and privacy assurances have suffered setbacks on two principal fronts. In the first place, there is the lack of UAS-specificity in privacy regulation; it has to some extent been addressed by judicial activism to buttress the existing UAS framework. Secondly, there is elusive Sense and Avoid technology, which occurs to some UAS despite America's comparatively advanced technology. Other challenges to full potential for safety, security and privacy assurance are understaffing of aviation safety inspectorate; conflicts on regulatory framework between State laws and the federal law; and ineffective data collection and sharing.

[209] Federal Aviation Administration https://www.faa.gov/news/updates/?newsId=84369 (Date of use: 2 August 2023).

Bibliography

Books

Carr B (2014) Unmanned aerial vehicles: examining the safety, security, privacy and regulatory issues of integration into US airspace. National Centre for Policy Analysis Dallas

Cavoukian A (2012) Privacy and drones: unmanned aerial vehicles. Information and Privacy Commissioner of Ontario Canada.

National Research Council (2007) Engaging privacy and information technology in a digital age. National Academies Press

Parker R (2017) A definition of privacy. Routledge, London

Journal Articles

Choudhry S (2004) The Lochner era and comparative constitutionalism. Int J Const Law, 1–55

Cracknell AP (2017) UAVs: Regulations and law enforcement. Int J Remote Sens, 8–10

Fallon Jr, Richard H (1990) Enforcing aviation safety regulations: the case for a split-enforcement model of agency adjudication Adm Law J 389–404

Henshon M (2014) Case notes: *FAA v. Pirke*. Syracuse Law Rev, 26

Heymann PB (2001) Civil liberties and human rights in the aftermath of September 11. Harv J Law Public Policy, 441

Ison DC (2014) Privacy, restriction, and regulation involving federal, state and local legislation: more hurdles for unmanned aerial systems (UAS) Integration? J Aviation/Aerospace Edu Res, 41–80

Jiang T et al (2016) UAS traffic management: concept of operation and system architecture. Int J Transp Sci Technol, 123–135

Logan GB (2013) The present status and the development of aviation law. J Air Law, 510

MacCracken WF (1930) The growth of aeronautical law in America. Int J Air Law, 418

Ron R (2011) Improving Airline Security in the United States. Combating Terrorism Center, 1–24

Chapter 5
Legal, Policy and Institutional Framework for Regulation of UAS in South Africa

5.1 Introduction

This Chapter provides an analysis of the regulatory framework for regulation of the UAS in South Africa. It specifically examines how the framework has been effective in addressing safety, security and privacy concerns arising from use of UAS as seen in Chap. 2. This is achieved through a brief background, overview of the legal and institutional framework under the South African Civil Aviation Act, 13 of 2009, and the South African Civil Aviation Authority (SACAA) respectively. A critical analysis of the salient regulatory provisions vis-à-vis their efficacy in addressing safety, security and privacy concerns is also provided.

5.2 Background of Regulation of UAS in South Africa

South Africa has a history of use of RPAs for military and civilian applications, which include the Denel Aerospace for surveillance missions and high-speed target practice, Advanced Technologies and Engineering for artillery fire correction missions.[1] It is in civilian application that remotely piloted aircraft continue to grow, for instance, in election monitoring, crime prevention and weather forecasting.[2] Growing demands have been recorded in firefighting, health, disaster management, pollution control, radio broadcasts and regulation of poaching.[3]

[1] Republic of South Africa Department of Transport White Paper on National Civil Aviation Policy of 2017, p. 119.

[2] *Oliver* (2015), pp. 1–5.

[3] Republic of South Africa Department of Transport White Paper on National Civil Aviation Policy of 2017, pp. 119–121.

M. Wanyonyi Rodgers, *The Law Regulating Unmanned Aircraft Systems in the United States, South Africa and Kenya*,
https://doi.org/10.1007/978-3-031-49927-2_5

The growth has presented South Africa with challenges as regards the need to ensure that remotely piloted aircraft are operated safely, without harming the public and affecting national security, and in a way that protects areas of national, historical, or natural importance.[4] Some of these challenges arise from the fact that the UAS has to operate in a national airspace, previously dominated by manned aircraft regulation.[5] Other challenges like privacy concerns emanate from the use, structure and formation of the UAS.

The shift towards civilian applications is a fairly recent phenomenon in South Africa and continues to face challenges that impact UAS regulatory framework. The framework was in its formative stage in early 2015, a fact that was detrimental to efforts at integration. The slow pace with which the regulation of UAS took root was partly the result of lack of similar structures that shaped regulation of manned aircraft. Despite the initial setback, integration of the UAS into the national airspace has progressively gained momentum given its ubiquity and heightened use.

Development of specific regulation of unmanned aircraft systems in South Africa began when the Air Traffic and Navigation Services published a guidance document to regulate UAS movements in 2002.[6] Two years later, the South Africa Joint Aviation Authority Committee and the EUROCONTROL UAS Taskforce developed guiding principles to advance the 2002 concepts.[7] The Taskforce recommended that development of UAS was to be guided by the laid down applicable principles of the regulations outlined in Chap. 3 of this book. The principles include fairness, equivalence, responsibility and accountability, and transparency.[8] This path is beneficial because once agreed upon, the principles aid in ensuring that the UAS are airworthy and operate efficiently in terms of sharing of responsibilities and improving overall chances of safety and security in use and operation.[9]

Building on the works commenced in 2002, a roadmap to UAS integration and regulation started in earnest in 2006 with the establishment by the SACAA of a Co-ordination Committee.[10] The Committee brought together stakeholders in the UAS sector (air traffic controllers, manufacturers, academia and operators) to provide input in formulating UAS regulatory framework.

Today, the regulatory framework is founded on regulations adopted by the national, provincial and local governments as enshrined in the Constitution of the

[4]Levush (2016), p. 1.

[5]Ingham et al. (2006), p. 698.

[6]Ingham (2009), p. 5.

[7]Unmanned Aerial Vehicle Operations in the RSA – Guidance, ATNS/HO/UAV WF, Johannesburg, 2002.

[8]Ingham et al. (2006), p. 698.

[9]South African Civil Aviation Authority UAV Task Force Final Report of 11 May 2004, pp. 11–14.

[10]Ingham (2009), p. 11.

Republic of South Africa.[11] The three spheres are both separate and interdependent entities. This is best articulated by Goitom when he states that the distinct governments are interdependent since they conduct both legislative and executive functions.[12] Accordingly, regulation of UAS is within command of the national government but with some delegated authority.

5.3 Overview of Current South African Framework for Regulation of UAS

That South Africa is an active participant on the global scene as appertains to regulation of UAS cannot be gainsaid.[13] The pace with which the country moved in ratifying and domesticating the Chicago Convention demonstrates its commitment to the framework of laws provided by the Convention and Agreement. It has remained committed to subsequent framework developed by the ICAO.

As a member of ICAO, South Africa was fronted to the Remotely Piloted Aircraft Systems Panel that was established in 2014.[14] The Panel coordinates, develops standards, recommends practices, supports air navigation services and guidance materials, and facilitates a safe, secure and efficient integration of UAS into the civilian airspace.[15] South Africa has at some point been Chair of the ICAO Aviation Security Panel. As member of the panel that coordinates and develops SARPs and Procedures on safety, security and integration, South Africa has a moral obligation to comply matters of UAS regulation with a view to integrating them into civil aviation.

The international framework as a matter of fact imposes on South Africa the obligation to domesticate the conventions contained therein into its own national law. This is explicitly expounded in Chaps. 2 and 3 of this book. Further, bilateral and multilateral trade agreements are binding documents among member States. In this regard, South Africa is a signatory to, among others, the Convention for

[11] Constitution of the Republic of South Africa, 1996, Section 40. See also Chaps. 6 and 7 establishes provincial and local levels of government respectively.

[12] Goitom H "Regulation of drones: South Africa" https://www.loc.gov/law/help/regulation-of-drones/south-africa.php (Date of use: 2 August 2023).

[13] South Africa is a State party to the Chicago Convention, having appended her signature in 1 March 1947, about a month after the convention's inception on 4 April 1947.

[14] Goitom https://www.loc.gov/law/help/regulation-of-drones/south-africa.php (Date of use: 2August 2023).

[15] Goitom https://www.loc.gov/law/help/regulation-of-drones/south-africa.php (Date of use: 2 August 2023).

Suppression of Unlawful Acts against the Safety of Civil Aviation,[16] and the Cape Town Convention of 16 November 2001.[17]

Emanating from the aforementioned international legal regime, there was need for specific measures to address emerging challenges to UAS in South Africa. The Cape Town Convention aimed at offering international protection to all member States against dangers associated with the airspace.[18] The Convention gave effect to international standards in certain categories relating to mobile equipment and associated rights, which include flying equipment such as UAS.[19]

At the sub-regional level, SADC member States are yet to develop a specialised agency to deal with security and safety of civil aviation in the region.[20] Although SADC was not essentially a focus of this publication, it is established that each SADC member State is left do develop her own local regulations, based on the framework provided by ICAO. The international conventions and treaty provisions apply to South Africa by virtue of their ratification, meaning that they do apply and are domesticated as sources of law.

The Constitution of the Republic of South Africa, 1996 is the supreme law, outlining the functions of bodies with legislative authority including parliament, provincial and local governments or general spheres.[21] Hence these bodies must act within the constitutional principles when making, applying and interpreting aviation laws. The Constitution also provides for fundamental human rights, which UAS regulation must not overlook.[22] For example, it provides that everyone has the right to privacy, which includes the right not to have (a) their person or home searched, (b) have their property searched, (c) have their possessions seized, or (d) have the privacy of their communications infringed.[23] This means that while undertaking regulation for integration of UAS into civil aviation, the South African Parliament, in addition to performing its legislative role, must take cognizant of the Bill of Rights.

The South African UAS legal framework is generally designed to address safety, security and privacy in the aviation industry. The supreme legislative framework is the Civil Aviation Act,[24] which evidences the legislative commitment to safety and security.[25] The Act allows for enactment of regulations and other subsidiary

---

[16] Convention on Suppression of Unlawful Seizure of Aircraft, Convention relating to Unlawful Acts Relating to International Civil Aviation of 10 September 2010 (entered into force on 1 July 2018).

[17] Cape Town Convention on International Interests in Mobile Equipment of 16 November 2001 (entered into force 1 March 2006).

[18] Goode (2012), p. 599.

[19] Goode (2012), p. 599.

[20] Abeyratne (1998), pp. 30–49.

[21] Constitution of the Republic of South Africa, 1996, Chaps. 4 and 6 on the role of Parliament and of local Government respectively.

[22] Constitution of the Republic of South Africa, 1996, Section 14.

[23] Constitution of the Republic of South Africa, 1996, Section 14.

[24] Civil Aviation Act 13 of 2009 (hereinafter referred to in this Chapter as the Civil Aviation Act).

[25] Civil Aviation Act, Section 72(1).

legislation to supplement and provide more details on implementation of the Act. In particular, Section 163 of the Civil Aviation Act is the legal basis for the SACAA to develop technical standards and rules for civil aviation in a manner that provides opportunities for UAS to operate in a safe and responsible environment. Operators are required to use manuals and other documents to prove their viability to SACAA. The regulations are introduced to pilots of remotely piloted aircraft, who are trained and familiarized with aviation rules and regulations and to the theoretical framework of remotely piloted aircraft and all practical training.[26]

The Civil Aviation Act of 2009 as amended from time to time makes provisions for aviation safety, accidents and investigations procedures, approvals of land rights for reconnaissance, and establishment of the institutional frameworks. The Act mandates the Minister responsible for aviation to make provisions regarding qualifications of operators, designation of functions to bodies, restriction of airspace, and institutions, classification, identification and development of appropriate technical, safety, security and development standards.[27] An overview of the Act reveals that it does not contain UAS-specific provisions. This despite the clamour for UAS integration having kicked off seven years before the Civil Aviation Act was enacted.

Under Section 1 of the Civil Aviation Act, an aircraft refers to:

> any machine, which can derive support in the atmosphere from the reactions of the air.

By implication, the above definition includes any UAS. To include UAS in the definition is supported by circumstances surrounding the Amendment Act, which resulted from efforts of the development of the Guidance Document in 2002, Principles of the Taskforce Report in 2004, and a roadmap for integration in 2006. This is proof that the drafters of the Act had in mind UAS regulation in crafting the definition of aircraft.[28] The approach, therefore, was to spell the general applicable rules but with necessary modifications.

The commitments under the Amendment Act reflect the international framework as it seeks to achieve the objectives in the Standards and Recommended Practices of the ICAO, whilst considering the local context. It is thus safe to conclude that the SACAA mandate relates to aviation safety, security and by extension privacy during oversight of airspace, airports, operations and personnel.

[26] Civil Aviation Act, Section 163.

[27] SACAA Act, Section 163.

[28] See Unmanned Aerial Vehicle Operations in the RSA – Guidance, ATNS/HO/UAV WF, Johannesburg, 2002 and South African Civil Aviation Authority UAV Task Force Final Report of 11 May 2004 already provided in the prior historical analysis.

5.4 Institutional Framework of South Africa Civil Aviation Authority and Other Institutions

The South African Civil Aviation Act[29] established the SACAA. On amendment in 2009, the Civil Aviation Act made provisions for the institution and specifically recognized it under Section 71. The institution has mandate to draft civil aviation regulations, technical standards for airworthiness and operation of non-type certified aircraft. It is clear from the preamble of the Civil Aviation Act that it targeted expansion of SACAA's mandate as regards safety and security oversight. These functions are handled at policy making level and day-to-day functioning of the SACAA that rests in the office of the Director General.[30] The Director General is answerable to the Minister of Transport on matters of civil aviation, safety and security, and also reports to the Board on matters within its jurisdiction.[31] The functions of SACAA are performed by the Director General and staff appointed by the former.[32]

The SACAA contributes to the overall regulation of South Africa's domestic air law through development of UAS regulatory requirements in the form of Aeronautical Information Circulars, Technical Standards, strategies, licencing, and oversight of flight inspections and conducting regular reviews.

The regulatory requirements, standards, procedures and strategies under Section 73 of the Civil Aviation Act are the basis of implementation of the provisions of the South Africa Civil Aviation Act as progressively amended. The SACAA plays a key role in the implementation of the aviation law insofar as it relates to UAS. Through the regulatory requirements, it can go beyond what the law prescribes like providing specifics on the regulation for practical application. In particular, SACAA provides an avenue for the South African domestic regulatory framework to redeem itself by taking a differential approach as opposed to the general approach adopted by the Civil Aviation Act, 2009 in which no UAS-specific provisions on safety, security and privacy have been made. In establishing these regulatory requirements, SACAA collaborates with other institutions boasting international best practices, particularly the FAA and the European Union (EU).[33]

SACAA has a further mandate of conducting comprehensive aviation industry audits and surveillance such as assessment of decisions taken by industry management at all levels for their impact on aviation safety and security.[34] The mandate is

[29] South African Civil Aviation Authority Act 40 of 1998 (hereinafter in this Chapter referred to as Civil Aviation Authority Act).

[30] Civil Aviation Act, Section 85.

[31] Civil Aviation Act, Sections 86(3) (a) and (b).

[32] Civil Aviation Act, Sections 73(4) and Sec 87(a)-(f).

[33] https://www.icao.int/environmental-protection/pages/ICAO_EU.aspx (Date of use: 4 August 2023).

[34] Civil Aviation Authority Act, Section 73(1)(d).

complemented by the monitoring role, as well as implementation and enforcement of aviation policies like the National Aviation Security Programme.[35] In addition, the SACAA is involved in conducting regular and timely assessment of international safety and security trends and developments, together with ensuring compliance with ICAO Annexes and Rules.[36]

Other than providing oversight on safety and security of remotely piloted aircraft (UAS) and national enforcement, SACAA[37] oversees enforcement of regulation in relation to safety and security operations in the process of integrating UAS into the national airspace, in line with ICAO Guidelines. In doing this, it develops enforcement mechanisms to ensure compliance with existing international and country laws, guidelines, orders, circulars and other standards.

The principal regulation at the ministerial level is the Remotely Piloted Aircraft Systems Regulations.[38] The Ministry of Transport issued regulations governing UAS in May 2015, which became effective on 1 July 2015.[39] The same was a product of the consultative structures of the SACAA as envisaged by Section 156 of the Civil Aviation Act after successful amendments to the South Africa's Civil Aviation Regulations[40] that had deficiencies as the Civil Aviation Act in as far as specificity in regulation of UAS was concerned. The regulations make provisions that border on safety, security and privacy concerns of UAS operation. They prescribe areas for UAS operation, prohibited places, the operational weight and distance above the earth's surface.

The development of RPAs Regulations through the Civil Aviation Regulation (Eighth Amendment) in conjunction with the Ministry of Transport was a clear indication of SACAA's commitment to enacting UAS legal frameworks. It led to universal recognition and was a show of South Africa's preparedness in this endeavour. The only challenge facing the framework appears to be the ubiquity of number and uses that to creation of toy aircraft.

Over and above development of regulations, SACAA has mandate to make requisite proposals to Parliament for legislation.[41] In this regard, SACAA is called upon to invest heavily in research for effectiveness. It employs an inclusive approach when dealing with issues appertaining to UAS. This includes involvement of local stakeholders[42] such as State organs, the military, airport operators, universities,

---

[35] Civil Aviation Act, Section 73(1)(f).

[36] Civil Aviation Act, Section 72.

[37] Civil Aviation Act, Section 73(1) (b).

[38] Eighth Amendment of the Civil Aviation Regulations of 2015, Government Notice R444/2015 of May 27, 2015 (hereinafter referred to as the Civil Aviation Regulations (Eighth Amendment).

[39] Civil Aviation Regulations (Eighth Amendment), Part 101.

[40] South Africa Civil Aviation Regulations of 2011 (effective June 2012) (hereinafter referred to as Civil Aviation Regulations).

[41] Civil Aviation Act, Sections 42 (1) (a) & (b), 42(2), 43 & 44.

[42] Constitution of the Republic of South Africa, 1996, Sections 118 and 152 (e). It provides for Local Government structure and States that local communities and community organization need to be encouraged to be involved in matters of local government.

research institutions, UAS manufacturers, UAS associations and prospective operators in general.[43]

The above enumerated mandates are expansive and are reflective of the role played by ICAO in providing international framework for aviation regulation. SACAA is undoubtedly the backbone of formulation, adoption, implementation and monitoring of UAS-specific laws in South Africa. It has seen South Africa post good reports on corporate governance, which translates to prudent financial performance in compliance with the requirements of Section 71 of the Civil Aviation Act. The SACAA is credited with the rise in the South Africa's level of compliance with the international framework as urged by scholars before the enactment of the Civil Aviation Act.[44]

There are other governmental institutions created under the Civil Aviation Act to implement and enforce South Africa's legal framework on civil aviation, and UAS in particular. They include the Department of Transport, and the Civil Aviation Authority Board, with mandate provided by the SACAA.[45]

These institutions work together through issuance of regulations, technical standards and circulars. Section 73 of the Civil Aviation Act mandates the Department of Transport and the Civil Aviation Authority to develop regulations, technical standards, guidance materials and circulars with import to govern UAS. Under Section 163 of the Civil Aviation Act and Part 101 of the Civil Aviation Regulations, the Director of Civil Aviation is mandated to provide other technical standards on UAS known as the South African Civil Aviation Technical Standards (SA-CATS)[46] that took legal effect in July 2015.[47] The Director also provides a number of Aeronautical Circulars that relate to remote pilot licensing, requirements for application of remote pilot licenses, training and aviation examinations applicable to UAS.[48] These instruments make it possible for regulation of operation by private, commercial, corporate and non-profit operators.

Complementing these bodies are provincial and local governments that regulate the use of public areas by UAS and ensure safety of citizens. This is achieved through enactment of local laws touching on safety and other UAS aspects. A key area is development of regulation on permission to operate. UAS operators are required to comply with provincial and local authority laws pertaining to permission

---

[43] https://www.icao.int/Meetings/RPAS/RPASSymposiumPresentation/Day%202%20Workshop%206%20National%20Regulations%20Sam%20Twala%20%20South%20African%20Civil%20%20Aviation%20Authority%20(SACAA).pdf (Date of use: 8 August 2023).

[44] Ingham (2009), p. 45.

[45] Civil Aviation Act, Section 75.

[46] South Africa Civil Aviation Technical Standards 101 (SA-CATS 101) of 1 July 2015 (hereinafter referred to as SA-CATS 101).

[47] Civil Aviation Regulations (Eighth Amendment), Section 5.

[48] http://www.caa.co.za/RPAS%20AICs/AIC%20007-2015 (Date of use: 10 August 2023).

Table 5.1 Operation requirement of commercial, corporate and non-profit UAS

	Commercial	Corporate	Non-profit
Air Service License (ASL)	X	–	–
RPAS Operator Certificate (ROC)	X	X	X
RPA Letter of Approval (RLA)	X	X	X
RPA Certificate of Registration (CoR)	X	X	X
Remote Pilot License (RPL)	X	X	X

to operate.[49] It is expected that the provisions of the permissive laws shall not violate the framework provided by SACAA.

5.5 Classification of UAS

Unmanned aircraft systems in South Africa take the form of commercial, corporate and non-profit UAS operations. The impact of the difference is subjection to different standard of regulation of safety, security and privacy.

5.5.1 Commercial, Corporate and Non-profit Operators

A commercial operation is one where the use of a UAS is concerned with commercial outcome, interest or gain. Corporate operations are by firms. Non-profit use can be for no economic gains, whether by individual or by corporate body[50] Whereas private operators of UAS are in a class of their own, the commercial, corporate and non-profit UAS are exposed to stricter regulations. The three operators share certain rules and restrictions but some technical and operational requirements depend on the type of operation as shown in Table 5.1.[51]

5.5.2 Private Operations

The Civil Aviation Regulations define private operations as "the use of remotely piloted aircraft for an individual's personal and private use, where there is no commercial outcome, interest or gain."[52] There are additional restrictions under

[49] Constitution of the Republic of South Africa, 1996, Chaps. 6 and 7 establishes provincial and local levels of government respectively.

[50] Ingham (2009), p. 45.

[51] Civil Aviation Regulations (Eighth Amendment), Section 101.01.5.

[52] Civil Aviation Regulations (Eighth Amendment), Section 101.01.5.

Table 5.2 Classification of UAS

	UAS classification			
Class	Line-of-sight	Energy (kJ)	Height (ft)	MTOM (kg)
Class 1A	Restricted visual line of sight/visual line-of-sight	Less than-15	Less than-400	Less than-1.5
Class 1B	Restricted visual line of sight/visual line-of-sight	Less than-15	Less than-400	Less than-7
Class 1C	Visual line-of-sight/extended visual line-of-sight	Less than-34	Less than-400	Less than-20
Class 2A	Visual line-of-sight/extended visual line-of-sight	Greater than-34	Less than-400	Less than-20
Class 2B	Experimental/research			
Class 3A	Beyond visual line-of-sight	Greater than-34	Less than-400	Less than-150
Class 3B	Visual line-of-sight/extended visual line-of-sight	Any	Less than-400	Less than-150
Class 4A	Beyond visual line-of-sight	Any	Less than-400	Less than-150
Class 4B	Any	Any	Any	Less than-150

the regulation including private operations being conducted with class 1A or class 1B only. Class 1A comprises UAS of less than 1.5 kg, while class 1B is a UAS that is not more than 7 kg in weight.[53] The Civil Aviation Act and UAS regulations (SA-CATS 101) require the two classes to fly at a height less than 400 m.

To facilitate regulation, South Africa has further classified the UAS in terms of weight, impact, energy, operational height above the ground, rules of flight and areas of operation.[54] UAS regulation in South Africa classifies UAS operatives under operators, pilots and persons who maintain them.[55]

Example of Table 5.1 validates and summarizes Operation requirement of Commercial, Corporate and Non-profit UAS under 2015 SACAA RAPS Regulation.

Example of Table 5.2 provides a summary on classification of UAS under 2015 SACAA RAPS Regulation.

---

[53] Civil Aviation Regulations (Eighth Amendment), Section 101.01.5.

[54] Civil Aviation Regulations (Eighth Amendment), Section 101.01.5. The classification criterion of UAS is defined in the South Africa categories.

[55] Civil Aviation Regulations (Eighth Amendment), Section 101.01.1.

5.6 Responses to Challenges Identified as Safety, Security and Privacy

5.6.1 South Africa's Response to Safety Concerns of UAS

Aviation safety as provided for under ICAO Annex 19 and Safety Management Manual (Doc 9859) arises from the design and capability challenges regarding sense and avoid technology, hence the need to mitigate safety risks. The safety of aircraft and people on the ground is an important attribute of civil aviation in South Africa through myriad provisions of laws including Part 101 of the Civil Aviation Regulations, inserted through the Civil Aviation Regulations as (Eighth Amendment) and other SACAA Circulars and Standards.[56] The regulatory framework for operation of UAS aims at managing them in the civilian airspace with emphasis on safety and training.[57]

Under the Civil Aviation Regulations (Eighth Amendment), anyone who desires to operate a commercial, corporate or non-profit UAS should have a valid remote piloting license.[58] A remote piloting license falls into three categories, namely: remote pilot license (airplane), remote pilot license (helicopter) and remote pilot license (multi-rotor).[59] The remote pilot license is rated in three ways depending on the mode and nature of operations. These categories are visual line-of-sight operations; extended visual line-of-sight[60] operations and beyond visual line-of-sight operations.[61] The three categories ensure that the regulatory system is able to respond to the unique safety issues arising from the various classifications of UAS operations.

The applicable general rules for one to be granted a licence have certain safety underpinnings. According to SACAA, for example, the applicant must be 18 years, have requisite training from an approved school, whether local or approved and validated foreign training.[62] The validation of foreign training is critical to ensure harmonization of skills and competencies to licenced UAS pilots. The South African system has put in place a Recognition for Prior Learning (RPL) Assessment, which

[56] Timothy (2016), p. 302.

[57] Hofmeyr CD "Here is why South Africa's new drone regulations are ridiculous" https://businesstech.co.za/news/general/92072/here-is-why-south-africas-drone-regulations-are-ridiculous/ (Date of use: 8 July 2023).

[58] Civil Aviation Regulations (Eighth Amendment), Section 101.03.1.

[59] Civil Aviation Regulations (Eighth Amendment), Section 101.03.1.

[60] SA-CATS, Section 101.01.1 defines an extended visual line of sight as an operation below 400 feet above ground level in which an observer maintains direct and unaided visual contact with the remotely piloted aircraft at a distance not exceeding 1000 m from the pilot.

[61] SA-CATS, Section 101.03.1.

[62] SACAA "Remotely Piloted Aircraft Systems: Pilot Licensing and Instructor Rating" http://www.caa.co.za/Pages/RPAS/RPAS%20pilot%20licensing.aspx (Date of use: 7 August 2023).

aids in determining whether the applicants have the requisite qualifications.[63] These assessments are essential given the UAS are likely to attract a number of users with training from foreign aviation schools. UAS licensing for commercial operations is issued under three categories, that is, airplane, helicopter and multi-rotor.[64] Additional rating may be endorsed on a license just like in manned aircraft in terms of visual line-of-sight operations, extended visual line-of-sight operations and beyond visual line-of-sight operations.

Equally inherent to safety is communication, whereby the regulations premise remote pilot licencing on satisfaction by an applicant of the requirement for radiotelephony communication and English proficiency.[65] This is made explicit by Krivonos, who observes that the overall objective of communication is to prevent aviation accidents by ensuring free and efficient flow of correct and ideal aviation information.

The requirements for communication were formulated against a backdrop of reports that most aviation accidents arose from communication mismatches.[66] Accordingly, the South African framework adopted a similar regulatory approach to ICAO's when it introduced English Proficiency tests in March 2011 through Advisory Circular 153AN/56.

The periodicity of the UAS pilot license is also relevant for effective monitoring. The licence has a lifespan of two years and one year for commercial and private operators respectively.[67] The differentiation recognizes bureaucracies to obtain the licence for the former. Anyone wishing to extend the deviation is required to re-submit application for purposes of renewal.[68] Ordinary renewals are done on an annual basis whereby applicants take refresher courses that aid pilots to be conversant with changes introduced by SACAA. These courses are not centralised, meaning they are offered at various training centres. The regulatory approaches to licencing remote pilots is a step towards achievement of the safety of navigation obligations under Article 3(3) of the Chicago Convention.

The institutions created under the Act and the general framework are pivotal in aiding the South African framework to match the approach by ICAO Circular No. 328-AN/190 and ICAO Annex 1, which view training as part of the larger licencing and thus important for aviation safety.[69] The Civil Aviation Act gives prominence to training as a means of achieving the overall aim of safety. Under

[63] SACAA "Remotely piloted aircraft systems: pilot licensing and instructor rating" http://www.caa.co.za/Pages/RPAS/RPAS%20pilot%20licensing.aspx (Date of use: 7 August 2023).

[64] SACAA http://www.caa.co.za/Pages/RPAS/RPAS%20pilot%20licensing.aspx (Date of use: 7 August 2023).

[65] See SACATS, Section 101.03.2 on Remote pilot license: training, examination and application for RPL requirements.

[66] http://aviationenglishway.com/2019/03/31/the-importance-of-an-effective-communication-in-aviation/ (Date of use: 4 August 2023).

[67] https://www.droneitsa.co.za/remote-pilots-licence-rpl/ (Date of use: 7 August 2023).

[68] Civil Aviation Regulations (Eighth Amendment), Section 101.03.6.

[69] See Burger and Jones (2011).

Section 31(9) of the Act, training of the Aviation Safety Board staff is essential for there to be objective investigation of accidents and formulation of workable safety recommendations as outlined in Section 30 of the Act.

Part 101 of the Regulations introduced by the Civil Aviation Regulations (Eighth Amendment) requires implementation and training to be conducted by recognized institutions. Training standards and requirements are aligned to include aeronautical information and operational components, as envisaged under Part 7.9 of the ICAO Circular No. 328-AN/190. SACAA Aeronautical Information Circular in particular makes provisions for aviation training organizations that conduct UAS training. It prescribes the scope of procedure manuals for such institutions, training curricula, and extends it to apply to UAS with necessary modifications.[70] These requirements are monitored through systems for any extension beyond the scope of approval. Other than the trainings, test centres are only those approved by the Director of SACAA.[71]

It is critical to train observers alongside the pilots. Under the Civil Aviation Act, an observer is "a trained and competent person designated by the operator who, by visual observation of the remotely piloted aircraft, assists the remote pilot in the safe conduct of the flight."[72] It follows that the training requirements and extension of use of flight curricular in Advisory Circular 008/2015 is important in harmonising manned and unmanned aircraft systems as envisaged by Part 2.12 of ICAO Circular No. 328-AN/190. This extension, however, does not appear to take cognizance of the differential training needs for UAS operators. Perhaps for expediency, the framework should adopt the spirit of Part 7.4 of ICAO Circular No. 328-AN/190 where the training for UAS operators is done on a need basis.

UAS certification is a critical aspect of safety regulation in South Africa. 'Operator' according to the Civil Aviation Act includes a remote pilot and other persons involved in air services. With regard to UAS, certification is to be granted to operators, whether individually or by artificial entities. The Regulations require that any person who operates a commercial, corporate or non-profit UAS should have a UAS operator certificate.[73] Operating a UAS is a heavily restricted affair as one needs first to be registered, obtain a number of licenses, approvals and certificates before being allowed into the airspace.

Commercial operators undergo a stringent certification process since they are required to apply for and obtain air service license from the Air Service Licence Council as a pre-condition for obtaining a UAS operator certificate.[74] The application for the UAS operator certificate is a five-step process, akin to that followed by ICAO. It involves pre-application, formal application, document evaluation,

[70] SACAA Aeronautical Information Circular No 008/2015 of 23 July 2015 (hereinafter referred to as the AIC 008/2015), Paragraph 2.

[71] South Africa Civil Aviation Act, Section 88(5).

[72] Civil Aviation Act, Section 2(g).

[73] Civil Aviation Regulations (Eighth Amendment), Section 101.04.1.

[74] Civil Aviation Regulations (Eighth Amendment), Section 101.04.1.

demonstration and inspection, and certification. Compliance with safety and security is monitored through an annual renewal process. As Dalamagkidis, Valavanis and Piegl observe, this period appears to be the standard for renewal of most licences for ease of planning by the State.[75]

Implementation of the certification regulation for commercial operations has come under scrutiny in the recent past. In July 2018, for instance, Ragongo and Caboz, questioned whether the Drones' Fireworks that was organized by Absa and Intel had the requisite permission from SACAA.[76] The public was of the view that the fireworks consisting of 300 drones were incongruent with the twenty licences that had been issued to commercial operators in that year. This arose from the fact that in order to achieve the goals of safety, it was envisaged that each drone for commercial purpose should be individually licenced prior to certification.[77] The move led to a realization that the certification process could be abused by a possibly liberal approach, which could peg it on an operator and not the number of drones.

The conditions in the certification exercise have safety underpinning. It is the holder of a UAS operator certificate's responsibility to develop an operator's manual, which is forwarded to the Director of Civil Aviation for approval.[78] The regulations state the components of the manual such as type and scope of operations, including the manner in which it is to be safely conducted. Operators are required to strictly comply with any changes as approved by the Director General of SACAA. Compliance with the manual provisions is complemented with development of a commensurate safety management system. The safety standards and requirements are the basic minimum guide to respective staff of UAS operators. It is worth noting that these prospects are dimmed by bureaucracies in the application and approval processes. For instance, O'Connell, owner of a drone company called Timeslice, had at one point to wait for nearly two years[79] before obtaining a letter of approval. Such delays could open avenues for non-compliance with the safety requirements.

The regulations recognize various entities and complexities of their operations, and require that the safety programme system reflects such complexities. From an analytical point of view, the regulations would be more effective if safety management is based on the type of UAS rather than the size of the operator. Such a system would ensure assurance of identification of potential safety hazards and risks, appropriateness, and effectiveness in safety management activities as envisaged by ICAO Circular No. 328-AN/190 and ICAO Air Safety Manual AN/959.[80]

---

[75] Dalamagkidis et al. (2011), p. 2.

[76] Ragongo T and Caboz J "Was Absa's drone show illegal" https://myofficemagazine.co.za/was-absas-drone-show-illegal/ (Date of use: 7 August 2023).

[77] Ragongo T and Caboz J https://myofficemagazine.co.za/was-absas-drone-show-illegal/ (Date of use: 7 August 2023).

[78] Civil Aviation Regulations (Eighth Amendment), Section 101.04.5.

[79] https://www.businessinsider.co.za/absa-has-been-breaking-sa-drone-laws-and-is-about-to-put-on-an-illegal-spectacular-for-its-big-reveal-today-2018-7 (Date of use: 4 August 2023).

[80] See Chap. 3, Sect. 3.4.1 of this book on analysis of these instruments regarding safety of UAS use.

As for registration of certified private UAS operators wishing to engage in commercial, corporate non-profit operation, the Civil Aviation Regulations require an application for, and approval by the Director of Civil Aviation Authority, a letter of approval and certificate of registration.[81] An operator applying for a letter of approval should submit a standard design, safety level documentation and demonstration of the safety systems. Operator who wishes to apply for approval to operate UAS should submit the UAS manufacturers' operating manual to the Director of Civil Aviation.[82] For UAS in Classes 1 and 2, it is mandatory that the operator provides information on UAS type, structure, composition, flight envelope capability, UAS dimensions/measurements and mass, together with drawings, mass and balance, payloads (specific or generic), use of frequencies, remote pilot station, ground support equipment and flight recovery system.[83] As Mashinini rightly observes, these levels of documentation mean that when the change of use occur, the major consideration for the Director should be the safety that the shift in use has on identifiable group of people and the general public.[84]

It is advised that information pertaining to actual performance of the UAS is submitted together with the above-mentioned documentation. The information includes maximum altitude, maximum endurance, maximum range, airspeed (take-off, cruise, landing, stall, maximum), maximum rate of climb, maximum rate of descent, maximum bank angle, turn rate limits, propulsion system (such as engine/motor, fuel, electrical, hydraulic, pneumatic, gas, solar).[85] The thoroughness with which this is done helps in discouraging change of use from the original design.

There is also the issue relating to safety in the regulation of UAS operation to the line-of-sight of the remote pilot or underground flight manager. A visual line-of-sight is a straight line within which a UAS operator can maintain a clear human or mechanical view of the UAS operating in the airspace. Maintaining the UAS within the visual line of sight ensures optimal safety by reducing accidents and collisions with other aircraft. UAS is said to be beyond the visual line-of-sight when it operates outside the prescribed visual range. This phenomenon is a safety challenge that requires legal framework to manage and maintain a critical balance between safety interests and the need for autonomy of operation of UAS.

A remote pilot is expected to maintain direct unaided visual contact with the UAS in order to manage the flight and satisfy separation and collision avoidance requirements.[86] Under Section 2(i) of the Civil Aviation Act, a restricted visual line-of-sight refers to an operation within 500 m of the remote pilot and below the height of the highest obstacle within 300 m of the UAS, in which the remote pilot maintains direct

---

[81] SA-CATS, Sections 101.02.1 and 101.02.4.

[82] SA-CATS, Sections 101.

[83] SA-CATS, Sections 101.02.2.

[84] Mashinini (2020), pp. 140–158.

[85] Mashinini (2020), p. 142.

[86] Mashinini (2020), p. 144.

unaided visual contact with the UAS to manage its flight and meet separation and collision avoidance responsibilities".[87]

The Civil Aviation Act, 2009 does not define Beyond the Visual Line-of-Sight,[88] but the definition was addressed in the 2015 Regulation after the Eighth Amendment[89] as an operation in which the remote pilot cannot maintain direct unaided visual contact with the UAS to manage its flight and to meet separation and collision avoidance responsibilities visually. The Amendment Regulation extended visual line-of-sight to mean operation below 400 feet above ground level in which an observer maintains direct and unaided visual contact with the remotely piloted aircraft at a distance not exceeding 1000 m from the pilot.[90]

It is a legal requirement that private operations are carried out in restricted Visual-Line-of-Sight.[91] An operation within the restricted Visual-Line-of-Sight is one conducted within 500 m of the UAS pilot and below the height of the highest obstacle within 300 m of the UAS. As Linchant *et al* observes, the purpose of this restriction is to minimise chances of air crashes amongst unmanned aircraft or with the manned aircraft. It is a requirement intended to ensure safety of the airspace.[92] In more specific terms "within 500 m of the remote pilot and below the height of the highest obstacle within 300 m of the UAS, in which the remote pilot maintains direct unaided visual contact with the UAS to manage its flight and meet separation and collision avoidance responsibilities."[93]

The import of the provisions is that a UAS that operates beyond the Visual-Line-of-Sight may cause air accidents with manned aircraft plying the same flight path. As such, operations are prohibited unless conducted within controlled airspace devoid of other flying aircraft. For this reason, Section 101.05.11 (1) of the South Africa Civil Aviation Technical Standards prohibits UAS operation beyond Visual-Line-of-Sight unless the holder has UAS operator certificate and with approval of the Director. The Director has powers to approve beyond Visual-Line-of-Sight operation, subject to meeting the RPAs operations requirements under Subpart 5 of the South Africa Civil Aviation Regulations on Technical Standards.[94]

Section 101.05.11 (3) of Regulation 101 provides that persons approved by the Director to operate beyond Visual-Line-of-Sight should only conduct their activities below 400 feet above surface level. At this level, they are noticeable and easy to control, and thus prevent accidents and collisions. The operator is expected to operate within strict compliance of the permitted height. These express limitations

[87] See also Mashinini (2020), p. 143.

[88] Civil Aviation Act, Section 2.

[89] Civil Aviation Regulations (Eighth Amendment).

[90] Civil Aviation Regulations, Regulation 2(f).

[91] Civil Aviation Regulations (Eighth Amendment), Section 101.01.

[92] Linchant et al. (2015) *Mammal Review* 239–252.

[93] Civil Aviation Regulations (Eighth Amendment), Section 101.01.

[94] Civil Aviation Regulations (Eighth Amendment), Section 101.05.11 (2).

and restrictions operate to ensure that there is no abuse of power by the Director, which can pose a threat to the safety of the people.

Despite the requirement for licencing, certification, training, approvals and caution through visual line-of-sight, the South African legal framework recognizes the inevitability of accidents and collisions. As such, it imposes insurance obligations on UAS operators. Under the framework, a UAS operator certificate holder should carry third party liability insurance to enable him or her pay compensation for any damage caused to a third party.[95] The insurance is an assurance against security risks that could arise from the use of UAS.

There are other threads of general safety considerations that run through the web of regulatory framework in South Africa. Flowing from the jurisdiction of SACAA to develop technical standards provided under Section 163 of the Civil Aviation Act, 2009, it has developed standards on safety.[96] The standards address issues on who can operate a UAS, how and when. Under this framework, a person who operates UAS should ensure that it is in a fit-to-fly condition, and the pilot is a license holder.[97] The fitness to fly for UAS is different from manned aircraft since it lacks a cockpit and crew. Thus fitness to fly is in consideration of the planned travel vis-à-vis how far the UAS can fly, ability to return home, ability to fly with low fuel or power, as well as the status of inbuilt software.

Other external considerations that influence the fitness to fly are weather conditions, the guarantee of compatibility and only one pilot should control interoperability with which the aircraft is connected to in all phases of flight, and remotely piloted aircraft at any given moment.[98] Interoperability is the ability to communicate with diverse types of UAS within the airspace and air traffic control systems for manned aircraft. This requirement is a significant step for integration and harmonization calls in the ICAO UAS Circular since it gears towards creation of a singular unmanned aircraft system traffic management (UTM) with that of manned aircraft. While these requirements are evidently aimed at addressing safety measures as per the requirement of ICAO Annex 19, they also address the challenges associated with aviation security as provided for under ICAO Annex 17 to curb acts of unlawful interference with civil aviation or criminal activities.[99]

Another factor is the language of the air training and education. Radio communication is an important safety requirement for UAS operations, bearing in mind that communication and information are key to aviation safety. The type of operation being undertaken by the UAS operator determines the restrictions relating to radio

---

95 South Africa Civil Aviation Technical Standards (SA-CATS), Section 101.04.12.

96 SA-CATS, Section 101.04.12.

97 SA-CATS, Section 101.04.12.

98 SA-CATS, Section 101.05.9(1).

99 See Chap. 3, Sect. 3.4.2 of this book on the analysis of the ICAO Annex 17. It may be recalled that Section 2.1.2 of the Annex provide that provides that each contracting State shall establish an organization and develop and implement regulations, practices and procedures to safeguard civil aviation against acts of unlawful interference taking into account the safety, regularity and efficiency of flights.

communication. Except for restricted Visual-Line-of-Sight operations, no UAS shall be operated unless the pilot has a functioning air-band radio in his or her possession, tuned to the frequency or frequencies applicable to the air traffic service unit providing services or controlling such area or airspace or to aircraft in such area or airspace.[100] The entire operation of the UAS is to be conducted using a radio line of sight,[101] which is a direct electronic, point-to-point contact between a transmitter and a receiver.

Other requirements are necessitated by the prevailing circumstances of the operation.[102] Section 101.05.16 (2) of the Regulation requires that the air-band radio has the required output and be configured in such a way that the range, strength of transmission and quality of communication extends beyond the furthest likely position of the UAS from the pilot.[103] For Visual-Line-of-Sight, Extended Visual-Line-of-Sight and Beyond Visual-Line-of-Sight operations, the pilot is obligated during the registration of the UAS as a call-sign, to make the required radio calls, indicating the altitude, location and intended operation of the UAS in the area and at such intervals as are required in order to ensure adequate separation from other aircraft is maintained.[104]

The regulatory framework in South Africa encompasses certain prohibitions in addition to the above general considerations in safety precautions for operation of different categories of UAS. Prohibited UAS-related activities include using unmanned aircraft systems to tow other aircraft; performance of acrobatic displays, and flying in formations.[105] Operators of private UAS are further restricted from using them for certain purposes that would endanger the public.[106] They are prohibited from flying within 10 km of an airfield or restricted airspace (sensitive areas such as nuclear power stations, police stations, crime scenes or courts of law).[107] Other restrictions are with respect to releasing, dropping, delivering or deploying of objects. Due to advancement in technology, UAS are likely to be used for delivery of items like drugs and foodstuff to remote areas, hence prohibition on delivery falls short of the intended legislative purpose.

If outside a controlled airspace, the operator should comply with the technical requirements for operation using command inputs, ability to remain clear from obstacles or any other hazards, and take appropriate action to execute collision avoidance from such obstacles or other aircraft wherever necessary. These are vital precautions aimed at reducing air crashes and civil liabilities to the owners who could be at fault, if the area is void of other air traffic or the operation occurs in

---

[100] Civil Aviation Regulations (Eighth Amendment), Section 101.05.16 (1).
[101] Civil Aviation Regulations (Eighth Amendment), Section 101.05.16 (1).
[102] Civil Aviation Regulations (Eighth Amendment), Section 101.05.16 (1).
[103] Civil Aviation Regulations (Eighth Amendment), Section 101.05.16 (2).
[104] Civil Aviation Regulations (Eighth Amendment), Section 101.05.16 (2).
[105] Civil Aviation Regulations (Eighth Amendment), Section 101.05.10.
[106] Civil Aviation Regulations (Eighth Amendment), Section 101.05.10.
[107] Civil Aviation Regulations (Eighth Amendment), Section 101.05.10.

specifically segregated airspace; or measures to mitigate other aircraft, obstacles or hazards. In addition, the Director of Civil Aviation can command and control data link frequency appropriate for effective operation and data gathering.[108]

Further, the framework prohibits a commercial, corporate and non-profit UAS from using a public road or public grounds as take-off or landing grounds. A UAS may be allowed to operate within 50 m of a public road so long as the operator is a UAS operator's certificate holder with permission of the Director General.[109] In South Africa, it is prohibited to operate (UAS) overhead or at a lateral distance of 50 m from any person, unless one is a qualified UAS operator with a valid certificate.[110] A UAS operator must show operational capabilities, ability to command the UAS, to control airspace that follows a predetermined course or group of waypoint inputs.[111] The efficacy of these provisions is left to implementation of the institutions created under the framework.

Generally, no person is allowed to operate a UAS over a public road, along the length of a public road or at a distance of less than 50 m from a public road. There are, however, three exceptions to the rule: the person should be a holder of a UAS operator's certificate; the operation should be approved by the Director in the operator's operations manual; in the case of operations over a public road, such road is closed for public use and reasonable care taken to ensure the safety of road users and pedestrians in the event of loss of control of the UAS. It appears that the regulatory limitation is generally a safety and security measure aimed at safeguarding the lives of road users.

The above-mentioned general regulatory prohibitions and relaxations have safety and security underpinnings. A review of the prohibitions in other countries and States such as Nevada shows their effects on the public, which explains why they can only be relaxed when a UAS operator certificate holder receives approval of the Director of Civil Aviation. In approving the operations or granting waivers, the requirements reflect the international regulations of drones that prevent use of UAS in highly populated areas. In South Africa, therefore, the Director of Civil Aviation is guided by requirements that are determined by whether the operation takes place in a controlled or uncontrolled airspace.[112]

Equally relevant are standards relating to regulation of night operations. These are UAS operations conducted between 15 min after sunset and 15 min before sunrise, as provided in the publication *Times of sunrise, sunset and local apparent noon of the South African Astronomical Observatory* or a similar publication issued by a recognized astronomical observatory.[113] The general rule is that UAS may not be operated at night except in restricted Visual-Line-of-Sight operation or by a qualified

[108] Civil Aviation Regulations (Eighth Amendment), Section 101.05.11.

[109] Civil Aviation Regulations (Eighth Amendment), Section 101.05.15 and 101.05.2.

[110] Civil Aviation Regulations (Eighth Amendment), Section 101.05.12.

[111] Civil Aviation Regulations (Eighth Amendment), Section 101.05.12.

[112] Civil Aviation Regulations (Eighth Amendment), Section 101.05.11.

[113] https://www.esrl.noaa.gov/gmd/grad/solcalc/ (Date of use: 4 August 2023).

person who is a holder of UAS operator's certificate, and as approved by the Director in terms of sub-regulation 101.05.12 (1).[114] At the very minimum, such operator intending to operate at night shall only do so subject to compliance with the requirements prescribed in the South Africa Civil Aviation Technical Standards.[115] Section 101.05.12 (2) of the Regulations specifically provide that "An UAS may not be operated at night in controlled airspace except as approved by the Director as prescribed in Regulation 101.05.3."[116]

The UAS are allowed to operate in airfields and controlled zones if fitted with transponder that is capable of displaying the unique code issued to them, unless otherwise exempted by the Director of Civil Aviation. For ease of monitoring compliance with waiver conditions, the UAS should be fitted with an altimeter capable of displaying to the operator its altitude above ground level. It should also be fitted with functioning lights, installed in such a way that they are visible from both below and above the UAS.[117] These components should at all times be "serviceable and functioning" and failure to meet any one of them can lead to cancellation of operation.[118]

In spite of the foregoing general prohibitions, authors such as Percy have opined that certain exceptions to the rule exist.[119] For example, it is not a requirement that private operations get approval and registration. Many people in South Africa possess unregistered UAS, which they use for recreational purposes. In that regard, they do not hold licensing operator certificates and are exempted from rules that regulate conveyance of dangerous goods among other safety requirements. For instance, they do not have to be in a "fit to fly" condition.[120] Exceptions extend also to regulations and reporting of flight time, use of flight logbooks, power services, first aid kit and fire extinguishers.

Operation in controlled airspace refers to designated dimensions with an air traffic control service provided to UAS pilots in accordance with the airspace classification in the Civil Aviation Regulations.[121] The regulations prohibit operations in airspaces where sensitive installations are situated[122] such as military bases, airports, police stations and State Houses.[123] The prohibition does not, however, rip off powers of the Director of Civil Aviation to waive any requirement in certain circumstances.[124] The power of the Director to exempt as provided under the Act is meant to aid

[114] Civil Aviation Regulations (Eighth Amendment), Section 101.05.12 (1).

[115] Civil Aviation Regulations (Eighth Amendment), Section 101.05.12 (2).

[116] Civil Aviation Regulations (Eighth Amendment), Section 101.05.12 (2).

[117] SA-CATS, Section 101.05.3.

[118] SA-CATS, Section 101.05.3.

[119] Percy (2013).

[120] Mashinini (2020), p. 142.

[121] SA-CATS, Section 101.05.3 (1).

[122] SA-CATS, Section 101.05.3.

[123] SA-CATS, Section 101.05.3.

[124] SA-CATS, Section 101.05.3.

efficient and effective UAS operations on case-by-case basis as applies in the US. The power is available where there is a visual meteorological condition, airfields traffic and controlled zones that are not more than 400 feet.

5.6.2 *South Africa's Response to Security Concerns of UAS*

Aviation security as regards UAS deals with protection from possible use in conducting acts that cause unlawful interference to the State or the UAS system itself. According to Abeyrante, security in use of UAS remains a challenge in South Africa even as the country devises measures to integrate UAS into civil aviation.[125] This section analyses Part 5 of the Civil Aviation Act of 2009 to determine how South Africa's requirements for nationality marks, registration and certification of RPAs pilots, training and approval systems, and framework for development of programmes aim at addressing the issues of actual and potential interferences.

As seen earlier, aviation security refers to safeguarding civil aviation against acts of unlawful interference. This is reflective of the approach taken by international air law specifically ICAO Annex 17 and ICAO Doc 8973. The framework upholds the principles of State sovereignty and territorial integrity under Articles 1 and 2 of the Chicago Convention through its requirement that all aircraft must have nationality marks for easy identification and registration.[126]

South Africa's regulatory frameworks recognize the need for aviation security by taking a number of steps like regulating registration of national marks of the UAS to address the challenge of unlawful interference. All UAS registered in South Africa are considered to have the nationality of South Africa.[127] The regulations require that an identification plate should be ingrained on the UAS, comprising the registration and nationality marks.[128] They also require display of marks, bearing the right colours and fonts, location, allocation and specification. It is only after ingraining and displaying these marks that an aircraft passing over the Republic of South Africa can be certified to operate.[129] The regulations directly underpin the Rules of the Air provisions under Article 8 of the Chicago Convention, which spells out the importance of nationality marks. This is a positive move towards compliance with the binding provisions of the Rules of the Air as contained in ICAO Annex 2 to address security issues.

The subsequent sub-section addresses civilian UAS operators who use the South African airspace and are regulated by the Civil Aviation Act and

[125] Abeyratne (2011), pp. 285–294.

[126] SA-CATS, Section 101.0.2.4.

[127] This is compliance with Section 101.02.4.

[128] SA-CATS, Section 101.02.4.

[129] SA-CATS, Section 101.02.4. 2 (1) (a)-(d).

Regulations.[130] The scope of the Civil Aviation Regulations extends to Classes One and Two as demonstrated in the tables under this chapter.[131] These regulations fall under three categories, namely, private operators, commercial, corporate and non-profit operators. It does not extend to autonomous unmanned aircraft,[132] unmanned free balloons and their operations, or other types of aircraft that cannot be managed on a real-time basis during flight. This includes aircraft operated in terms of Part 94 of the Civil Aviation Regulations, which addresses the operation of "non-type certificated aircraft",[133] model aircraft,[134] and toy aircraft.[135]

Training and authorization are important security measures in South Africa. The 2015 Regulations prohibit flying of UAS 10 km close to vital strategic installations such as military bases without permission from the Director of SACAA.[136] This rule prevents the possibility of use of UAS compromising the security of the State.

Instructively, the SACAA has a Certification and Training arm as well as a training department. The training department sets standards, regulates trainings and provides oversight. Under the standards, the training and training centres are required to focus on aviation security procedures and processes.[137] The training packages are tailored to ensure planning, coordination and conducting procedures under ICAO Annex 17. The design of courses pursuant to Parts 109 and 110 of the Civil Aviation Regulations are aimed at integrating ICAO SARPs to curb unlawful interferences within the meaning of ICAO Aviation Security Manual.[138]

On its part, the certification department undertakes the role of standard setting, reviewing of regulation and certification of screening. Like the screening processes developed under the US framework, the screening may not be effective for the regulation of UAS operations. The review mandate is relevant to ensure that the law tries, as much as possible, to keep up with technological development. Of relevance to security is that a UAS operator certificate holder has additional mandate to take

---

[130] SA-CATS, Section 101.02.4. 2 (1) (a)-(d).

[131] SA-CATS, Section 101.02.4. 2 (1) (a)-(d).

[132] Civil Aviation Regulations, Regulation 1.01.1 provides that an unmanned aircraft that does not allow intervention in the management of the flight.

[133] A non-type certificated aircraft is any aircraft that does not qualify for the issue of a certificate of airworthiness in terms of Part 21 and shall include any type of certificated aircraft that has been scrapped, of which the original identification plate should have to be removed and returned to the applicable aviation authority and is rebuilt as a full-scale replica.

[134] Civil Aviation Regulations, Section 1.01.1 defines a model aircraft" as a heavier-than-air aircraft of limited dimensions, with or without a propulsion device, unable to carry a human being and to be used for competition, sport or recreational purposes rather than UAV developed for commercial or governmental, scientific, research or military purposes, and not exceeding the specifications as set by the federation.

[135] Toy aircraft is a product falling under the definition of aircraft, which is designed or intended, for use in play by children.

[136] Civil Aviation Regulation (Eighth Amendment), Section 101.05.10 (3) (a)-(d).

[137] Civil Aviation Act, Sections 75 (m) (i), 103 (j), 155 (e) (i-v), f (i-iv). Also see SA-CATS, Regulation 101.03.3 (1-4), 101.03.4 (1-4), 101.03.5 (1-4) and 101.04.1 (i).

[138] Civil Aviation Act, Section 155 p (iii).

security measures while using the UAS. This mandate includes conduct of background and periodic criminal record checks on persons working with UAS.[139]

South Africa places a lot of significance on registration as a security measure. Part 101 of the Civil Aviation Regulations, introduced by the Civil Aviation Regulations (Eighth Amendment), recognizes security challenges that may be caused by proliferation of UAS into the airspace. It provides for registration of imported UAS. Under the Regulations, in case the UAS leave the airspace, they have to be re-registered.[140] The conditions for the re-registration are geared towards meeting security standards by accounting for UAS that re-enter the airspace of South Africa. The UAS can only be registered if it has not been registered in another State. It is the author's view that this condition is well calculated to prevent the susceptibility of the airspace of the Republic of South Africa to instances of espionage.

Ownership of the UAS is a critical element during registration. It serves to ensure that the UAS are not used to commit crime anonymously and enables ease of tracking for accountability by owners should they be used to perpetrate criminal activities. Further, it makes it possible that a person with a criminal record is restricted under the laws for the sake of the country's security. Part 101 of the Civil Aviation Regulations, 2015 approaches the security issue from a responsibility point of view in cases of corporate ownership of UAS operations. For instance, the Regulations require disclosure of directors and resolutions or founding statements for a company or a closed operation to acquire UAS respectively. In respect of according responsibility of security to an identifiable group, renewals of registration certificates require proof trusteeship granted by the High Court.

Related to cooperate ownership, firms must produce South African identity to be allowed to own UAS. It means, therefore, that a foreign national, save for one who owns a pilot licence, cannot be part of the directorship of a company that owns a licence. This restrictive approach is meant to weed out instances of foreign ownership that may compromise the security of the State.

While this is a plausible approach especially against the backdrop of the September 11 attacks in the US, the restrictive security approach may seem to be imbalanced with the development objectives of regulation of UAS that, as Nonnecke observes, are equally vital objectives of UAS regulations.[141] The limitation may also conflict with the practice since the nature of the UAS is such that it is more likely to be owned by foreigners, either individually or as a firm, than nationals.

Another security measure is inspection of UAS as per Part 101.04.9 of the Civil Aviation Regulations (Eighth Amendment). Under this framework, UAS are required to undergo tight inspections to ensure there are no armaments that threaten the security or sovereignty of the State. It is obvious that such inspections are heightened depending on the relationship with a country and prevailing

[139] SA-CATS, Section 101.04.8.

[140] Civil Aviation Regulations (Eighth Amendment), Part 101 Regulations.

[141] Nonnecke (2012), pp. 121–141.

circumstances. These prerogatives are granted to the Republic by virtue of Article 8 of the Chicago Convention.

Additional effort in ensuring security is a long-term requirement for carriers, operators, providers of traffic and navigation services in the aviation sector to develop their aviation security programmes.[142] The role of the Civil Aviation Security Department of the SACAA is critical in ensuring harmony in the provisions through its consideration and approval of the participants' security programme.

South Africa has developed a comprehensive National Security Programme in addition to the participants' security programmes developed under Section 111 of the Civil Aviation Act. The Programme maps out training and certification issues and ensures that instances of unlawful interference with aircraft, including UAS, are weeded out. It provides the basis for coordination of actions by international organizations, government departments and involvement of private actors such as carriers in aviation security. The Programme also provides for effective communication between bodies for effective regulation.[143] Its coordination is pivotal in arresting threats of terror attacks that require a multi-faceted approach, making it the surest way of dealing with current security challenges that entail technological sophistication.

The South African framework further strives to achieve the security objectives through certain general geographical restrictions and functional requirements regarding UAS operation. To comply with security measures, the regulations prohibit operations in controlled airspaces or grounds where sensitive installations are situated[144] such as adjacent to or above nuclear plants, prisons, military bases, airports, police stations, crime scenes, courts of law, State Houses and national key points of strategic installation.[145] These are areas that deal with matters touching on the territorial integrity of the State.

Although the Civil Aviation regulations prohibit UAS operations in controlled airspaces, the Director of Civil Aviation may waive this requirement in some circumstances.[146] This power is meant to aid in the efficient and effective operations of UAS only. The discretion is limited if it compromises the aviation security, which explains why the exemption is done on case-by-case basis. The intention to limit the discretion by the Director is evidenced by the express provision of instances to which it can be exercised as visual meteorological condition, airfields traffic and control zones that are not more than 400 feet. Even if the discretion is exercised in respect to these three areas, the permission to operate in airfields and controlled zones is subjected to statutory limitations requiring that the UAS be fitted with transponder capable of displaying the unique code issued to them, unless otherwise

[142] SA-CATS, Section 101.04.5.

[143] South African Civil Aviation Authority "National Security Programme" http://www.caa.co.za/Pages/Aviation%20Security/National-AVSEC-programme.aspx (Date of use: 9 August 2023).

[144] Civil Aviation Régulations (Eighth Amendement), Section 101.05.3.

[145] Civil Aviation Régulations (Eighth Amendement), Section 101.05.3.

[146] Civil Aviation Régulations (Eighth Amendement), Section 101.05.3.

exempted by the Director of Civil Aviation.[147] The restriction on the controlled airspaces and exercise of discretion under this framework follows the model of regulation in the US.

5.6.3 *South Africa's Response to Privacy Concerns of UAS*

The Civil Aviation Act does not expressly address the right to privacy in UAS use. It only sets out the provision as a right to be considered in its monitoring, unlike the objectives of safety and security that are specifically addressed in distinct parts of the Act. This is reflective of the international framework on UAS use, which is also comparatively marginal in respect to provision on privacy.

The right to privacy is mentioned in Chap. 7 of the Civil Aviation Act, which makes provision for monitoring of regulatory compliance. Section 145 makes provision on the powers and manner of conduct of searches and seizures, and powers of arrests for offences provided under the Act. Section 145(1) envisages monitoring of the Act through conduct of warrantless searches on aircraft. The Act obligates the monitoring officers to ensure that any search contemplated be conducted with strict regard for decency, order and with respect for each person's right to dignity, freedom, security and privacy.[148] This means that all entries and inspections under the Act must be conducted in a manner that upholds the right to privacy.

Mention of the respect for the right in the monitoring and enforcement sections of the Civil Aviation Act is indicative of the reactive approach taken in the respect for the right to privacy. It does not envisage taking of steps to ensure, for instance, that operators' manual contains provisions on the respect of right to privacy. A more proactive approach is found in the regulation that limits the operation of UAS to a lateral distance of 50 m from any structure or public road. This is aimed at helping to prevent clandestine uses of UAS to invade the right to privacy.[149]

There are other instances when SA-CATS addresses the issues of negligent and reckless operation of UAS. The second part of Section 101.05.9 of the Regulations prohibits anyone from operating UAS in a negligent or reckless way, as to jeopardize the safety of any person, property or other aircraft in the air or on the ground. Since privacy invasion is a means of jeopardizing property or a person, the right and its guarantee can be inferred. There are many instances that draw from this analysis of substantive provisions on safety operations that go a long way in ensuring there is no violation of people's right to privacy.

The requirement under Section 101.01.7 (d) of the Civil Aviation Regulations (Eighth Amendment) that obligates pilots to observe all statutory requirements relating to liability, privacy and other law enforceable by any other authorities

[147] Civil Aviation Régulations (Eighth Amendement), Section 101.05.3.

[148] Civil Aviation Act, Section 145(13).

[149] Civil Aviation Regulation (Eighth Amendment), Section 101.05.03.

exacerbate the conditions set out above. This part, therefore, invites all UAS operators to comply with the provision on the protection of the right to privacy as encapsulated in Section 14 of the Constitution of the Republic of South Africa.

The South African Constitution provides safeguards concerning the privacy of every citizen, which include the right not to have their person or home searched, their property searched, their possessions seized or their communications infringed.[150] Obviously, such rights can be limited by law, in case those limitations are reasonable in a just and open society based on human rights equality and freedom.[151] Further protection of these rights is discussed in the human rights instruments, both at the international and continental levels that are applicable to South Africa. As seen in the overview of the framework, the challenge that the African Charter on Human and Peoples Right does not have provisions for privacy specific to UAS is a limitation on continental efforts, as far as South Africa is concerned. However, the application of human rights treaties, which have codified the international custom, are buffer for protection of the right to privacy regarding the use and operation of UAS.

5.7 General Challenges in Regulation of UAS in South Africa

The steps set out above evidence significant legislative efforts in provision of the safety, security and privacy rights in South Africa, albeit with some inherent challenges. Existing gaps under the framework are discussed below.

5.7.1 Exclusion of Toy Operators

The South African UAS Regulatory framework only applies to RPAs, which under the Civil Aviation Regulations as amended in 2015 covers unmanned aircraft while expressly excluding toy and model aircraft. The regulations only apply to private, commercial, corporate and non-profit operations of certain players. That it excludes That it excludes autonomous UAS, non-type certified aircraft, model aircraft and toy aircraft, creates a challenge in the path of integration and harmonization of UTM for UAS. While the practice of exclusion of model aircraft is in line with the framework under the ICAO, the objective of excluding toys in South Africa is based on the fact that they are used for hobbies. With the ubiquity in UAS use, almost a decade after the laws were made and amended, toy aircraft can be used for clandestine activities irrespective of their weight and size. They, therefore, are a potential threat to safety, security and privacy of users and the public. The exclusion causes confusion

[150] Constitution of the Republic of South Africa, 1996, Section 14.

[151] Constitution of the Republic of South Africa, 1996, Sections 7(3) and 36(1) & (2).

amongst South African citizens, which leads to breaking aviation laws related to UAS.[152]

5.7.2 *Lack of Provisions on Community-Based Organizations*

Unlike the US, South Africa has no provision for community-based organizations to seek UAS approvals for its members. This leaves open a window through which unscrupulous operators can fly UAS to the detriment of safety and security of civil aviation in general, and UAS in particular. It is also a missed opportunity to complement the enforcement capacity of SACAA. It is the author's take, therefore, that SACAA should consider the practice and adopt it in the local community as once involved, they help in oversight and reporting incidences.

The exemption could pose the challenge of UAS interception for criminal activities, which in effect is a violation of the people's right to privacy as protected by Section 14 of the Constitution of South Africa. In comparison, the US has a way of dealing with the challenge by giving mandate to community-based organisations to partner with FAA on matters of recreation and approval of operations.

5.7.3 *Wide Powers of the Director of Civil Aviation*

The powers of the Director of Civil Aviation are limited with regard to granting permission to use UAS in controlled places, but are broad as appertains to publishing technical standards, and responsibility for safety and security.[153] These powers enable the exercise of discretion in exempting pilot licensing requirements, including allowing operation in controlled airspaces. Given the rapid rise in nature, classes and use of UAS, the powers should not be entrusted to just one person. Therefore, the author suggests that the exercise of such discretion should be limited to reduce exposure of civil aviation to the desires of an individual with potential of abuse to the detriment of the entire civil aviation sector. Formation of a security committee involving a multi-agency or appeal panel could suffice in cases where one is dissatisfied by decisions made by the Director General. The case of Absa drones' fireworks over Johannesburg is an example of a ticking time-bomb emanating from this challenge in the regulatory framework.

---

[152] Khyanyile N "Fun with a Warning" https://www.news24.com/SouthAfrica/News/fun-with-a-warning-20190204-2 (Date of use: 4 August 2023).

[153] Civil Aviation Act, Section 86(3)(a).

5.7.4 *Implementation Challenges*

The mandate to monitor and enforce compliance with the aviation law is provided in Section 113 of the Civil Aviation Act. The SACAA is empowered to enter, inspect and examine any aircraft, place and premises.[154] Further, it considers the information furnished by the operators, books and documents, and has power to conduct seizures and inspections, liaison with criminal enforcement agencies, among others for the proper administration of the Civil Aviation Act. Rise in the use of UAS means that there is commensurate increase in the number of engaged inspectors, investment in training and creation of awareness, all of which require substantial funding.

Despite the existing legal and institutional framework, regulatory provisions and implementation, certain challenges persist that could derail the regulation of UAS use.[155] The SACAA faces numerous hiccups including workforce constraints and resultant enforcement challenges. For example, many UAS are imported and declared at the port of entry; however, some are not declared at customs for registration and monitoring purposes, hence providing difficulties in effectively enforcing compliance of required civil aviation standards.[156]

The challenge is occasionally brought to the fore through the media, as was the case involving two Lebanese and two South African citizens who were arrested in January 2018 and arraigned in Kempton Park Magistrate's Court for allegedly illegally exporting components of drones to Hezbollah in Lebanon.[157] The case was yet to be determined at the time of writing this book. *Prima facie*, the case depicts some of the challenges experienced with the slow pace of implementation of UAS regulation, hence the urgent need for SACAA to put its house in order and get UAS integration into effective operations to avert and mitigate such risks. The existence of these challenges shows that SACAA has not been able to maintain a critical balance between integration and criminal law administration. Specific challenges in the implementation are expounded below.[158]

---

[154] Civil Aviation Act, Section 113(1)(a).

[155] Lindiwe Nchabelenga is a lawyer and an Inspector at South Africa Civil Aviation Authority. Ms Lindiwe, who is national civil aviation inspector for SACAA, traces the source of this challenge to the overstretching in the institutional capacity.

[156] Mngadi M "Two Lebanese brothers in court for Hezbollah drone export case" https://www.news24.com/news24/southafrica/news/two-lebanese-brothers-in-court-for-hezbollah-drone-export-case-20180226-2 (Date of use: 4 August 2023).

[157] Mngadi https://www.news24.com/news24/southafrica/news/two-lebanese-brothers-in-court-for-hezbollah-drone-export-case-20180226-2 (Date of use: 4 August 2023).

[158] https://mybroadband.co.za/news/gadgets/126654-12-things-you-need-to-know-about-south-africas-new-drone-laws.html (Date of use: 10 August 2023).

5.7.5 Absence of Southern African Civil Aviation Safety and Security Organization

The ICAO-led framework recognizes that safety and security activities and programmes can be better harnessed at regional and sub-regional levels. In other words, it makes a lot of sense for South Africa to have a higher compliance rating compared to its neighbours so as to harness regulatory peer influence amongst States. It is for this reason that ICAO has rolled out an initiative for Regional Aviation Safety Groups through the its Regional Offices.[159]

SADC member States lag behind when it comes to establishing a regional body to unequivocally deal with civil aviation within the sub-regional bloc. The establishment of the Interim South African Safety Organization was characterised by an aura of reluctance by the members. This sharply contrasts with their East African counterparts who have Civil Aviation Safety and Security Oversight Agency (CASSOA) at the sub-regional level. On top of this, Africa is yet to establish African regional UAS regulations. It needn't be overemphasised that a Southern African States' civil aviation body could be handy in regulating civil aviation within the SADC region by addressing safety, security and privacy challenges associated with movement of UAS across the region.

The potential negative effects of not having such regional bodies can be enormous. It could easily result in clandestine UAS movements into neighbouring countries within a regional economic block with less developed or no UAS regulations, and thus compromise safety, security and privacy in the use and operation of UAS in South Africa. It is projected that regulation at the regional and sub-regional levels would address issues including general aviation safety and security by formally addressing UAS registration, certification, and compliance.

5.8 Conclusion

It is worth noting that the move towards regulation of UAS in South Africa began mildly in 2002, and gained momentum around 2011. The regulatory framework has specific and express provisions for UAS as established in 2015. There are no reported conflicts between the State and federal laws on regulation in South Africa, which has a three-sphere government structure that enables it to adopt a US-like regulation structure, albeit with lack of community-based organizations. South Africa's active participation in ICAO Security Panel puts it ahead as regards moral obligation to comply with safety and security measures in the ICAO-based framework. This adds onto its adoption of the Chicago Convention, although

[159] https://www.icao.int/safety/SafetyManagement/Pages/Regional-Aviation-Safety-Groups-(RASGs).aspx (Date of use: 4 August 2023).

lack of SADC-based civil aviation regulations seems to derail sub-regional efforts in as far as safety and security are concerned.

The substantive provisions of the Civil Aviation Act, 2009, the regulations thereunder and robust framework of circulars issued by SACAA are particularly relevant in regulating safety, security and privacy issues. These significantly mirror the international approach envisaged under the ICAO framework. Despite the development of a robust legal and institutional framework, together with a high rate of ICAO-participation that gives rise to increased compliance with the ICAO framework compared to other African countries, South Africa is still grappling with lack of an efficient legal framework. For instance, the existing framework does not adequately address the UAS-specific issues of privacy. This is a challenge since the constitutionally backed right to privacy is too general and does not address the challenges caused by recent technological developments in aviation, which need to be captured under the Regulations. Regarding safety, exclusion of UAS toy operators from the Regulations has serious safety implications, which may surpass its justification.

The institutional legal frameworks for implementation of the law have played an important role in defining standards, guidelines, monitoring and licensing of UAS. Whereas the Regulations have gone a long way in providing a regulatory framework for UAS, its current design has loopholes regarding power of the Director of SACAA. The implementation challenges related to weak links in the institutional framework have overreaching effects in compromising safety and security. These challenges affect potential uses of the UAS. Consequently, the UAS legal and policy frameworks in South Africa, without the integration roadmap within the country and the region, do not fully speak to current needs and challenges in UAS operations, as well as integration development. Overall, South Africa has made fundamental progress towards integration of UAS into civil aviation.

References

Books

Dalamagkidis K, Kimon PV, Piegl LA (2011) On integrating unmanned aircraft systems into the national airspace system: issues, challenges, operational restrictions, certification, and recommendations. Springer Science & Business Media

Levush R (2016) Regulation of drones: comparative summary. The Law Library of Congress, Global Legal Research Center, Washington DC

Percy S (2013) Regulating the private security industry. Routledge

Contribution in Books

Timothy R (2016) A comparative global analysis of drone laws: best practices and policies. In: The future of drone use. TMC Asser Press, Hague, p 302

Journal Articles

Abeyratne R (1998) The future of African civil aviation. J Air Transp Worldwide, 30–49
Abeyratne R (2011) Civil unrest and airport and aviation security. J Transp Secur, 285–294
Goode R (2012) From acorn to oak tree: the development of the Cape Town Convention and Protocols. Uniform Law Rev, 599
Ingham LA, Jones T, Maneschijn A (2006) Considerations for UAV design and operation in South African airspace. Aeronaut J, 695–699
Mashinini N (2020) The processing of personal information using remotely piloted aircraft systems in South Africa. De Jure Law J, 140–158
Nonnecke BM (2012) Hitting or Missing African UAS Objectives? An evaluation of universal access and service (UAS) policy guidelines for developing countries. Commun Strateg, 121–141
Oliver D (2015) History of South Africa UASs. Afr Defence Rev, 1–5

Thesis and Dissertations

Ingham LA (2009) Consideration for a roadmap for the operation of UAV in South Africa Airspace. PhD Thesis Stellenbosch University

Workshops and Conference Papers

Burger CR, Jones T (2011) Adapting existing training standards for unmanned aircraft: finding ways to train staff for unmanned aircraft operations. Paper presented to the International Aerospace Symposium of South Africa (IASSA) Centurion South Africa 26–28 September 2011

Chapter 6
Legal, Policy and Institutional Framework for UAS in Kenya

6.1 Introduction

This Chapter provides a reflective analysis of the regulatory framework for regulation of Unmanned Aircraft Systems (UAS) in Kenya. It seeks to analyse how the Kenya Civil Aviation Authority (KCAA) addresses safety, security and privacy concerns arising from the use and challenges of UAS as a way of integrating UAS operation into civil aviation airspace. The Chapter approaches the analysis by providing a brief background, overview of the legal, policy and institutional framework, principally under the Civil Aviation Act No. 21 of 2013 and KCAA Amendment Act of 2016 respectively. It critically analyses the salient regulatory provisions within the regulatory framework vis-à-vis their efficacy in addressing the safety, security, and privacy concerns associated with UAS operations in Kenyan civil aviation. The term Remotely Piloted Aircraft Systems (RPAs) is used interchangeably with UAS because it is what featured in Kenya's previous legal and policy framework.

6.2 Background to Regulation of UAS in Kenya

Use of UAS is on the rise in Kenya, primarily for civilian applications.[1] UAS have traditionally been used in Kenya for various purposes, namely: remote sensing, aerial photography, surveying, disaster management, communication, protection of fisheries and forest resources, coastguard, locust control, research and development,

[1] The Civil Aviation Act (Remote Piloted Aircraft Systems) (UAS) Regulations of 6 October 2017 Legal Notice No 269 (annulled) (hereinafter referred to as the 2017 RPAs Regulations) had allowed Kenyans to own UAS for sports, private activities and commercial purposes. KCAA has now developed a roadmap on how to re-introduce the regulation back to operation. Also see Andae G "Kenya flies behind peers in drones regulation" *2019-9-18 Business Daily* https://www.

M. Wanyonyi Rodgers, *The Law Regulating Unmanned Aircraft Systems in the United States, South Africa and Kenya*,
https://doi.org/10.1007/978-3-031-49927-2_6

oil and mineral exploration.[2] Today, the uses cover issues of wildlife management and agriculture. Wildlife management pioneered the use of UAS technology from *Unmanned Innovation Inc* in Kenya at the Ol Pejeta Conservancy to control poaching.[3] This came about upon realization of timing inadequacies in traditional methods of poaching control.[4] Overall, the results have been very positive in terms of combating the vice.[5]

Another area that is increasingly gaining attention and traction is control of cattle rustling amongst nomadic communities such as the Pokot, Maasai, Turkana and the Samburu. [6] Attempts have been made to integrate UAS in tracking cattle, directing security personnel and surveillance to locate rustlers and stolen cattle. Researchers in Kenya such as Mbote and Muriungi project potential use the mapping and surveying in areas that are far from town.[7]

The increased civil use of UAS in Kenya is partly fuelled by the government's long-term and short-term development policies,[8] which are pegged on infrastructural, scientific, technological and innovation development.[9] In addition, Kenya has an ambitious agenda in land, human resource development, security and public sector reform.[10] However, these reforms encounter numerous obstacles such as identified sources of insecurity as conflicts and cattle rustling require government counter-measures to address them.[11] There are also 'traditional' conflicts, emerging crimes like terrorism, piracy and cybercrime that the government continues to fight. To fight growing insecurity, the police require sophisticated technology such as UAS. Increase in traditional uses causes concerns of safety, security and privacy of the members of the public and users of the UAS in these operations.

There are scattered instances of UAS use by the military in Kenya. In 2012, for example, the Kenya Defence Forces (KDF) acquired UAS at a cost of $9.86 million for use by the African Union Mission on Somalia (AMISOM)[12] for weakening the Al-Shabaab militia group camps, which were undertaking terrorist attacks against

---

businessdailyafrica.com/corporate/tech/Kenya-flies-behind-African-peers-in-drones-adoption/4258474-5278452-fvbplqz/index.html (Date of use: 6 August 2023).

[2] Andae https://www.businessdailyafrica.com/corporate/tech/Kenya-flies-behind-African-peers-in-drones-adoption/4258474-5278452-fvbplqz/index.html (Date of use: 6 August 2023).

[3] Wright (1916), p. 106.

[4] Odido and Madara (2013), p. 112.

[5] Odido and Madara (2013), p. 112.

[6] Odido and Madara (2013), p. 113.

[7] Kameri-Mbote and Muriungi (2017), p. 172.

[8] Government of Kenya Vision 2030 of 2007.

[9] http://www.president.go.ke/2017/12/12/speech-by-his-excellency-hon-uhuru-kenyatta-c-g-h-president-and-commander-in-chief-of-the-defence-forces-of-the-republic-of-kenya-during-the-2017-jamhuri-day-celebrations-at-the-moi-international/ (Date of use: 10 August 2023).

[10] See Ronald (2012), pp. 128–143.

[11] Wright (1916), p. 107.

[12] AMISSOM refers to the African Union Mission in Somalia.

Kenyans.[13] The US military has on a number of occasions used Kenya's airspace to launch attacks against terrorist targets in Somalia.[14] Kenya too, has made several strikes against Al-Shabaab hideouts in Somalia resulting in casualties, in an effort to eliminate piracy along the Kenya-Somalia border and stamp out terrorism in general. [15] The Kenyan framework has not attempted to adopt regulation on such military operations. The long title of the Civil Aviation Act is clear that the Act is only concerned with orderly development of civil aviation in Kenya.

6.3 Legal Framework and Foundation to Regulation of UAS in Kenya

Kenya ratified the Chicago Convention in May 1964. Accordingly, the country is bound by obligations of State parties concerning regulations as contained in Article 11 of the Convention. Kenya is a member of ICAO thus bound by the ICAO Annexes, Standards and Recommended Practices (SARPs) such as ICAO Annex 17 on security, and Annex 19 on Safety Management System (SMS): the Annexes are domesticated through development of National Civil Aviation Security Programmes and State Safety Programme (SSP) respectively. Kenya gets support through ICAO guidance materials such as Aviation Security Manual (Doc 8973), Aviation Safety Manual (Doc 9869), Manual on Remotely Piloted Aircraft Systems (RPAs) (Doc 10019 AN/507) of 2015, ICAO UAS Circular No. 328-AN/190 of 2011, and Circular 330 AN/189 on Civil/Military Cooperation in Air Traffic Management of 2011. Kenya has ratified several Conventions and numerous treaties in relation to civil aviation as highlighted below.

Pursuant to Article 2(6) of the Constitution of Kenya, the Conventions ratified before or after the promulgation of the Constitution in 2010 automatically formed part of Kenyan law. Kenya is a party to the Convention on Suppression of Unlawful Seizure of Aircraft, Convention relating to Unlawful Acts Relating to International Civil Aviation,[16] Protocols Relating to an Amendment to the Chicago Convention,

---

[13] Otuki N "Kenya buys Sh1bn pilotless aircraft in war on Al-Shabaab" *2012-2-25 Business Daily* https://www.businessdailyafrica.com/economy/Kenya-buys-Sh1bn-pilotless-aircraft-in-war-on-Al-Shabaab (Date of use: 4 July 2023).

[14] Olingo A "Kenya now drafts regulations, joins Rwanda to allow drones into its airspace" 2016-4-17 *The East African* https://www.theeastafrican.co.ke/news/ea/Kenya-joins-Rwanda-to-allow-drones-in-its-airspace-/4552908-3162800-13jswqt/index.html (Date of use: 10 August 2023).

[15] Olingo https://www.theeastafrican.co.ke/news/ea/Kenya-joins-Rwanda-to-allow-drones-in-its-airspace-/4552908-3162800-13jswqt/index.html (Date of use: 10 August 2023).

[16] Convention on Suppression of Unlawful Seizure of Aircraft, Convention relating to Unlawful Acts Relating to International Civil Aviation of 10 September 2010 (entered into force on 1 July 2018).

Convention on the International Recognition of Rights in Aircraft,[17] Convention on International Interests in Mobile Equipment (The Cape Town Convention), the Protocol on the Convention on International Interest in Mobile Equipment on Matters Specific to Aircraft Equipment (the Cape Town Protocol), Convention on Unification of Certain Rules Relating to International Air Carriage signed at Warsaw on 12 October 1929 as amended by the Hague Protocol of 1955 (the Warsaw Convention), the Convention for the Unification of International Carriage by Air, signed at Montreal on 28 May 1999 (the Montreal Convention) and Convention on Compensation for Damage Caused by Aircraft to Third Parties.[18] Kenya domesticated the Cape Town Convention and the Cape Town Protocol by enacting the International Interest in Aircraft Equipment Act No. 27 of 2013, which gives the High Court of Kenya jurisdiction in respect of claims brought under it. The provisions of these Conventions are binding on Kenya by virtue of the good faith principle and the principle of *pacta sunt servanda*.[19] Kenya, therefore, draws from the spirit of international law to provide guidance for State parties to develop regulations that enable integration of UAS operations in civil aviation in their respective jurisdictions and to assure safety, security and privacy concerns.[20]

At the continental level, Kenya is a member of the African Union and a party to the Africa Union (AU) Constitutive Act.[21] Kenya is guided by the Constitution, which recognizes the institutional framework under the Africa Civil Aviation Commission, a specialized agency of the African Union. The Commission takes lead in fostering liberalization of air transport and compliance with the ICAO framework.[22] The institutional framework of the Africa Civil Aviation Commission forms the basis of cooperation with regional economic blocs or communities and ICAO to ensure that aviation matters of mutual interests are settled.[23] It is worth noting that the Commission is mandated with the overall responsibility of safety, security and environmental protection in the aviation sector within the African continent among other functions.

At the sub-regional level, Kenya became a member of the East African Community (EAC) after it ratified the EAC Treaty of 1999. Article 92 of the EAC Treaty requires Kenya to harmonize its laws and policies on civil aviation in order to

[17] Convention on the International Recognition of Rights in Aircrafts of 19 June 1948 UNTS 4492 (entered into force on 17 September 1953).

[18] Convention on Compensation for Damage Caused by Aircraft to Third Parties of May 2009.

[19] Vienna Convention on the Law of Treaties of 1969, Preamble and Articles 2(1) (a) and 26. *Pacta sunt servanda* is a *Latin* idiom that may be translated to mean treaties must be complied with or agreements once made must be kept.

[20] See Chap. 3, Sects. 3.4.1–3.4.3 on the international law response to safety, security and privacy concerns to UAS use and operations.

[21] Constitutive Act of the African Union of 2001.

[22] Constitution of the Africa Civil Aviation Commission of 17 January 1969 (entered into force on 17 March 1972) (as Revised in 2009), Article 3.

[23] Constitution of the Africa Civil Aviation Commission of 17 January 1969 (entered into force on 17 March 1972) (as Revised in 2009), Article 17.

provide efficiency of the aviation sector in support of other sectors of the economy. It also requires Kenya to ensure that the aviation transport systems are safe and efficient. Further, the country is obligated to ensure maintenance of a high level of security for air operations, including joint searches.[24] The EAC has created a framework through the Civil Aviation Safety and Security under the EAC Civil Aviation Safety and Security Oversight Agency Act.[25] The only challenge regarding implementation is that the EAC laws do not have a direct applicability and absolute supremacy over national laws owing to the provision of Article 8(2) of the Treaty for the Establishment of the EAC of 1999, which requires States to develop domestic laws to give effect to those of the EAC.

At the domestic level, the substance of civil aviation law can be traced from as early as the 1970s. The Kenya Civil Aviation (Amendment) Act[26] was enacted in 1970 and underwent amendments in 1977 through to 1979, resulting in the establishment of the Kenya Civil Aviation Authority (KCAA) as an autonomous body taking over the functions of the Directorate of Civil Aviation.[27]

In terms of its regulatory approach post-2010, Kenya adopts a devolved governance structure with one national government and 47 county governments that operate distinctively, albeit interdependently.[28] Under the Fourth Schedule to the Constitution of Kenya, 2010, civil aviation, under the larger umbrella of transport and communications, is the function of the national government. Generally, the national government had not lived to regulation of UAS within this larger mandate up to 2017. Accordingly, the UAS integration into non-segregated (civilian) airspace in Kenya, for a long time and especially in the pre-2013 legal regime, remained a challenge due to a *lacuna* in a binding UAS regulatory framework in Kenya.

In 2013, there developed an urgent need for law reform in the response mechanism for safety, security and privacy provisions relating to, among others, UAS. This led to development of the principal civil aviation regulatory framework, primarily set out in the Civil Aviation Act of 2013.[29] The Act defines an aircraft as "any machine that derives support in the atmosphere from reactions of the air other than reaction of the air against the earth's surface, and includes all flying machines, aeroplanes, gliders, seaplanes, rotorcrafts, airships, balloons, gyroplanes, helicopters, ornithopters and other similar machines but excludes State aircraft."[30] This definition does not expressly provide for the regulation of operation of UAS. The application could, however, be drawn by implication owing to the inclusive nature of the definition

[24] EAC Treaty 1999, Article 92(3) (m).

[25] See EAC Civil Aviation Safety and Security Oversight Agency Act of 2007, Sections 1, 2 and 3 (a).

[26] The Kenya Civil Aviation (Amendment) Act, Chapter 394, Laws of Kenya.

[27] See Cap. 394 Lok now repealed that formed KCAA.

[28] Constitution of Kenya, 2010, Article 6(3).

[29] The Civil Aviation Act 21 of 2013 (hereinafter referred to as the Civil Aviation Act), Section 83 repealed the Civil Aviation Act Chapter 394 Laws of Kenya.

[30] The Civil Aviation Act, Section 2 (j).

which covered 'other machines' such as balloons and other aircraft. Regarding the exclusion of State aircraft, both the Civil Aviation Act, 2013 and the Civil Aviation (Amendment) Act, 2016 are categorical that the laws apply to civil aircraft. The application of the rules to State aircraft is possible through the direction of the Cabinet Secretary responsible for Transport as under Section 3(2) of the Civil Aviation Act, 2013 it applies only for expediency of regulation of State aircraft but does not in any way mean that military UAS are subjected to the regulatory frameworks under the Civil Aviation Act, 2013 and Civil Aviation (Amendment) Act, 2016.[31]

The principal law under the Civil Aviation Act, 2013 recognizes the application of international Conventions. The envisaged Conventions are numerous, and include protocols and Annexes thereto relating to civil aviation, to which Kenya is a party. It is upon the Board of the Kenya Civil Aviation Authority to make legislative proposals for giving effect to the international Conventions and instruments.[32]

Three years after the enactment of the Civil Aviation Act, 2013, Parliament enacted the Civil Aviation (Amendment) Act[33] which introduced a raft of legal changes in the regulation of civil aviation in Kenya. A notable change was the provision of the definition of unmanned aerial vehicle to mean:

> a pilotless aircraft is flown without a pilot-in-command on-board and is either remotely or fully controlled from another place (ground or another aircraft, space) or programmed and fully autonomous.[34]

This definition is expansive as it envisages both the manner of control and operations of UAS. For the first time in a legislative enactment, the 2016 Amendment Act provided an express recognition of UAS under Kenyan aviation law requiring regulation. Henceforth, the amendment law of 2016 represents a huge leap in as far as formal recognition and integration of the UAS into the Kenyan civil airspace is concerned in achieving the spirit of Article 3 of the Chicago Convention.

The Constitution of Kenya[35] provides fundamental safeguards with a bearing on regulation of use, manufacture and operation of UAS. Specifically, it has a Bill of Rights that recognizes and protects, among others, the right to privacy. Under Chapter Four of the Constitution (Bill of Rights), enforcement of the right can be done through a petition to the High Court on an allegation that the right has been infringed, breached or threatened.[36]

---

[31] Section 3(ii) of the Civil Aviation Act provides that: The provisions of this Act shall not, except where expressly included or if the Cabinet Secretary so directs by order published in the Gazette, apply to state aircraft or to any class or classes of state aircraft.

[32] The Civil Aviation Act, Section 15(3)(a)(ii).

[33] The Civil Aviation (Amendment) Act 42 of 2016 (hereinafter referred to as the Civil Aviation (Amendment Act).

[34] The Civil Aviation (Amendment Act), Section 2.

[35] Constitution of Kenya, 2010.

[36] Constitution of Kenya, 2010, Article 23(1).

The Kenyan legal framework gets support from a number of legislations that acknowledged regulation of civil aviation as far as it relates to use, manufacture and operation of UAS. Kenya has a specific law on enforcement of data protection. The Data Protection Bill was enacted into law after passing by Parliament on 7 November 2019, and assented to by President Uhuru Kenyatta on 8 November 2019. The Data Protection Act[37] enhances privacy rights as enshrined under the Kenyan Constitution.[38] The latest passage of the law comes against a backdrop of many reported instances in which human rights groups have reported excess surveillance over the Kenyan airspace by UAS.[39] Relevant national legislations relating to the implementation and enforcement of the integration of UAS into the Kenyan national aviation airspace are the National Security Council Act,[40] Kenya Airports Authority Act,[41] Security Laws (Amendment) Act[42] and Regulations made under them. Relevant Regulations are the Kenya Civil Aviation (Security) Regulations,[43] Civil Aviation (Air Operator Certification and Administration) Regulations,[44] and Civil Aviation (Operation of Aircraft) Regulations,[45] These Regulations were amended in 2018 to Civil Aviation (Operations of Aircraft for Commercial Air Transport) Regulations, 2018 and Civil Aviation (Rules of the Air) Regulations.[46]

Flowing from the legislative developments through the Civil Aviation (Amendment) Act, 2016, the Cabinet Secretary for Transport and Infrastructure, has mandate to enact civil aviation regulations including those for regulating UAS. The development of regulations on implementing particular provisions for UAS under the 2016 Civil Aviation (Amendment) Act was accorded urgent attention. In October 2017, KCAA developed the 2017 Civil Aviation (Remotely Piloted Aircraft Systems) Regulations. The Regulations applied to a wide spectrum of dealings in remotely piloted aircraft, ranging from manufacturing, assembly, procurement, importation, testing, operation and maintenance of the aircraft.[47] The scope of the Regulations covered all remotely piloted aircraft except State aircraft, unmanned free balloons or airships and toys that operate within an aerodrome, not less than 500 m from the aerodrome boundaries. Generally, the registration of the aircraft was based on categorizations and classification, which puts currency on use and weight

[37] Data Protection Act 24 of 2019.

[38] Constitution of Kenya, 2010, Article 31 (c) and (d).

[39] Privacy International "State of Privacy Kenya" https://privacyinternational.org/state-privacy/1005/state-privacy-kenya (Date of use: 29 August 2023).

[40] National Security Council Act 23 of 2012.

[41] Kenya Airports Authority Act No 3 of 1991.

[42] Security Laws (Amendment) Act 19 of 2014.

[43] Kenya Civil Aviation (Security) Regulations of 2015 as amended in 2020.

[44] Civil Aviation (Air Operator Certification and Administration) Regulations of 2013.

[45] Civil Aviation (Operation of Aircraft) Regulations of 2013.

[46] Civil Aviation (Rules of the Air) Regulations of 2013.

[47] The 2017 RPAs Regulations, Regulation 3.

respectively, from class 1A to class 3C.[48] The operations were categorized into personal, commercial and recreational purposes of use of RPAs.

The 2017 RPAs Regulations were short-lived as Parliament adopted a report of the Committee on Delegated Legislation on 26 June 2018 in its second session, and pursuant to the provisions of Section 15 of the Statutory Instruments Act[49] and Standing Order 210 (4) (b) of 2018, annulled them in their entirety for reasons of inadequate public participation during development, as required by the Statutory Instruments Act. The Kenya Civil Aviation Policy suffered a similar fate though not under Parliament's mandate for revocation. Its main objective is to support operation of UAS in a safe, secure, harmonized and seamless environment equal to manned operations.[50] The suspension was a missed opportunity for the security measures that were practically beefed up through authorization systems at the Ministry responsible for Transport and Department of Defence headquarters. It was also a missed opportunity for security measures through practical steps for cancellation of permits in light of State safety interests that were necessary to complement the Civil Aviation (Rules of the Air) Regulations and Civil Aviation (Safety Management) Regulations.

Despite the annulled 2017 RPAs Regulations, there are certain cross-cutting reassurances of safety, security and privacy issues relating to UAS that can be obtained from myriad Regulations that have been passed pursuant to provision of Section 82 of the Civil Aviation Act. They include the Civil Aviation (Rules of the Air) Regulations,[51] the Civil Aviation (Airworthiness) Regulations,[52] and the Civil Aviation (Personnel Licensing) Regulations.[53] Instrumental in the regulatory framework is the Kenya National Civil Aviation Security Programme, and Safety programmes.

From a historical perspective on development and law reform set out above, it is clear that the integration of UAS into civil aviation was thrown into limbo for the intervening period between end of June 2018 and March 2020. During this period, KCAA embarked on addressing the issues raised by Parliament such as observance of public participation in all counties, and providing measures to address safety and national security while adhering to the Constitutional right to privacy. In order to preserve the status quo in the intervening period, the Cabinet Secretary for Transport, Infrastructure, Housing, Urban Development and Public Works, through Kenyan Gazette Legal Notice No 76, on 26 March 2019 published prohibition to fly and operate Unmanned Aircraft, effectively stopping usage of UAS within the Kenyan airspace until such a time when new regulations were to be enacted.

[48] The 2017 RPAs Regulations, Regulation 4.

[49] Statutory Instruments Act 23 of 2013.

[50] Republic of Kenya Policy on Remotely Piloted Aircraft Systems of 2017.

[51] Civil Aviation (Rules of the Air) Regulations of 2013.

[52] Civil Aviation (Airworthiness) Regulations of 2013 (as amended in 2016).

[53] Civil Aviation (Personnel Licensing) Regulations of 2013.

As Captain Kibe[54] posits, after the nullification of the 2017 RPAs regulations, the first meeting by UAS Working Group was held on 11 September 2018 to provide a roadmap and strategy to the Cabinet Secretary for Transport, Infrastructure, Housing, Urban Development and Public Works, the Attorney General, and Parliament on how to expedite the UAS regulation. The roadmap took into account the views of Parliament such as enhancing security, privacy concerns, undertaking public participation in all counties, and adherence to the Statutory Instrument Act.[55]

By December 2019, KCAA had concluded the public participation exercise in compliance with Parliament's directive by capturing concerns raised and conducting a workshop in Nairobi.[56] In April 2020, the process of redevelopment and public consultations on the Regulations culminated in the Cabinet Secretary for Transport, Infrastructure, Housing, Urban Development and Public Works promulgating the Civil Aviation (Unmanned Aircraft Systems) Regulations,[57] 2020, through gazettement in the Kenya Gazette Supplement No. 34 Legislative Supplement No. 22, issued as Legal Notice 42 of 2020. This was in the exercise of the powers conferred on the office by Section 82 of the Civil Aviation Act No. 21 of 2013.

The 2020 UAS regulation enumerates various activities such as import, export, manufacture, assembly and testing of UAS. It contains five parts that address the various aspects of UAS operations in Kenya. Part I addresses categorization of operation and registration of UAS. Part II provides for categorization of operation and registration of UAS. Part III provides for the operation of UAS. Part IV addresses issues of security. Part V focuses on miscellaneous issues. The substantive contents make provisions for issues of safety and privacy.

6.4 Institutional Framework

6.4.1 Organs, Structure and Key Functions of KCAA

The Civil Aviation Act establishes certain institutions responsible for implementation of provisions relating to regulation of UAS. Part III of the Act makes provision on duties of operators and concerned stakeholders in ensuring safety of persons on board. These safety and security concerns are implemented through enforcement of criminal sanctions, most of which are robustly described in Part V of the Act. The Act also creates a National Civil Aviation Administrative Review Tribunal to deal with grievances on licensing and ensure consumer protection.

---

[54] This was an interview with Director-General KCAA that was conducted on 11 September 2018.

[55] Act No 23 of 2013.

[56] Authors' interview with Director-General during the Civil Aviation Safety and Security Oversight (CASSOA) 5th Symposium held in Burundi on 27–28 February 2020.

[57] Civil Aviation (Unmanned Aircraft Systems) Regulations Legal Notice No. 42 of 2020 (hereinafter referred to as the 2020 UAS Regulations).

Even more pivotal is the establishment of the KCAA, whose main objective is efficient and economic planning, developing and managing civil aviation, and regulation and operation of safe civil aviation systems in Kenya. The institutional discussion of the authority and its nexus with the above objectives as set out in Section 6 of the Civil Aviation Act is discussed below.

KCAA is established under Section 7(1) of the Civil Aviation Act. Established under Section 13 of the Act, the Board of Directors governs the Authority. The KCAA Board is composed of the following: the Chairperson, who is appointed by the President; the Director-General, appointed under Section 19 of the Act; Principal Secretary in the Ministry responsible for matters relating to civil aviation or his/her representative; Principal Secretary to the National Treasury or his/her representative, Principal Secretary in the Ministry responsible for matters relating to internal security or his/her representative. Other members of the Board are persons, not being public officers, who are appointed by the Cabinet Secretary through a competitive process, and who are to be independent upon appointment and maintain such independence during their term of service on the Board. To ensure efficacy in the discharge of their mandates in relation to the safety, security and privacy issues, the additional persons are brought on board on account of their demonstrable expertise, professional knowledge and experience in accountancy, auditing and aviation law or business and management.[58]

In addition to the Board, KCAA discharges its mandate through the support of four directorates, three operational and one support, namely: aviation safety standards and regulations, air navigation services, East African School of Aviation and corporate services. The first three provide the services, which are core to the mandate of KCAA, while corporate services provide support in services delivery. The directorates have departments, which though not a creation of the law, are designated for convenience in the day-to-day operations of civil aviation matters, and enforcement of the above explained mandate. The departments are critical in creation of assurance in the safety, security and privacy fronts for use of UAS.

The role of the Board, as is the case in South Africa, is policy formulation whereas the responsibility for the day-to-day running of the KCAA is bestowed upon the Director General of the Authority, who exercises all powers and discharge of all functions of the Authority with control over personnel and activities.[59] The other general duties of the Board are outlined in the Act to include oversight of KCAA in financial matters such as remuneration and general administrative matters. It ensures that the safety and security of civil aviation, and UAS in general, is done in accordance with existing legislation.[60] The specific duties of KCAA are establishment, co-ordination and maintenance of State safety and security programmes, certification of aircraft operators, enforcement of approved technical standards of aircraft, licensing and monitoring of aeronautical personnel, provision of technical

[58] Civil Aviation Act, Section 7.

[59] Civil Aviation Act, Section 20.

[60] Civil Aviation Act, Sections 15 and 16.

services for the design, installation, and modification of electronic, radio and other equipment used in the provision of air navigation services. [61] In execution of the mandates related to safety and security of aviation in Kenya, the KCAA Board and Management work in conjunction with the National Civil Aviation Security Committee and Airport Security Committees.

The conduct of KCAA's duties is done within two broad mandates, namely,` oversight and a mandate of enforcement. The oversight mandate includes ensuring integrity of the systems, equipment and facilities of the Authority, issuance and dissemination of publications referred to in the regulation, production of accurate, timely, comprehensive and relevant air transport information for planning and decision-making. The Authority is also responsible for approving, certification and licensing of aircraft maintenance organizations and regulation of aviation training institutions in Kenya. This is in addition to the establishment, management and operation of training institutions for purposes of the Authority, registration of rights and interests in aircraft, planning, development and formulation of the airspace master plan for safe and efficient utilization of the Kenyan airspace, establishment, co-ordination and maintenance of State aviation safety and security programme, licensing and certification of aerodromes, regulated agents and air navigation service providers.[62]

The oversight mandate of KCAA, on the other hand, takes an economic perspective as it includes protecting consumer and environmental rights, and ensuring fair trading practices by giving effect to the Chicago Convention and other international agreements relating to civil aviation, to which Kenya is party; and performance of such other functions as may, from time to time, be conferred on it by the Cabinet Secretary or by any other written law. [63]

The double package of mandates grants KCAA power to execute its legislative functions. KCAA has made steps to tailor-make its mandate and functions to achieve safety and efficiency. For instance, KCAA's consumer protection initiative is based on its commitment to provide a safe and efficient civil aviation environment that contributes to the achievement of Kenya's developmental objectives, as articulated in Kenya Vision 2030.[64] Despite the optimism, scholars like Waithera note that

[61] Civil Aviation Act, Sections 15 and 16.

[62] Civil Aviation Act, Sections 15 and 16, Section 7(P-U).

[63] Civil Aviation Act, Sections 15 and 16, Section 7 (V-AA).

[64] The Aviation Consumer Protection Section of KCAA was established in 2004 with the objective to ensure that all Aviation Consumers obtain the best services and value from the service providers within the aviation industry. The section is also responsible for informing, educating and protecting consumers and thus ensuring services provided in the aviation industry are of the highest standards, comparable to that in other parts of the world and hence consumers are informed of their rights and responsibilities. See more information on https://www.kcaa.or.ke/about-us/consumer-protection (Date of use: 4 August 2023).

The Kenya Vision 2030 as launched in 2008 by President Mwai Kibaki aims to transform Kenya into a newly industrializing, middle-income country providing a high quality of life to all its citizens by 2030 in a clean and secure environment.

likely challenges of lack of adequate funding has potential to compromise the achievement of this mandate.[65]

The listed modes of appointment to the KCAA Board confirms the position of Section 4(3) of the 2013 Act, as a State agency, with the mandate to ensure safety, security and privacy concerns regarding aircraft including UAS.[66] Should the government seriously consider plans for privatization in future, it ought to follow the ICAO Privatization Policy, which Kesharwani notes has significant benefits once all the safeguards are met.[67]

KCAA has since its establishment in 2002 continued to implement its mandates. This is, however, not without challenges, chief among them being inadequate funding.[68] Be that as it may, KCAA is recognized as playing a critical role of ensuring that an appropriate civil air transport framework is established and sustained as an enabler of air transport infrastructure.[69]

Further, and in order to overcome these challenges in discharge of its mandate, KCAA is undertaking various projects with the aim of delivering on its part to Kenya Vision 2030 national development blueprint that targets to make Kenya a middle-income nation by the year 2030. It is doing this through aligning organizational structure to strategy, recruitment, training and retention of competent staff, right-sizing and resourcing the organization appropriately, achieving international safety and security compliance, re-organization of the airspace and modernization of air traffic management systems. [70] KCAA is in the process of providing infrastructural development for aviation medical centre for aviation medical examination training, medical examiners for licensed medical doctors to conduct examination for medical fitness of pilots who are eligible for issuance of medical certificates as required under the current UAS 2020 Regulation second schedule r 20 (3) r. 1(c) & r 3.

As far as implementation is concerned, KCAA's mandates include licensing of air services, provision of air navigation services, establishment and maintenance of a system for the registration and marking of civil aircraft, securing sound development of the civil aviation industry in Kenya, advising the government on matters concerning civil aviation, and co-ordination and direction of search and rescue services. KCAA is mandated to facilitate and provide support for aircraft accident and incident investigations conducted by the Chief Investigator, carrying out investigations on incidents that are not classified as accidents and serious incidents, the safety, security, economic and technical regulation of civil aviation and dealing with incidents of unlawful interference with aviation security. [71]

---

[65] Waithera (2015), p. 3.

[66] https://www.iata.org/en/pressroom/pr/2018-06-05-04/ (Date of use: 13 August 2023).

[67] Kesharwani T "Privatization in the Provision of Airport and Navigation Services" https://www.icao.int/Meetings/AMC/MA/1999/aps/01_kesharwani.pdf (Date of use: 13 August January 2023).

[68] Waithera (2015), p. 3.

[69] Kenya Civil Aviation Authority Strategic Plan 2012/13-2016/17, p. 6.

[70] Kenya Civil Aviation Authority Strategic Plan 2012/13-2016/17, p. 6.

[71] Civil Aviation Act, Section 7 (a-k).

6.4.2 Partnership with ICAO

Under Section 8(2) (d) of the Civil Aviation Act, the KCAA is mandated to enter into partnerships with any person, agency or authority within and outside Kenya for the purposes of achieving its objectives and delivering on its mandates. Pursuant to this provision, KCAA as an appropriate authority on civil aviation, has partnered with ICAO with a view to addressing safety and security issues arising from the civil aviation management. Consequently, KCAA staff have been active participants in the ICAO meetings on regional aviation safety.[72]

The partnership extends to training at the East Africa School of Aviation (EASA) that has a curriculum addressing safety and security issues in civil aviation operations. ICAO uses the school directorate of KCAA as centres of excellence worldwide. EASA has the following training departments; aviation business management, aviation safety and security, air navigation, services maintenance and curriculum development unit.[73] The school is also the training wing of KCAA as an Approved Training Organization. Other institutions are the ICAO Aviation Security Training Centre and the Government Safety Inspector Training Centre that is endorsed by ICAO, and accredits the school, both as an institution and its curriculum.[74]

6.4.3 KCAA and Regional Cooperation

KCAA is an active player in the development of regional efforts for regulation of safety and security aspects of civil aviation at the East African Community level. It works closely with the East Africa Civil Aviation Safety and Security Oversight Agency (CASSOA). At the sub-regional level is the EAC Air Transport Facilitation Committee that oversees the harmonization of national laws of EAC Partner States towards reflecting the ICAO Annex 17 on Aviation Security and Annex 19 on Safety.[75] Going by statistics, CASSOA is ranked as a high performer in oversight of safety issues in the world and is only second to its European counterpart.[76]

Other than in the East African Community, KCAA has made significant strides in aviation security through partnerships with other aviation stakeholders. For example, it partners with International Air Transport Association (IATA) through the latter's safety and security programmes. Kenya is a partner to the IATA Secure Freight Pilot

[72] See ICAO "Report of the Fourth Meeting of the Regional Aviation Safety Group for Africa-Indian Ocean" (Nairobi 12–13 October 2017) 1–32.

[73] East Africa School of Aviation "East Africa School of Aviation-ICAO Regional Training Centre of Excellence" easa.ac.ke (Date of use: 18 August 2023).

[74] KCAA "About EASA" https://www.kcaa.or.ke/easa/about-easa> (Date of use: 11 August 2023).

[75] Makau (2014), pp. 1–10.

[76] CASSOA (2018), p. 5.

Program, which aims at security of flights and cargo.[77] KCAA, through EASA, partners in training with IATA, the institution that provides training associated with airlines.

6.5 Response to Safety, Security and Privacy Challenges in UAS Operations

6.5.1 Kenya's Response to Aviation Safety in UAS Operations

It shall be recalled that safety challenges principally arise from the design of UAS regarding the sense and avoid technology. Safety of aircraft has been a key legislative regulatory issue since the development of the KCAA Aviation Policy. The Policy made further safety assurances by requiring any person operating or controlling UAS operations to undergo training and familiarize themselves with relevant rules and procedures applicable within any airspace through which the aircraft may be flown.[78]

The Policy required that any UAS be operated in a manner that minimizes hazards to persons, property or other aircraft, and in accordance with conditions specified by the Authority from time to time. [79] Such rules are critical to ensure that operating a UAS in the civilian airspace is controlled to limit danger to civil aircraft in accordance with the Civil Aviation (Rules of the Air) Regulations and the UAS Regulations.

Under the Civil Aviation Act, it is clear that KCAA's mandate includes establishing, coordinating and enhancing State Safety Programmes. Part III of the Act lays prohibitions on all persons from engaging in acts that imperil aircraft safety. This provision was implemented through criminal sanctions of a fine to the tune of two million shillings.[80] Under Section 20 of the Act, the Director General was to audit the performance of the State Safety Programmes and hold executives accountable to such programmes. Section 10 of the Civil Aviation (Amendment) Act, 2016 amended Section 20 of the 2013 Act to introduce the power of the Director to establish a safety oversight system and to prohibit flights in unsafe conditions.[81]

Additionally, the regulation of aviation trainings had underpinnings of safety. The Civil Aviation Act imposes an obligation on KCAA to approve, licence and certify training institutions.[82] The Director General is mandated to establish schools

[77] Makau (2014), p. 5.

[78] The 2017 RPAs Regulations, Regulation 29. Also see the annulled aviation policy.

[79] 2020 UAS Regulations, Regulation 54.

[80] Civil Aviation Act, Section 46(1)-(2).

[81] Civil Aviation (Amendment) Act, Section 10(b) and (c).

[82] Civil Aviation Act 2013, Section 3B (q).

to offer training in the aviation industry.[83] The Authority has come up with the Civil Aviation (Approved Training Organizations) Regulations,[84] 2013 that govern the application, issuance, renewal, suspension and revocation of licences and certificates to the Approved Training Organizations. A review of the criteria for training institutions, which is Appendix 18 of the National Safety Programme, shows that authorizations of government agencies and other safety agencies must be obtained. Besides EASA, other licenced training institutions that consider safety as a key aspect of their training programmes are the Kenya School of Flying, Moi University School of Aerospace and Sciences, Think Aviation Training, Nairobi Flight Training, Mombasa Aviation Training Institute, Valentine Air Services, Ninety-Nine Flying School and KQ Pride Centre.

Under the 2020 UAS Regulations, safety of UAS use and operation is a key consideration in registration and licensing in Kenya.[85] This explains why UAS categorization is the basis of licensing due to safety risks posed by their operations.[86] Any amendment to the Remote Aircraft Operators Certificate can only be approved, if necessary, for the safety of commercial operations of the UAS. It is a general requirement for operation of UAS that requests for authorization should include aeronautical safety communications frequencies equipment.[87] Safety is also considered when KCAA reviews and takes the decision for cancellation, revocation, or variation of such authorizations.[88]

The 2020 UAS Regulations offer myriad assurances of safety in all operations provided in its scope. For instance, it is incumbent upon operators and owners to ensure that the remote piloted aircraft system is airworthy.[89] This means that all the UAS operating in the Kenyan airspace are required to meet the standards of safe operation depending on type and design. The goal is achieved by providing an additional general obligation on owners and operators to operational control and safety of operations as well as compliance with the request for information by KCAA, which include issuing certificate of aircraft's airworthiness, licences, authorization certificates, operations speeds, and capabilities such as communication, frequency and sense and avoid systems.[90]

The provision of sense and avoid systems set out above represents a notable improvement in the 2020 UAS Regulations as they were not provided under the annulled 2017 RPAs Regulations. Despite this effort, challenges persist as the regulation refers to adherence to rules of the air mainly applicable to manned aircraft. In appreciating the fact that not all UAS have capability to detect and avoid other

[83] Civil Aviation Act, Section 5A(2)(v).

[84] Civil Aviation (Approved Training Organizations) Regulations of 2013.

[85] 2020 UAS Regulations, Regulation 4(c).

[86] 2020 UAS Regulations, Regulation 5.

[87] 2020 UAS Regulations, Regulation 23(2)(l).

[88] 2020 UAS Regulations, Regulation 22(1)(a).

[89] 2020 UAS Regulations, Regulation 12.

[90] 2020 UAS Regulations, Regulations 23(1)(a) and (d).

aircraft, the regulation provides for remote pilots to maintain awareness so as to see and avoid other aircraft and yield the right of way to all aircraft and vehicles, which may not be practical in some incidences where UAS fly beyond sight of the operator. The challenge is exacerbated by challenges arising from lack of unmanned traffic management (UTM) system that could help collision avoidance with capability to detect where command and control centre of UAS operation are located,[91] the communication link enhances both safety and security of the airspaces by way of interception of unauthorised intrusion of UAS.

Despite the challenges regarding sense and avoid systems, it is not lost that the obligation on operators demonstrates an approach the KCAA is laying out at the lowest level of compliance, which is with the operators and owners whose safety considerations are supposed to complement its requirements when exercising the oversight mandate. The general compliance ensures that there is reduction of accidents and collisions with other UAS and manned aircraft.

In order to practically overcome these safety concerns, the 2020 UAS Regulations impose certain limitations on safe operations of UAS. For instance, Regulation 24 provides the vertical height limit of operation of UAS. It specifically prohibits the operation of UAS 400 feet above ground level or at night, and must be fitted with cameras and operate with Visual Meteorological Conditions. The Regulation also requires that the distance from other vessels, buildings, trees in lateral and vertical distances must not fall below 50 m. This provision imposes reasonable care on UAS operators to ensure the safety of road users and pedestrians. The Air Navigation Service Providers are mandated to provide for procedures that ensure integration of UAS as regards aviation safety.[92] The KCAA has mandate to impose further operating restrictions on UAS in the interest of safety.[93] These restrictions were evidently geared to preventing accidents that can be caused by collisions with things borne of nature.

During operations, UAS operators are obligated to use sight to ensure they avoid collisions with other aircraft and must at all times yield the right of way.[94] This rule guides how the UAS integrates into the civil aviation airspaces in relation to other manned aircraft and is based on the rationale that their way can be easily diverted by the pilot in command with ease in comparison to that of manned aircraft. The pilots too, through the UAS owners and operators, are obligated, apart from medical compliance, to ensure that they do not consume alcohol or psychoactive substances less than 8 h prior to reporting on duty.[95] In addition, the pilot must have UAS system pilot certificate issued pursuant to Regulation 19.

In an apparent realization of the inevitability of accidents even with strict adherence to the above safety means, the Regulations make provisions on

[91] Jeanneret and Rambaldi (2016), p. 14.

[92] 2020 UAS Regulations, Regulation 36(2).

[93] 2020 UAS Regulations, Regulation 38(1)(a).

[94] 2020 UAS Regulations, Regulation 31(1).

[95] 2020 UAS Regulations, Regulation 44.

obligations during the happening or after the occurrence of an accident relating to UAS. The Regulations envisage use of emergency procedures, command and control, and air traffic control communication by UAS operators.[96] A challenge that may don the achievement of this requirement is that Kenya has not established a command and control system (CCS), which is a necessary element in integration of UAS into the national civil airspace. CCS is a technological system used by security agencies to ensure that UAS flying in the national airspace are identified immediately they enter the country's national airspace.[97] The technology is important for Kenya to ensure that her airspace is safe from acts of unlawful interference to civil aviation.

The operations in aerodromes are restrictively regulated by KCAA.[98] Should accidents happen, there arises an obligation to report the same to KCAA so as to aid the investigations.[99] Another reactive approach is through provision of insurance. The current framework for regulation of UAS at Regulation 40 addresses issues of insurance against third party injuries. Regulation 40(4) appears to provide some exemption, by providing that KCAA may dispense with the requirement for insurance depending on the category of UAS, meaning small UAS may operate without comprehensive insurance. Insurance protection is important, otherwise non-observance of liability means other aircraft, persons and property on the ground are exposed to unnecessary danger linked to lack of third-party claims and compensation by insurance companies.

The safety requirements permeate the organizational arrangements for commercial UAS operators. For example, in terms of staffing, a commercial UAS operator is required to have an accountable manager responsible for its SMS.[100] Such a system is an approach to managing safety of UAS use and operation, through organizational structures, policies, and procedures.[101] In developing the system, the regulations address adequacy issues by requiring certificate holders to design the system in a manner that is commensurate with the size and complexity of their operations.[102] The Regulations are definitive as stipulates the standards of an effective safety management system. For instance, the system must identify actual and potential safety hazards, develop remedial actions and mechanisms for continuous assessment of its appropriateness.[103]

The Regulations also have provisions for the training of persons undertaking private UAS operations only through authorized training centres.[104] In an apparent recognition of risks that result in the operation of commercial UAS, the Regulations

96 2020 UAS Regulations, Regulations 23(2)(n), 35(1) & 36.

97 Jeanneret and Rambaldi (2016), p. 14.

98 2020 UAS Regulations, Regulation 26.

99 2020 UAS Regulations, Regulation 25(1).

100 2020 UAS Regulations, Regulation 38.

101 2020 UAS Regulations, Regulation 2.

102 2020 UAS Regulations, Regulation 19.

103 2020 UAS Regulations, Regulation 2.

104 2020 UAS Regulations, Regulation 21(1).

provide additional requirements for training of pilots of UAS for commercial use.[105] Commercial operators are required to comply with additional requirements of the Remote Aircraft Operators Certificate (ROC) including adequate staffing, ownership and safety requirements.[106] Generally, training as provided for under Regulation 21 of the 2020 UAS Regulations is expected to equip one with the competencies for award of the remote pilot certificate. An applicant for a remote pilot certificate under Regulation 20(1) of the Regulations must demonstrate a level of knowledge appropriate to privileges granted to such holder in the following disciplines: air law, UAS general knowledge, flight performance, planning and loading, human performance, meteorology, navigation, operational procedures, and principles of flight related to UAS and radiotelephony. In addition, he or she must pass a skills test to demonstrate ability and competency to perform as a remote pilot of the specific UAS category and associated UAS, the relevant procedures and manoeuvres appropriate to the privileges granted.[107]

Overall, KCAA is responsible for the implementation of the safety provisions and requirements. It reserves the power to conduct surveillance and inspections to ensure compliance accountability. The provisions of the Act are implemented through offences and general penalties of fines not exceeding one million shillings for each offence or to imprisonment for a term not exceeding one year, or to both.[108]

6.5.2 *Kenya's Response to Aviation Security in UAS Operations*

As seen in Chap. 2, security concerns principally arise from the threats of national interference caused by the traffic management and command control challenges. In response to this, the KCAA developed an Aviation Policy in relation to UAS. Kenya's Aviation Policy was designed to promote and facilitate civil aviation by ensuring provision of an effective regulatory framework for UAS operations throughout the country. Its main objective is to support operation of UAS in a safe, secure, harmonized and seamless environment equal to manned operations.[109] However, just as the 2017 RPAs Regulation, the Policy suffered the same fate when Parliament recommended that until the questions raised on security, public participation, and privacy were addressed, the Policy remained suspended. In the author's analysis, a Policy is an internal KCAA document and not a law made by Parliament, hence Parliament had no *locus* to nullify it. Consequently, such action was *null and void ab initio* and *ultra vires*.

[105] 2020 UAS Regulations, Regulation 45.

[106] 2020 UAS Regulations, Regulation 14(1)-(3).

[107] 2020 UAS Regulations, Regulation 20(1) as read with the Second Schedule of the Regulations.

[108] 2020 UAS Regulations, Regulation 51(2).

[109] Republic of Kenya Policy on Remotely Piloted Aircraft Systems of 2017, p. 1.

Despite the uncertainty, certain perspectives are derivable from the Policy. a discussion of these glimpses is necessary since the adopted Regulation did not deviate much from the Policy. Overall, Kenya's Policy on UAS was consistent with the country's proposed legislation framework, which provides, *inter alia,* that all persons, institutions or entities with intent to import, test, operate, procure, manufacture or assemble UAS must apply for authorization from the KCAA as provided under the then 2017 RPAs Regulations.[110] The authorization could only be subject to prerequisites of security clearance and approval by the relevant ministry.[111] Evidently, the focus of the authorization was on maximization of security in the use of UAS.

Further security measures were placed in the Policy with a requirement of approval from the Department of Defence headquarters, including UAS for civil use. The purpose of the Ministry of Defence involvement is to ensure that there are background checks on UAS owners. This condition could obviously prove difficult for private applicants seeking registration of UAS as the facility is a restricted area where civilian visitors are subjected to stringent security clearance before placing their requests.[112] From this analysis, the provision appeared to be a policy and administrative problem invented by government officials within military circles for fear of the insecurity that UAS could pose in the national airspace if they were allowed lenient approval status.

Regarding exports and general removal of UAS out of the country, the Policy proposed prohibition of any Kenyan registered UAS from being taken out of the country without authorization by KCAA. All UAS are expected to have adequate security to protect the system from unauthorized modification, interference, corruption or control/command action.[113] In other words, UAS were to operate strictly in accordance with rules governing the flight of manned aircraft and meet infrastructure requirements applicable to the class of airspace within which they intended to operate, save for where KCAA provides otherwise.

An analysis of the Policy leads to the conclusion that it placed more prominence on regulation of imports and exports than on the actual operations of the UAS in the country. Accordingly, the stringent measures and obstacles that it introduced to deter applicants or importers did not, and does not, in any way address the central problem of UAS operation. What follows is illegal importation of UAS and unauthorised use. The possible consequences are that Kenya could experience an influx of unlicensed UAS operating in her airspace. Moreover, the Department of Defence does not have clearly outlined procedure of vetting applicants. Lack of such procedures may be ground for possible arbitrary action. The arbitrariness may be exacerbated by lack of coordinated databases between authorities dealing with crime and criminal investigations and the Ministry of Defence. Once the Policy comes back to life,

[110] 2017 RPAs Regulations, Regulation 6 (2).

[111] 2017 RPAs Regulations, Regulation 6 (2).

[112] See Wanjala (2015) *KJLJ-JBSD* 62–78.

[113] Republic of Kenya Policy on Remotely Piloted Aircraft Systems of 2017, p. 1.

stakeholders can take opportunity and ensure it is synchronised with the yet to be established National Security Policy and the National Security Strategy on UAS. Specifically, they should at the earliest opportunity ensure that the security Policy on UAS has convergence with the civil aviation policy on UAS to avoid conflict of polices and eliminate any *lacuna* in law relating to operation of UAS in Kenya.

Currently, the principal legislation is clear that the mandate of the KCAA is expressly recognized under Section 7(1) (j) of the Civil Aviation Act to include dealing with incidents of unlawful interference and ensuring aviation security.

With regard to the regulatory support to the principal statute, it is noted that prior to the development of the 2020 UAS Regulations, general security issues in civil aviation were dealt with under the Civil Aviation (Security) Regulations of 2015 as amended in 2020, which set of Regulations was undergoing review at the time of writing this book.[114] Part III of the Regulations in particular imposed obligations on aircraft operators to develop security and security training programmes. These programmes would be aligned to the National Civil Aviation Programme developed by KCAA.[115] Regulation 35 provided that the responsibility for security rested with the operator who was under an obligation to ensure that its staff and personnel are trained, aware of and comply with the National Civil Aviation Security Programme. Additionally, Regulation 47 recognized the enforcement power of the KCAA in preventing acts of unlawful interference in respect of aircraft when the Authority acts are based on reliable information.

The 2020 UAS Regulations have established a raft of UAS specific security measures. They, for instance, provide that only adult Kenyan citizens or residents or persons, and both levels of government have capacity to own UAS.[116] This means that anonymous ownership that could compromise the security of the country is not allowed.[117] For non-nationals, it is the residence of that particular person at the time of application that matters; meaning that the person's stay in Kenya must be authorized under any written law. The change of ownership amongst the permissible groups must be notified to KCAA. KCAA is required to approve importation and exportation of UAS through issuance of permits.[118] This too is an opportunity to weed out imports that are used for espionage.

Under Regulation 8, UAS manufacturers must obtain prior authorization with additional requirement for security clearance. Although the Regulations are not express on how the clearance should be done, it is expected that the NIS, which is the disciplined civilian intelligence agency under the Constitution of Kenya, 2010,[119] would handle the clearance aspect.

[114] Civil Aviation (Security) Regulations of 2015 as amended in 2020.

[115] Civil Aviation (Security) Regulations of 2015, Regulations 9, 10, 13, 14, 21 and 22.

[116] 2020 UAS Regulations, Regulation 6(1), (b)-(c) and 3.

[117] 2020 UAS Regulations, Regulation 6(1) (a).

[118] 2020 UAS Regulations, Regulation 7(2).

[119] See Constitution of Kenya, 2010, Article 242 on the role of NIS.

Apart from permit and approval systems for manufacture, imports and exports, security assurance is provided for through requirement of prior registration for operation or ownership of the UAS. With regard to prior registrations issued by KCAA, the Authority considers security clearance similar to that of the manufacturing processes.[120] Regulation 43 mandates holders of remote aircraft operator's certificate to complement KCAA's mandate of conducting background checks, checks on criminal records of its personnel, develop interference detection systems, and protect integrity of their UAS. Further, they are mandated to train personnel and designate a coordinator responsible for security issues.[121]

Registration is not final in itself as a registration status may be changed by KCAA for reasons known to the law pursuant to the provision of Regulation 10. The Regulation offers an avenue for the consideration of provision of other legislations as set out earlier in the discussion on domestic framework that aims at safeguarding national security interests to deregister UAS when it compromises the security of Kenya.

Other than the security approvals provided in dealing with applications under the Regulations, there are additional security requirements for operators to meet security procedures.[122] The procedures must be developed in accordance with the Civil Aviation (Security) Regulations, 2013 (as reviewed in 2015 and 2020) requirements set by KCAA.[123] In particular, they must show the practice to be taken to avoid interference. Compliance with the procedures is to be boosted with security surveillance by KCAA that target avoidance of unauthorized use and unlawful interference.[124]

6.5.3 *Kenya's Response to Privacy Challenges Associated by Operations of UAS.*

The privacy concerns of UAS arise from their ability to flow close to buildings, properties and homes. Kenya addressed its mind to this challenge in its Aviation Policy, which was advanced in the protection of the right to privacy. The Policy required that UAS operations be such that they do not cause an infringement on privacy of individuals or entities.[125] The protection of the right to privacy, however,

[120] 2020 UAS Regulations, Regulations 8(1) and (2).

[121] 2020 UAS Regulations, Regulation 43(a)-(h).

[122] 2020 UAS Regulations, Regulation 45.

[123] 2020 UAS Regulations, Regulation 45.

[124] 2020 UAS Regulations, Regulation 47.

[125] See Constitution of Kenya, 2010, Article 31 on right to privacy and safeguard. The policy and regulation should therefore provide that any person conducting operations using UAS fitted with cameras shall operate them in a responsible way to respect the privacy of other persons and their property as outlined in the Constitution.

birthed a huge gap since the Policy excluded issues pertaining to State aircraft, unmanned free balloons or airships, and operations in which more than one UAS is managed by a remote pilot station at the same time. [126] Under the Policy, in the interest of aviation safety, authorization given for operation of UAS may be withdrawn or cancelled.[127]

The Constitution of Kenya, 2010 is the principal law on the protection to right to privacy. Article 31 of the Constitution provides that:

> Every person has the right to privacy, which includes the right not to have, their person, home or property searched, their possessions seized, information relating to their family or private affairs unnecessarily required or revealed or the privacy of their communications infringed.[128]

Unlike the case with safety and security as set out above, the Civil Aviation Act did not make specific provision on how respect to this right ought to converge with UAS operation. The Civil Aviation (Amendment) Act did not remedy the situation either. It was not until the 2020 UAS Regulations were developed that the privacy provision was made regarding regulation of UAS operations in the Kenyan airspace. Regulation 53 of the 2017 RPAs Regulations had provisions on privacy of persons and property.[129] It provided a general provision requiring any person conducting operations using remotely piloted aircraft system fitted with cameras to operate them in a responsible manner, and in a way as to respect the privacy of other persons and their property. Under the defunct Regulations, surveillance was required to be with the consent of the persons or owners of property unless the same was for newsgathering. With respect to privacy protection, imaging technology fitted on the UAS should be used for investigations, research, and no other purposes that can breach privacy.

The UAS 2020 Regulations make provisions for the protection of privacy rights on various activities related to UAS. Specifically, the Regulations prohibit equipping a UAS system with an imaging device to conduct surveillance.[130] Any use of such a system for taking images of persons must be done with written consent of the subject.[131] The same prohibition extends to use of such imaging device to record an image of a privately owned or leased real property or such owner, licensee, invitee with intent to conduct surveillance.[132]

The Regulations resolve the difficulty of testing intention by setting the standard of a reasonable expectation of privacy upon UAS operators. Such a reasonable expectation arises where a person or property is not observable by a person located

---

[126] Republic of Kenya Policy on Remotely Piloted Aircraft Systems of 2017.

[127] Republic of Kenya Policy on Remotely Piloted Aircraft Systems of 2017. Also see the aviation policy on authorization.

[128] Privacy International https://privacyinternational.org/state-privacy/1005/state-privacy-kenya (Date of use: 29 August 2023).

[129] 2017 RPAs Regulations, Regulation 54(1).

[130] 2020 UAS Regulations, Regulation 41.

[131] 2020 UAS Regulations, Regulation 41.

[132] 2020 UAS Regulations, Regulation 41(2).

at the ground level in a place where they have a legal right to be.[133] The Regulations also recognize instances of exception to the general protection of the reasonable expectation of privacy, which include mapping and evaluation of the earth's surface, investigations of forests, search and rescue, and investigation of vegetation or wildlife.[134] There is a rider, however, that each of the exemptions can only be exercised with prior approval of KCAA.[135] Authors such as Nader *et al* imply that these scanty provisions on privacy in respect of UAS regulation is suspect owing to recent technological changes.[136] It seems to be a carry-over of concerns arising from the annulment of the 2017 Regulations. It, therefore, misses the ideal situation where the focus is that the safety, security and privacy should be addressed in a balanced manner, which does not compromise any one aspect.[137]

As for its implementation, there exists scepticism regarding the impact of the use of UAS on privacy. This particularly arises from the Kenyan legal and legislative history in respect of rights. Privacy International that shed more light on this issue has noted the Kenyan trend is increasingly giving a chance for conduct of surveillances that have real potential to further limit the right to privacy.[138] The organization attributes the trend to the coming into force of the National Intelligence Service Act,[139] the National Security Council Act, Cap. 206 (Act No. 23 of 2012), and the Prevention of Terrorism Act, No. 30 of 2012. The NIS Act allows the NIS to limit privacy in the course of its investigations and monitoring activities.[140] The Prevention of Terrorism Act (POTA) on its part provides the authorities with wide powers to limit the right. For instance, it provides that the right can be limited in cases of investigations into terrorist acts, detection and prevention of terrorism.[141]

The challenges in practice were evidenced when Parliament, in what was arguably a chaotic process, passed the Security Laws (Amendment) Act in 2014.[142] The Act grants powers to national security organs to intercept communications, which powers have an effect of limiting the right to privacy as guaranteed under the Constitution of Kenya, 2010. As a countermeasure, constitutional courts are always open to strike down any infringement of privacy rights as protected under Article 31 of the Constitution of Kenya, 2010.

---

[133] 2020 UAS Regulations, Regulation 41(3).

[134] 2020 UAS Regulations, Regulation 41(4) (a)-(d).

[135] 2020 UAS Regulations, Regulation 42(4).

[136] See 2017 RPAs Regulations, Regulations 47, 48 and 49 on security provisions and Regulation 53 on privacy.

[137] See Nader et al. (2020), pp. 1–17.

[138] Privacy International https://privacyinternational.org/state-privacy/1005/state-privacy-kenya (Date of use: 29 September 2019).

[139] National Intelligence Service Act 28 of 2012.

[140] National Intelligence Service Act 28 of 2012, Section 6.

[141] Prevention of Terrorism Act 30 of 2012, Section 35.

[142] Security Laws (Amendment) Act 19 of 2014.

Even more worrying is the refrain by the Civil Aviation (Unmanned Aircraft Systems) Regulations, 2020 from making positive obligations regarding protection of the right to privacy. The provisions on respecting the right to privacy are too general and may be the origin of poor implementation by stakeholders while interacting with the law.

These limitations are, however, cured by the robust provision on data protection provided through the Data Protection Act.[143] Since the Act is clear on the obligation of collectors of personal data including such issues as disclosure, it provides a good tool for privacy reassurance with respect to current technological advancements pending promulgation of the UAS Regulations. Another positive development to the protection of privacy is development of the Computer Misuse and Cybercrimes Act.[144] This Act has set out certain constitutional objectives at Section 3 that are geared towards achieving, among others, respect for the right to privacy. It provides for offences against the integrity, confidentiality, and availability of data, computer-related and content-related offences that may impact negatively on the privacy of data in the computer systems and networks. These bodies of law protect citizenry rights to ensure that information relating to their families or private affairs are not unnecessarily required or revealed, and complement the existing framework under the 2020 UAS Regulations.

6.5.4 Implementation of the Response Mechanisms

Generally, the Regulations are implemented through criminal sanctions. Failure to comply with the directions under the Regulations attracts a fine not exceeding one million shillings for each offence or to imprisonment for a term not exceeding three years, or to both. Contravention of the provisions of the Third Schedule attracts fines in millions of shillings and imprisonment terms, or both.[145] The general penalty provided for under the Regulations is a fine not exceeding two million shillings or an imprisonment term not exceeding three years, or both. It is the author's view that the fines may not be effective in deterring commission of crimes by the owners or operations of UAS that are engaged in large commercial enterprises who may end up paying the fine without much difficulty. Again, the penalty may also not be proportionate to the extent of harm caused. It is worth noting, however, that this view is only theoretical since no such instance has manifested itself in the Kenyan jurisdiction. The oversight role of KCAA and CASSOA, and the Kenyan courts is pivotal in the implementation of the provisions set out in this Chapter.

[143] Data Protection Act 24 of 2019.

[144] Computer Misuse and Cybercrimes Act 5 of 2018.

[145] 2020 UAS Regulations, Regulation 51.

6.6 Other UAS Integration Challenges

6.6.1 *Institutional and Operational Challenges of UAS Integration*

Whereas Kenya has made tremendous progress towards regulating UAS through promulgation of regulations and active participation at the international level, this has not been without its fair share of challenges. Kenya's policy and regulatory framework related to UAS have been in existence for a shorter period compared to the United States and South Africa.

KCAA is the sole Authority or institution with oversight mandate over aviation matters in Kenya. Its Board of Directors is constituted under the Act to complement and implement the process of integrating UAS into civilian airspace. But since the Board does not work on full-time basis, the technical civil aviation functions are handled by a Director General and his/her technical staff. The import of Section 10 (3) of the Civil Aviation Act is that the Director General of KCAA retains wide powers in respect of oversight, safety and security, while carrying out administrative functions. The section further explains that the Director General is at the core of the creation, operationalization and implementation, and monitoring of the safety oversight system. The system has expansive roles including licensing, development of technical guidance, surveillance and resolution of safety concerns.

Despite these wide roles that relate to UAS, KCAA has six staff members currently stationed in an established office, specifically dedicated for registration of UAS.[146] Their greatest challenge at the time of writing this book was lack of capacity to undertake registration of the UAS. As at May 2020, KCAA had not made progress concerning integration of UAS into civil aviation. There is need, therefore, to create awareness or campaign to be undertaken with the view of ensuring that the UAS in possession of the public are registered. It should concern everyone that the pace at which the regulation is being implemented compromises the safety of users, stakeholders, UAS operators and operations, and manned aircraft in general.

6.6.2 *Inadequate County Governments' Involvement*

The Constitution of Kenya, 2010 establishes 47 County Governments, which are listed in the First Schedule of the Constitution. The Fourth Schedule of the Constitution recognizes transport and communication as a mandate of the National Government, with no such mandate being granted to the 47 devolved units. The legal framework too does not apportion any clear role and responsibility to the county governments with regard to UAS operation oversight, the reason being aviation is

[146] Author's interview with the Director General KCAA on 11 September 2018.

not a devolved function. This phenomenon is exacerbated by inadequate enforcement machinery, as KCAA is yet to benefit substantially from the capacity of the devolved units. Accordingly, KCAA has not been able to factor into the 2020 UAS regulation Community Based Organizations for self-regulation as is the case with the US.

There is recognition, though, that the devolved units ought to play a role in this regard. Parliament, courtesy of the Hansard dated 26 June 2018, clarifies the need for involvement of county governments, citing lack of stakeholder participation in all counties while annulling the established 2017 UAS Regulations,[147] despite the fact that most UAS activities occur in areas under the jurisdiction of the devolved units or county governments. These sentiments resonate with the provisions of Part 2 of the Fourth Schedule of the Constitution, which mandates the county governments to be at the forefront in organizing communities for participation at various levels of governance.

6.6.3 Insufficient Framework for Public Participation in UAS Regulation

That public access and participation is a requirement as per Article 118 of the Kenya Constitution, is perhaps the clearest testimony that citizens in the rural areas and who are likely to be most affected by UAS operations, must be given a chance to give their views with regard to legislation of UAS regulations. The Constitution places public participation as a Constitutional principle of good governance.[148] This is incorporated and elaborated in statutes[149] as well as case laws in Kenya.[150] It would appear that involvement in cases concerning the aviation sector would be by way of availing them to create an opportunity for the citizens to air their opinion or present the same by way of memorandum.[151] It is expected that if members of the public were involved, they would air their views on matters to do with the fees they are levied regarding registration and operation of UAS, which include reporting authorised operations.

The intent and purpose of the participation is both to fulfil the Constitutional requirements as well as to ensure that KCAA develops a document that captures the aspirations of stakeholders such as the public, military, police, aviation operators, manufactures, policy makers, institutions of higher learning among others.

[147] Constitution of Kenya, 2010, Article 118. The provision facilitates public participation and involvement in the legislative and other business of Parliament and its committees. Also see Article 189 which calls for cooperation between national and county Governments.

[148] Constitution of Kenya, 2010, Article 10(2) (b).

[149] See Statutory Instruments Act 23 of 2013.

[150] See *Robert N Gakuru & another v Governor Kiambu County & 3 others* [2013] eKLR.

[151] https://www.afrocave.com/public-participation-kenya/ (Date of use: 4 August 2023).

A review of the Civil Aviation Act of 2013 as amended in 2016, reveals tardiness in substantive provisions for public participation. While this book appreciates that Kenya has an elaborate, albeit inadequate, framework for public participation,[152] the analysis projects that having such substantive provision would be necessary given the unique positioning of civil aviation and most importantly, the use and operation of UAS. As such, the practice does not even evidence realization of the full potential of consultation of communities especially in designing the rescue missions and accident management and response. The lack of such enthusiasm within the civil aviation led to the annulment of the 2017 RPAs Regulations.

It is instructive to note that Parliament cited non-compliance with provisions of the Statutory Instruments Act, No. 23 of 2013, which is the statute that creates the basis for public participation in the promulgation of statutory instruments such as UAS Regulations.

6.7 Conclusion

It is undeniable that Kenya has actual and potential of more civil uses of UAS. It has robust legal, policy, and institutional framework for the civil aviation. In recognition of safety, security and privacy concerns related to aviation, research has established that Kenya has made significant legislative efforts to integrate UAS into the civilian aviation airspace through adoption of the Civil Aviation Act, amendments in the Civil Aviation (Amendment) Act and a myriad of other Regulations. The legislative and institutional frameworks form the basis for domestication and consequential compliance with international standards of civil aviation as established under the Chicago Convention and further elaborated by frameworks developed under the auspices of ICAO.

The establishment of the Kenyan institutional framework and coordinated by the KCAA is an important milestone. Institutionally, KCAA has responded positively in terms of addressing the general civil aviation safety and security through provision of legislative rules and policy formulations. Although the larger fabric of the regulatory framework is not specifically dedicated to UAS operations, it governs the day-to-day operations in the Kenyan airspace. Previous lack of UAS-specific framework had a major setback on the achievement of the full potential of aviation safety and security, and at the same time adhering to safeguards of right to privacy as identified in Chap. 2 of this book.

The Chapter credits the KCAA for showing great interest in regulation of UAS through the RPAs 2017 Regulations, though as noted, the credit suffered a major setback when the interest expressed through gazettement of the Regulations was shot down in Parliament in June 2018. It concludes that the events of 2017 challenged the achievement of Kenya's roadmap for integration of UAS into the civil airspace,

[152] See Mwenda et al. (2012), pp. 130–135.

creating a catch-22 situation in which for a number of years, the country did not have UAS regulation in place to check the increasing number of UAS in her airspace.[153] Evidently, the lack of regulations posed a threat to safety and security, coupled with actual violation of the right to privacy due to the potential of existing illegal operations of UAS in her airspace. Of these challenges, privacy concerns seem to be more prominent due to the government's approach of increasingly limiting the right to privacy through adoption of legislation on national security. KCAA on its part responded quickly and positively to the issues raised by Parliament, culminating in the Cabinet Secretary finally gazetting the new UAS law on 30 March 2020. The regulation considers adherence to safety, security and privacy concerns with a view to smoothening the legal path to integration.

References

Books

Jeanneret C, Rambaldi G (2016) Drone governance: a scan of policies, laws and regulations governing the use of unmanned aerial vehicles (UAVs) in 79 countries. CTA Swiss Foundation

Journal Articles

Kameri-Mbote P, Muriungi M (2017) Potential contribution of drones to reliability of Kenya's land information system. Afr J Inf Commun, 159–169

Mwenda AN et al (2012) Trends in consultation and public participation within environmental impact assessment in Kenya. Impact Assessment Project Appraisal, 130–135

Nader M, Al-Jaroodi J, Jawhar I, Idries A, Mohammed F (2020) Unmanned aerial vehicles applications in future smart cities. TFSC, 1–17

Odido D, Madara S (2013) Emerging technologies: use of unmanned aerial systems in the realization of Vision 2030 goals in the counties. Int J Appl Sci Technol, 107

Ronald HK (2012) Managing the public sector in Kenya: reform and transformation for improved performance. J Public Adm, 128–143

Wright W (1916) The Wright Brothers' Aeroplane. Aeronaut J, 100–106

Thesis and Dissertations

Waithera EN (2015) Factors influencing aviation safety: the case of Kenya civil aviation authority. Master of Arts thesis University of Nairobi

[153] Kenya did not have an effective UAS regulation after annulment of RPAs regulation of 2017 in June 2018 until 30 March 2020.

Workshops and Conference Papers

CASSOA (2018) Aviation Safety: A Collaborative Approach. In Symposium Report. Paper Presented in the 4th EAC Aviation Symposium, Crowne Plaza Nairobi 1-2 February 2018

Makau H (2014) Best Practices to Enhance Cooperation and Collaboration between Aviation Security and Customs. In: Enhancing Air Cargo Security and Facilitation (Paper presented to the ICAO-WCO Joint Conference Manama Bahrain 16–17 April 2014

Chapter 7
Synthesis of Outcomes Regarding Integration of UAS into Civil Aviation in the US, South Africa and Kenya

7.1 Introduction

As a secondary lens, this book Chapter looks at frameworks from the perspective of International Aviation Law (IAL) and its adoption to domestic, legal, policy and institutional framework. It analyses how the current legal responses were developed separately to deal with UAS' associated challenges of safety, security and privacy rights assurances in South Africa and Kenya. It is clearly established that the US has had a long history of interaction with UAS, hence the approach to discuss the legal responses of the two African States at different stages of developing UAS regulation against lessons from the US. The Chapter also analyses the notable safety, security and privacy challenges experienced by the States under inquiry.

7.2 Lessons Learned

Though there is no unified international legal instrument that deals with all aspects of UAS, the Chicago Convention at Article 8 makes an explicit recognition of UAS. The framework is complemented with soft laws developed by ICAO such as SARPs, with varying levels of biding effect towards implementation of its provisions of regulation, and play a key role towards the integration process. The international framework is aimed at inspiring regional and domestic response to, among others, challenges concerning integration of UAS into respective national aviation airspaces. From the analysis of how the three States considered in this book have developed and adopted the international framework, it is clear that other than other commonalities including establishment of regulatory authorities, there is incongruence in the domestic response to regulation of UAS in terms of legislative history

M. Wanyonyi Rodgers, *The Law Regulating Unmanned Aircraft Systems in the United States, South Africa and Kenya*,
https://doi.org/10.1007/978-3-031-49927-2_7

and developments, timelines and reasons for amendments of aviation laws.[1] The incongruence, notwithstanding, it is clear that the States can learn from one another, or may showcase to other States certain lessons towards effective integration of UAS into their respective national aviation systems. These are divided into three limbs as discussed below.

The first limb relates to the lesson that the States can learn from each other. The first lesson regards the need for public participation. Though the three States covered herein had general constitutional frameworks for public, private sector and stakeholder engagement, the same is wholly inadequate in the regulation of UAS issues. Instructively, UAS has unique stakeholders such as manufacturers, developers, exporters, importers, owners, pilots, operators of different categories, members of the public and the Government. Their involvement is necessary since redress for UAS safety, security and privacy concerns mainly targets them or they interact with UAS in one way or another.

The Kenyan framework can borrow from South Africa, for instance, regarding the participation of the public in the nomination and evaluation in the appointment of members to the Aviation Safety Investigations Board. The decision by the Kenyan Parliament to annul the 2017 RPAs Regulations for reasons of non-compliance with public participation exposes the need for Kenya to consider public participation in regulation, use, monitoring and operation of UAS.

South Africa too can learn a variety of lessons to make the public participation aspect more meaningful. Of particular concern is with respect to provision for public participation on substantive procedural and rule-making processes. This provision requires and limits the rates of participation in rule-making to accredited representatives, advisers, experts and observers but leaves out key stakeholders in the value chain of UAS, including members of the public in whom the safety, security and privacy concerns converge.

The second lesson regards the need for enhancement of capacity at the regulatory authorities of the three States. Unlike the US which has a long history of dealing with UAS, it is established that both SACAA and KCAA have less than six staff each stationed in their offices and overseeing UAS applications and registration.[2] These countries need to take cue from the US in order to overcome often-glaring logistical problems for effective oversight and enforcement of the provision of the framework on safety, security and privacy regulations.

The third lesson has to do with the devolution of the regulatory phenomena as a pivotal approach in ensuring efficacy. This, however, depends on the constitutional framework for such devolution functions. For instance, in the US, the regulation is done at Federal and State levels. The same is true for South Africa, which does regulation of UAS at the national and local government spheres. Kenya, on the other

[1] See Chaps. 4, 5 and 6 of this book on analysis of the history and substantive provisions of principal laws under FAA Modernization Reform Act, South Africa's Civil Aviation Act and Kenya's Civil Aviation Act respectively.

[2] See SACAA & KCAA organizational structure (Date of use: 30 August 2023).

hand, has a different constitutional make-up where civil aviation is the sole mandate of the national government and not devolved to county governments.

The fourth and final lesson is on the need for development of regional and sub-regional agencies dealing with UAS regulation. This is necessary both to complement the regulatory work of ICAO and to aid in harmonization of approaches among sub-regional organization participants. The East Africa Civil Aviation Safety and Security Oversight Agency (CASSOA) in particular, has proved to be effective in respect of Kenya in supplement operations of the institutional frameworks for implementation of UAS regulatory framework within East Africa. South Africa could take the cue within the regional organization of Southern Africa Development Community (SADC) to provide mechanisms of obtaining regional consensus on regulatory and oversight issues. For SADC, doing so may start with expression of political goodwill through ratification of Interim Southern Africa Safety Organization (ISASO).

The second limb comprises lessons that may be learnt from the US' framework for assurance of safety, security and privacy concerns related to UAS. These lessons are particularly important because the US has longer experience with UAS use and established UAS-specific regulations.

First, the general classification of UAS depends on their performance specifications, endurance, maximum altitude, altitude and wing loading capacity among other considerations. The US regulatory framework adopts a unique classification of UAS in a manner that upholds robust classification with different classes attracting varying safety and security obligations.[3] The South African and Kenyan systems can emulate the framework for certificate of waivers in order to ensure that at all material times the regulation of UAS is proportionate to the risk of the operation in question. This focus will ensure a safety risk assessment based approach, which avoids use of a lot of resources in monitoring UAS, whose operations and circumstances pose no obvious safety risk as contemplated under the ICAO Circular 330 AN/189 on Civil/Military Cooperation in Air Traffic Management of 2011.[4]

Secondly, there is need to ensure gradualism and pragmatism in the approach for integration of UAS into the civil airspace. From the US' perspective, the lesson relates to focus on safe rather than full integration through the US' phased-in approach. For instance, despite interacting with the UAS in the early 1900s, the FAA Modernization and Reform Act, which provides for operation of the model aircraft, was only adopted in 2012. The pragmatism involves the information of policy and legal development with history to ensure that the country does not get it wrong. From the regulation of UAS in the US, it is clear that their proper integration into civil aviation systems works on the understanding that UAS operations should

[3] See Chap. 4, It explains that Section 333 of the FAAMR Act and the cuurent FAA Reauthorization Act of 2018 allows an operator of a UAS weighing less than 50 pounds to apply for a certificate of waiver, which allows the equipment to deviate from certain operating rules where the FAA is satisfied that the proposed operation does not pose security challenges.

[4] See Chap. 3 of this book which analyses the Circular as requiring that the operation of UAS be regulated in a manner that is proportionate to the risk of the operation in question.

not increase risk to other airspace users, persons and properties on the ground. That is why the US premises its process on a safe rather than full integration. In other words, full integration that is not safe is self-defeatist and at all times the two objectives should be simultaneous. South Africa and Kenya can learn to ensure that they do not wait for disaster attacks such as the September 11 attacks in the US to shape their policy, legal and regulatory discourse regarding UAS security countermeasures.[5] Given their relatively lower levels of experience of UAS, the US practice offers a best learning opportunity for South Africa and Kenya to embrace pragmatics in their laws and regulations, or at least in the implementation of their UAS policy formulation and laws.[6]

Thirdly, is the flexibility-related lesson. From the US' perspective, flexibility is reflected in the recognition of community-based organizations that are allowed to form local units through which FAA allows them to establish guidelines on the operation of small model UAS with the regulator retaining overall mandate. The approach allows the FAA to concentrate on regulation of huge commercial UAS and other recreational UAS that pose serious safety, security and privacy risks and leave the rest that require less supervision to community-based-organizations like clubs.

Fourthly, the US boasts more robust and proactive frameworks on redress of the sensitive matter of security in aviation, something worth emulating.[7] FAA is comparatively more creative in developing relevant Committees, frameworks under Advisory Circulars, Orders and Programmes that complement the provision of principal legislations aimed at addressing UAS safety and security challenges.[8] No wonder, therefore, South African and Kenyan frameworks have borrowed from the US system to varying degrees.[9]

Lastly, judicial activism plays a critical role in filling the void and inconsistences in the substantive provision for redress of privacy concerns in international and domestic frameworks. Analysis of the US regime reveals that the country's courts

---

[5] See Chap. 4, of the book on legislative gradualism through development of Air Commerce Act of 1926 Air Commerce Regulations of 1928, Civil Aeronautics Act of 1938 the Federal Aviation Act of 1958 and the Department of Transportation Act of 1966 and the latest FAA Reauthorization Act of 2018.

[6] See Chap. 5, on the book on the history of the US civil aviation industry.

[7] Chapter 4, discussion on Title 49 of the US Code and FAA Modernization and Reform Act, 2012. and FAA Reauthorization Act of 2018.

[8] Chapter 4, of the book provides analysis of Advisory Circular on Reporting Laser Illumination of Aircraft and orders such as FAA Order JO 7110.65, FAA Order No. JO 7210.3, FAA Order JO 7110. See also South Africa's and Kenya's National Civil Aviation Security Committee (NCASC), National Civil Aviation Security Programme (NCASP) and National Civil Aviation Quality Control Programme (NCAQCP).

[9] Chapter 4, of the book provides analysis of the South African Framework under National Civil Aviation Security Committee (NCASC), National Civil Aviation Security Programme (NCASP) and National Civil Aviation Quality Control Programme (NCAQCP). See also Chapter Five on Kenyan Framework under Security Amendment Act 19 of 2014, National Police Service Act Chapter 84 Laws of Kenya, Prevention of Terrorism Act 30 of 2012, South Africa Police Service Act 57 of 2008.

have risen to the occasion and been able to interpret the law in a manner that protects the right to privacy. In the wake of worrying trend of legislations that restrict the right to privacy, Kenyan and South African courts could learn to protect the rights of the vulnerable with regard to breach of privacy in UAS operations.

The third limb concerns the lessons that can generally be learnt by States, but not covered herein. Firstly, there is an urgent need for clear and harmonized domestic standards for policy and regulation of UAS in all States to achieve their integration into civil aviation. This arises not merely from the emergence of issues around sense and avoid technology, command control, UAS traffic management (UTM) and protection of privacy, but also UAS' unique physical capabilities, actual and potential uses. Development of standards is necessary to complement the international framework for proper functioning and implementation. Bearing in mind the envisaged regulation, States may adopt different naming for the UAS since it is the relevance and efficacy of regulation, and not merely the name, that is important.

Secondly, adopting the regulatory approaches in respect of UAS, an outright ban should not be an option for addressing their safety, security and privacy concerns.[10] Research identifies a three-step approach of segregate, accommodate and integrate, depending on UAS capacity and the risks it poses. While the US, South Africa and Kenya attach immense significance to UAS cost and efficiency, it is projected that it could find its way into human and cargo transportation, thus heightening the concerns raised herein.[11]

Thirdly, owing to the elusive nature of UAS regulation, States must strive to adopt the international framework for regulation, including use of guidance materials developed by ICAO, entrench partnerships with ICAO and other international agencies as contemplated under Article 65 of the Chicago Convention. This will offer a vital complementary system for efficient implementation of programmes and approaches towards integration of UAS into the national airspace of the respective States. States could borrow a leaf from South Africa's active participation in the ICAO Council that imposes on it a moral obligation to comply with effective implementation index of the existing regulatory framework and providing continual policy and legislative improvement.[12]

The fourth lesson is on the direct correlation between economic development and regulation of aviation including UAS, given that policy, regulatory mechanisms and approaches for integration of UAS require intense planning and huge monetary injection. A developed country like the US has managed to develop sense and avoid systems, and address the technological bases of safety, security and privacy of UAS with comparative ease.[13]

[10] Chapter 1, of the book on the explanation of 'outright ban' regulatory approach.

[11] See discussion on the justification for regulation of UAS use in Chap. 1, of the book.

[12] Chapter 5 of the book analyses the institutional framework of SACAA which provides details of SACAA's partnership with ICAO.

[13] Chapter 4, of the book provides the history and background of regulation of civil aviation recognizes the technological and economic developments of the US.

7.2.1 Safety Challenges

With respect to the safety challenges, the international law under the Chicago Convention and ICAO framework of Annex 19 has robust provision on the safety assurances. Where necessary, in respect of the States, the framework is complemented by other international instruments that are differentially ratified by States.[14] At the domestic level, the three States considered in this book have adopted the legislative frameworks that regulate certification, authorization, remote pilot licencing, training and maintenance of visual line of sight to ensure the safety of UAS operations.[15] In other words, the States to varying degrees and through their respective aviation regulatory institutions regulate skills and behaviour of operators as tools for ensuring that safety of UAS use is assured as a means of achieving integration of UAS into civil aviation airspace.

In both South Africa's and Kenya, necessary filings of safety levels and systems precede the authorization for use of UAS. The licensing of the skills is classified depending on the level of risks associated with the weight and use of the UAS. Moreover, the licensing requires authorized training, medical examination and attainment of majority age. South Africa licensing classification is comparatively more robust since it recognizes additional safety parameters.[16] Another difference is the measurements regarding the maintenance of the visual line of sight.[17]

Analysis of the regulatory regimes reveal that the States have developed some form of regulation regarding the design of the UAS together with the development for the sense and avoid technologies to ensure avoidance of collision as the UAS is integrated into the respective national aviation systems. Simply put, the States to a varying degree regulate the design, specifications and the operational systems of the UAS in order to ensure compliance with the set safety standards as well as management of UAS systems. Both South Africa and Kenya regulate the carrying of dangerous materials.[18] Although they recognize the need for the sense and avoid in the UAS integration plans, the technology presents implementation challenges to

[14] See Chap. 3 on analysis if international framework, Chicago Convention, ICAO Annexes 2 & 19, ICAO Circular No 328 AN 190, and complementary framework under Hague Convention on the Suppression of Unlawful Seizure of Aircraft, 1970.

[15] See respective analyses under Chaps. 4, 5 and 6 of the book.

[16] Chapter 5, of the book expounds the classification based on parameters such as impact, energy, operational length above the ground, rules of flight and air operation.

[17] Chapter 5, of the book explains that in South Africa, the UAS operation within restricted Visual-Line-of-Sight is an operation conducted within 500 m of the UAS pilot and below the height of the highest obstacle within 300 m of the UAS. Under the discussion in Chap. 6, of the book, the Kenyan minimum which is set at the minimum of 400 feet from the ground level.

[18] Chapter 5, 1 of the book expounds the South Africa's provisions on regulation of dangerous goods with only private UAS is exempted. Same is the case for Kenya as under Chap. 6, of the book albeit with focused on the impact on aviation insurance.

the two jurisdictions for small UAS.[19] Another common challenge is non-regulation of environmental concern of noise arising from UAS in both States.

With respect to the authorization, design and specifications as well as systemic requirements, the States are inspired by the ICAO Regulations. It will be recalled that South Africa and Kenya have domesticated ICAO Annex 19 on Safety Management System that regulates safety among member States, supported by ICAO Safety Management Manual and ICAO circular 328-AN/190 that serves as a sources of information and guidance in development of aviation State Safety Programme (SSP), safety regulation and policies.

7.2.2 *Security Challenges*

With respect to aviation security challenges, the international law asserts State sovereignty in regulation of civil aviation matters in international instruments as enshrined in the Chicago Convention Articles 1 (sovereignty) and 2 on territoriality. In safeguarding aviation security, States operate under customary international law based on general State practices such as right of overflight.[20] The frameworks provide for commitments in providing authorization mechanisms, programmes and audit processes to address security challenges as provided for under ICAO Annex 17 and Aviation Security Manual (Doc 8973). At the domestic levels, the US, South Africa and Kenya have developed rules to create a balance between recognition of lawful use of UAS and the regulation of related unlawful acts that pose a threat to national security. Principally, rules such as the National Civil Aviation Security programmes relate to the assertion of State sovereignty as the basis for authorization. South Africa and Kenya provide for mandatory provisions for UAS registration and authorization as well as adherence to security programmes. In Kenya there is an even more robust multi-agency approach where the active involvement of security agencies and the Department of Defence is pivotal in the regulation of UAS. This high-level security measure is akin to the US' approach that takes the form of the Department of Homeland Security.

It is established that the two States take other pro-active security approaches to conduct background checks on operation and regulation of storage of UAS.[21] Both jurisdictions demand that UAS not in use be stored and prepared for flight in a secure

[19] For Kenyan implementation challenges are explained under Chap. 6, South African challenges relating to toy and community-based organizations are at Chap. 5, of the book.

[20] Chapter 3, of this book provides a background of analysis on the international framework for regulation of UAS.

[21] Compare SA-CATS 101 r 101.04.8 discussed in Chap. 5, of this book and the Kenya Aviation Policy, Kenya Civil Aviation (Remote Piloted Aircraft Systems) Regulations 2017, reg 6(2) (now annulled) and Regulation 43 of the 2020 UAS Regulations discussed in Chap. 6, of the book.

manner.[22] It is noted that a further step in the development of requirements for organizational arrangements requires operators to ensure security measures and programmes are established and implemented.[23]

As regards security controls through registration, background checks, regulations of UAS storage and organizational tools, the States have domesticated ICAO guidance materials on security such as ICAO Circular 328-AN/190. This commitment is evidence that South Africa and Kenya have ratified the Chicago Convention and domesticated ICAO Annex 17, which is demonstration of the desire to ensure aviation security in the chain of UAS regulation through national legislations and policies.

7.2.3 Privacy Challenges

With regard to privacy challenges, the international framework provides comparatively less aviation-related safeguards compared to other safety and security concerns.[24] This is reflected in the domestic frameworks of the States that adopt differential levels of effective implementation index as evidenced in the differential levels of legislative steps and judicial activism in the United States, South Africa and Kenya.[25] The domestic frameworks are also heavily dependent on the national constitutional frameworks for protection and enforcement. The States' reliance on such protection in the international system is, therefore, placed on the International Bill of Rights and several countries' Constitutions. Although Constitutions are fundamental with safer protections against breach, they are too general for specific protections save for the US, which has proved to offer far better protection, at least from the analysis of jurisprudence.[26]

That notwithstanding, the legal frameworks of the three States covered herein have tended to adopt domestic rules that complement UAS-specific rules regarding

[22] See Chap. 5, on discussion on the content of the General restrictions SA- CATS 101, Section 101.05.3 in South Africa and part 5.2.

[23] See Chap. 6, on the description of Kenya's National Civil Aviation Security Programme Section 4.3 on partnership with IATA through the latter's safety and security programmes. South Africa's programme functioning through analysis of SA-CATS 101, r 101.04.5 and part 4 on the role of Civil Aviation Security Department of SACAA and Section 111 of the Civil Aviation Act 2009 on development of National Security programme under Chap. 5, of this book.

[24] See Chap. 3 of this book on the analysis of International Bill of Rights instruments on assurance of piracy and tardiness of such provision on the Chicago Convention, 1944.

[25] US, South Africa and Kenya's frameworks on regulation of privacy is discussed under Chaps. 4, 5 and 6, respectively.

[26] The Fourth Amendment to the Constitution of the US discussed under Chap. 4, and the Constitution of Kenya, 2010 discussed under Chap. 6, provide for general protections. Analysis of key highlights of the US jurisprudence is under FAA Reauthorization Act of 2018.

privacy concerns.[27] In particular, they focus on distance as a tool to balance UAS freedom and respect for the privacy of others. In other words, all three legal systems, to varying degrees, regulate the distance from persons or property at which a UAS may be used or operated. The distances vary of course,[28] but appear to be integral in protecting the right of privacy under the UAS regulations.

Analysis of the regulatory regimes suggests a trend in favour of regulating the components of UAS as a means for achieving balance between integrating them into civil aviation and protecting privacy rights of the people on the ground and their properties, although it varies in degree. For example, while the US and Kenya have rules on the attachment of cameras, South Africa's rules are less clear and have to be inferred.[29]

Finally, with regard to the distance regulation and the component requirement, the regulatory frameworks in the three States adopt the principal legislative framework under the Chicago Convention, which places emphasis on prohibition of use of photographic apparatus in an aircraft over the territory of another State.[30]

7.3 Conclusion

UAS global regulation is moving towards a non-restrictive approach, which is dictated by factors like the legislative development levels of States. As such, developing States should not get stuck with the wait-and-see approach but consider regulation on an *ad hoc* basis. For developed countries like the United States, the way forward is to adopt legislation to cover for emerging situations of possible use of UAS to transport cargo and people. However, the two set of countries should monitor the general trajectory of development of UAS technology and adopt the best approach, while embracing flexibility to improve on integration. Emphasis should be placed on approaches that do not compromise safety and security, as well as violate the universal fundamental human right to privacy.

The legislative processes in South Africa and Kenya may be different, but they have made phenomenal progress in developing policies aimed at aviation regulation and integration of UAS into civil aviation. The two States' regulatory frameworks recognize the general need to regulate UAS operations towards achieving integration of UAS into civil airspace despite there being no consensus amongst members of the

[27] While South Africa has developed Civil Aviation Regulations of 2015, Kenya has developed UAS 2020 Regulations. The US on its part utilizes the Academy of Model Aeronautics Safety Code of 2018 as read with FAA Reauthorization Act of 2018.

[28] In US, the Academy of Model Aeronautics Safety Code of 2018 generally prohibit flying the UAS closer than 25 feet to an individual. In South Africa, there is a limit the operation of UAS to a lateral distance of 50 m from any structure or public road.

[29] For example, See Chap. 6, on the analysis of 2020 UAS Regulations, Regulation 24(1)(e) and its provision on regulation of imaging devices. The SA-CATS do not have express provision on such.

[30] Chicago Convention Art 36.

regional economic bodies they are members of. Kenya UAS 2020 Regulation is evidence of similarity of approaches in ensuring safety and adoption of State safety programmes, effective licensing, and authorization, categorization of UAS, public participation frameworks, security standards and observance of people's privacy. Other similarities occur in the regulatory approaches and enforcement of UAS Regulations such as criminal sanctions.

The jurisdictions face challenges resulting from lack of unanimity in Sense and Avoid technology, and tardiness in having UAS-specificity in privacy provisions in the existing legislation. Others relate to concerns in environmental, enforcement, privacy, licensing and authorization. It is established that the US has had long-standing involvement in UAS, thus serving as a model from which South Africa and Kenya can pick vital lessons. Key among these are safe and pragmatist integration of UAS, integration, flexibility in the regulation of safety and privacy concerns arising from use of UAS, use of community-based organizations and introduction of certificate of waiver framework.

Chapter 8
Conclusion, Recommendations and Way Forward

8.1 Introduction

This book chapter provides a one-stop-shop repository of all that is covered in the preceding seven chapters. It is acknowledged that there is absence of unified international UAS regulatory framework that significantly hampers their integration into civil aviation. This happens against the backdrop of increased technological use of UAS without effective integration into the national airspace. Inquiry is made into how and to what extent the existing international regulatory frameworks viz., the Chicago Convention and ICAO address current UAS-related challenges of safety, security and privacy. Of focus in this regard is how the US, South Africa and Kenya through institutional, policy and legal frameworks have responded to UAS regulation in addressing current needs and challenges in operation within their domestic frameworks.

Investigation is made of the rights and obligations of States in addressing UAS challenges under international and domestic laws, with a view to providing recommendations to aid faster and safer integration of UAS into civil aviation by the States under study. Practical recommendations and opportunities for improvement in operations of UAS to international, regional, sub-regional, domestic frameworks and stakeholders towards addressing safety, security and privacy challenges are also offered.

8.2 General Conclusions

Chapter 1 of the book provides expansion of UAS use, increased safety, security, privacy concerns and advancement in technology as the basis for an array of regulatory approaches regarding UAS. It offers the general implementation and

M. Wanyonyi Rodgers, *The Law Regulating Unmanned Aircraft Systems in the United States, South Africa and Kenya*,
https://doi.org/10.1007/978-3-031-49927-2_8

enforcement challenges experienced by States that have opted to regulate UAS in their domestic frameworks.

Chapter 2 demonstrates that States are faced with circumstances that make regulation of UAS almost inevitable. It emphasizes that in choosing to take up the challenge, States have to decisively deal with the unique safety, security and privacy concerns arising from the use of UAS.

Chapter 3 traces the international air law response to the thematic areas of safety, security of the ICAO framework, and is complemented by other international human rights instruments, international customary law and general principles of law to address concerns in the three thematic areas. It emerges that the concern for privacy is unevenly addressed compare to safety and security.

Chapter 4 analyses the response to UAS integration by the US, a jurisdiction with a longer history with UAS regulation; it has advanced framework to address the three thematic areas through a more proactive regulatory agency, namely FAA. The challenge of unbalanced focus on privacy concerns as well as lack of sense and avoid technology in some UAS appears to take a toll on enforcement and regulatory framework.

Chapter 5 analyses South Africa's framework and its approach to safety, security and privacy concerns. It is established that the framework is cognizant of and addresses these thematic areas. The least of the focus is on privacy. South Africa is lauded for her active participation in ICAO despite the challenges occasioned by a lack of support by Southern Africa Development Community (SADC) in her endeavours to integrate UAS into civil aviation.

Chapter 6 takes a critical review of Kenya's approach to the three thematic areas enumerated above. It is established that Kenya has made notable strides, for example, via legislative amendments in 2016, the development of UAS policy, and the 2017 RPAs Regulation that was initially annulled but re-enacted as 2020 UAS Regulations to address the challenges of safety, security and privacy. At its nascent stages, however, Kenya faces challenges related to sense and avoid technologies, UTM, command and control, lack of involvement of county governments for effective enforcement and categorization of UAS regulation.

Chapter 7 provides a synthesis of the scenarios in the three States, that is, the US, South Africa and Kenya. That the three jurisdictions have certain common elements in their approach to UAS regulation, common and peculiar challenges, and the lessons they can learn from each other on matters of classification, training, authorizations, integration planning and regional efforts. It is established that pragmatism, flexibility, gradualism and UAS classification are the key areas for redress as regards UAS regulation in the three thematic areas outlined above.

8.3 Recommendations

The recommendations contained in this section are based on the foregoing general and specific conclusions. They target the ICAO and relevant structures, bodies and institutions within the domestic jurisdictions of the US, South Africa, Kenya and, by limited extension, regional and continental agencies for implementation towards successful integration of UAS into civil aviation as they endeavour to address safety, security and privacy challenges associated with UAS operations.

8.3.1 ICAO

Firstly, there is need to broaden the meaning and scope of aircraft in the Chicago Convention. Enacted in 1944, the Chicago Convention was designed to specifically address international law for manned aircraft and by extension unmanned aircraft as provided for under Article 8. For States without UAS-specific laws, the treaty law can only be made by implication, which is not sustainable as it only promotes a wait and see approach in regulation of UAS at the domestic level. Some authors affirm the conundrum by suggesting that the implication of its application has not been without controversy.[1] Adoption and remodelling of the Chicago Convention on UAS in the manner envisaged for amendment under Article 94 and having State parties ratify it, has the potential to boost commitment of State parties such as South Africa and Kenya that developed regulation and others that are yet to develop UAS legislation. Alternatively, though not quite ideal, ICAO State parties could consider adoption of a new Convention or additional protocol tailored to address UAS, considering the ever-changing technological and operational landscapes.

Secondly, although Annex 6 Part IV provide for development for UAS operations, ICAO uses the term RPAs because its main focus is on large UAS that fall in the category of manned aircraft. Hence, ICAO limits itself to UAS above 25 kg. This means there is need for ICAO to consider developing ICAO Annex 20 for UAS. The Annex should be binding to all member States so that UAS application is well regulated to address global emerging technological trends appearing as moving target, on uses, designs and capabilities of UAS. Alternatively, the conditions and standards set out under the ICAO Circular 328.AN/190 on UAS could be revised and adopted through an amendment then ratified as the Annex. The Annex will be prominent for parties who comply for purposes of international obligation, best practice, moral authority to external forces of international power politics or other reasons. It is envisaged that this recommendation to the ICAO is relevant in the short-term, pending the complete execution of the other made above to ensure that UAS has equal prominence as that under Annex 6 that deals with Operation of

[1] Marshall (2009), p. 693.

Aircraft with a view to giving more emphasis on expected increase of UAS operation.

It is also recommended that security and safety mechanisms are enhanced. To meet the security and safety standards provided for under ICAO Annexes 17 and 19 respectively, UAS should be enhanced with modified global positioning system data to avoid possible manipulation by hackers who use such data for criminal activities like terrorism and cyber-attacks among a host of other unlawful interference with civil aviation. Communication between UAS, other aircraft, control towers and ground crew should also be improved via sharing UAS operational frequencies, UTM, common data, and video links through the development of counter-jamming technologies and providing background security and safety checks.

Finally, ICAO should ensure a robust framework for regulation of UAS-specific privacy concerns. In seeking to level the concern of privacy with that of safety and security, it is recommended that ICAO considers development of Annex 20 as suggested above to make provision for privacy associated challenges. In the alternative, provide additional amendments to Annex 2 and 6 to expressly address issues identified under this book for UAS unified integration into civil airspace.

8.3.2 South Africa and Kenya

With regard to the two African States, ten recommendations are made as outlined below. Firstly, they should strengthen aviation institutions to make them efficient and able to cope with technological advances regarding UAS. To guarantee the desired efficiency, there should be public participation, upholding the independence of regulators, and establishment of permanent regulatory units that deal with UAS. This would help to address existing challenges such as regulatory independence, capacity building and ability to issue policy statements in the dynamic civil aviation sector for sustainable development.

Secondly, the States should consistently review UAS regulations through relevant departments with a view to strengthening them, taking into consideration new technological advancements. These departments should also consider the appropriate times to collaborate with community-based organizations and to adopt classification models that distinguish model aircraft and regulated aircraft in respective national aviation systems. It is envisaged that such clarity in categorization shall aid the aviation regulators in determining the extent to which UAS are allowed to operate within the airspace, the information they are likely to collect about individuals, their uses, disclosure requirements, as well as possible impact on individual privacy. The States should emulate the US in developing efficient categorization of UAS for a more focused regulatory approach regarding the differential rates of safety, security and privacy risks they pose.

Thirdly, the States should develop minimum standards for operator dynamic training with curriculum focus on proficiency and safety in UAS control and interaction with other aircraft in the national airspace. This will go a long way in ensuring the safety of civil aviation given the exponential growth of the UAS sector (as identified in Chap. 1 of this book).

Fourthly, the executive and legislative authorities should develop or maintain a balance between protection of human rights including right to privacy and public security regarding use and operation of UAS to ensure that the former is not sacrificed at the altar of the latter. Countries such as South Africa can borrow from Kenya's annulled 2017 RPAs Regulations and the current Kenya 2020 UAS that has provisions devoted to provisions on privacy protection. This is a sure way of complementing the International Bill of Rights assurances on privacy protection. To further entrench these efforts, it is recommended that courts adopt judicial activism akin to that in the US in order to bridge the gap in the provisions and implementation of the same at the domestic, sub-regional and regional jurisdictions; and across the African continent.

Fifthly, the States should enact legislation to give requisite mandate to individuals to mitigate potential impact on personal privacy such as protecting UAS against unauthorized disclosure. Licenses issued should specify those individually responsible for safe use of UAS and the information collected thereof.

Sixthly, the States should endeavour to expand opportunities for citizens to air their grievances or complaints through legally recognized fora. A statement of the UAS operators that is accessible online should accompany all licenses granted by State agencies with possible frameworks or timelines in handling such complaints.

Seventhly, South Africa and Kenya should adopt lessons of pragmatism, gradualism and flexibility from the US on integration of UAS into civil aviation. This requires formulation of effective UAS regulation enforcement mechanisms and development of implementation roadmaps with achievable deadlines. Priority should be placed on ensuring there is proper listing of all unmanned aircraft irrespective of size or use for data compilation and information sharing with relevant agencies or countries. Clear sanctions for violators of UAS regulations as established should be effectively enforced.

Eighthly, it befits to aver here that the importance of UAS should not be ignored with the rising globalization, coupled with rapidly changing technology. The States should devote more resources and funding for research in a discipline that is, without doubt, the future of civil aviation. UAS has potential to impact how people work, live, move and associate as technology advances.

Ninthly, the States should consider UAS traffic management (UTM), which has capacity to detect where command and control centre for the UAS in operation is located. The purpose is for the enforcement officers to ensure compliance through monitoring of UAS hovering in civil airspace for effective oversight. The implementation will support regulation in addressing the safety and security challenges in the civil aviation industry.

Lastly, South Africa and Kenya should consider allocating resources for command and control system (CCS), which is essential for civil aviation to control UAS movement within their airspace. It is proposed that such improved system be available in at least every regional security or civil aviation office or at the county level. The technology, once established, will go a long way in providing countermeasures in dealing with emerging crime trends.

8.3.3 Kenya

With respect to Kenya, five recommendations are made herein:

Firstly, Kenya should make regulatory requirements for UAS operators to mitigate risks against other airspace users, ground property and people in general. This is in addition to the 2020 UAS Regulation having provision and requirement to take up insurance before they are allowed to operate within the national airspace to mitigate civil liability issues and claims.[2] There is a glaring lack of proper guidance on how insurance applies; the *lacuna* in the regulations is the assumption that the aircraft premium computation would work for UAS, which may not be appropriate due to their varied sizes.

Secondly, Kenyan should consider developing a policy to co-ordinate and progressively harmonize matters relating to civil aviation, and UAS in particular, in line with the Chicago Convention. Of prime concern is an appeal to integrate UAS as emerging technology into the national airspace, complete with safety and security regulation of their operations. Other than complementing what the Kenya National Security Policy and the National Security Strategy provides, the Policy should address environmental management, disposal of ruined UAS, safety and security, air traffic management, training, research, innovation, policy direction on protection of privacy rights, involvement of county government structures, monitoring and evaluation of UAS systems.

Thirdly, the Government should provide the KCAA with adequate funding to undertake research in the field of UAS, which could ultimately help achieve Kenya's dream of full integration of unmanned aircraft system into civil aviation. This is because, the study has revealed that UAS has the potential of significant evolution due to technological advancement.

Fourthly, the East Africa School of Aviation (EASA) should be fully funded and equipped to offer state-of-the-art training in UAS, and certification to those who qualify. Progressively, the institution should evolve into the Aviation University of East Africa so as to contribute more effectively in requisite research and technology that is critical towards realising integration of UAS regulation into civil aviation. This is together with other contribution to the aviation industry.

Fifthly, since the KCAA cannot oversight itself; it is high time the East Africa School of Aviation, is delinked from the directorate of KCAA to concentrate on providing learning and research in the aviation industry.

---

[2] Legal Notice No. 42. KCAA UAS Regulation 2020 r. 40.

8.3.4 USA

Fully cognisant of the fact that the US has interacted with UAS for much longer, it is recommended that it shares the experience with other countries for capacity building and effective enforcement. The FAA should take the lead in this endeavour, which is a recipe for strengthening UAS regulation and boosting international trade with other member States across the world.

With UAS' potential to transcend domestic jurisdictions and create safety, security and privacy risks, there is need for institutionalized partnership between the US and other countries to safeguard its airspace from unlawful intrusion.

8.3.5 Regional/Sub-regional Economic Communities: EAC, SADC and AFCAC

It has emerged all through this book that UAS use is not the preserve of any one country. For this reason, there is justification to make some recommendations for regional bodies, namely, EAC, SADC and AFCAC with a view to streamlining UAS operations across their jurisdictions.

With regard to the EAC, the Civil Aviation Safety and Security Oversight Agency (CASSOA) should, as a matter of priority, consider a framework for establishment and creation of a specific office dealing with UAS, complete with qualified staff. Doing so will increase harmonization of regulation within the region and improve coordination of UAS integration in East Africa and domestic jurisdictions such as Kenya.

As for SADC, South Africa should step up support of other member States in establishing a regional civil aviation body with a view to preserving and propagating the regulatory and institutional frameworks it has developed towards integration of UAS into civil aviation. In so doing, it can borrow a leaf from the EAC's Civil Aviation Safety and Security Oversight Agency. This will significantly boost the interim Southern Africa Safety Organization (iSASO), which is yet to realise its full operational potential.

Both EAC and SADC should consider harmonizing procedures and standards with like bodies within the African continent. Such a move would create the ideal ground for effective oversight and enforcement of UAS. By benchmarking with other countries where UAS is long entrenched into regulation encompassing several States, Kenya and South Africa stand to benefit immensely.

The African Civil Aviation Commission (AFCAC), established under the AFCAC Constitution that was adopted on 16 December 2009, should consider establishing structures within its UAS operations to progressively and incrementally complement interventions for addressing safety, security and privacy challenges at the African continental level. This is in addition to amendment and revision of the AFCAC Constitution as provided for under Article 22 (of the Constitution) to strengthen the oversight role and provide regulations for general civil aviation. An office dedicated specifically for UAS, modelled on the framework of the FAA, should be created by taking similar measures.

8.4 Areas for Further Research

The compilation of this book is aptly informed by a study of safety, security, privacy, policy, institutional, legal and regulatory issues of UAS under international air law, the US, South Africa and Kenya. These are geographical regions that are considered not volatile, hence the need for research on UAS regulation and integration into civil aviation in volatile States. Other areas worth exploring concern is the future prospects of UAS (with capacity to carry people and cargo), projected effects on current conventional civil aviation architecture, and UAS use in marine operations. Although, this research area of UAS operations currently appear underdeveloped, there is need for researchers to move with speed to attempt catch up with technological revolution associated with ever increasing capability and development of UAS.

Reference

Journal Articles

Marshall D (2009) Unmanned aerial systems and international civil aviation organization regulations. North Dakota Law Rev 85:693

Legislation

Chicago Convention 1944
Vienna Convention on the Law of Treaties 1969
EAC Treaty 1999

M. Wanyonyi Rodgers, *The Law Regulating Unmanned Aircraft Systems in the United States, South Africa and Kenya*,
https://doi.org/10.1007/978-3-031-49927-2

Case Law

Air Evac EMS, Inc. v Robinson, 486 2007 F. Supp. 2d US 713, 722 (MD. Tenn.)
American Airlines v City of Audubon Park 1969 407 F.2d US 1306 (6th Cir.)
American Airlines v Town of Hempstead 1968 398 F.2d US 369 (2d Cir.)
Carpenter v the United States 2018 No. 16-402, 585 US (SC)
City of Burbank v. Lockheed Air Terminal, 1973 411 US 624 (SC)
Dow Chemicals v the United States 1986 476 US 227 (SC).
Electronic Privacy Information Centre (EPIC) v FAA 2018 No 16-1297 US (D.C Cir.)
FAA v Raphael Pirker 2013 EA-5730 (NTBS)
Green v. Bock Laundry Machine Co. 1989 490 US 504 (SC)
Katz v. United States 1967 389 US 347 (SC)
Libyan Arab Jamahiriya v United Kingdom 1992 88 (ICJ) Rep
Lochner v. New York 1905 US 198 (SC)
Media Council of Tanzania an Others v Attorney General of the Republic of Tanzania App 5 EA 2019 (EACJ)
Med-Trans Corp. v Benton 2008 581 F. Supp. 2d US 721 (EDNC)
Montalvo v. Spirit Airlines 2007 508 F.3d 464 US 471 (9th Cir.)
R v Burgess (1936) 55 CLR (HCA)
Robert N. Gakuru & another v Governor Kiambu County & 3 others 2013 KE 532 (HC)
Philadelphia Indemnity Insurance Co v Hollycal Production Inc et al 18-768 SA (2018) 7 (SC)
Skysign International Inc. v City and County of Honolulu 2002 276 F.3d 1109 US (9th Cir.)
Smith v Maryland 1979 442 US 735 (SC)
Smith v State 1999 238 US 605 (Ga. App)
United States v Miller 1939 307 US 174 (SC)

M. Wanyonyi Rodgers, *The Law Regulating Unmanned Aircraft Systems in the United States, South Africa and Kenya*,
https://doi.org/10.1007/978-3-031-49927-2

Kenya

Constitution of Kenya, 2010
Computer Misuse and Cybercrimes Act 5 of 2018
Data Protection Act 24 of 2019
Kenya Airports Authority Act No 3 of 1991
Kenya Civil Aviation Act 21 of 2013
Kenya Civil Aviation (Amendment) Act 42 of 2016
Kenya Information and Communication Act (KICA) Cap 411A
National Intelligence Service Act 28 of 2012
National Security Council Act 23 of 2012
Statutory Instruments Act 23 of 2013
Prevention of Terrorism Act 30 of 2012
Security Laws (Amendment) Act 19 of 2014
KCAA RPAs regulation 2017
Legal Notice No. 133 - The Civil Aviation (Surveillance and Collision Avoidance Systems) Regulations, 2018
Legal Notice No. 129 - The Civil Aviation (Certification, Licensing and Registration of Aerodromes) Regulations, 2018
Legal Notice No. 91 - The Civil Aviation (Safety Management) Regulations, 2018
Legal Notice No. 94 - The Civil Aviation (Aircraft Nationality and Registration Marks) Regulations, 2018
The Civil Aviation (Security) Regulations, 2020
The Civil Aviation (Unmanned Aircraft Systems) Regulations, 2020

M. Wanyonyi Rodgers, *The Law Regulating Unmanned Aircraft Systems in the United States, South Africa and Kenya*,
https://doi.org/10.1007/978-3-031-49927-2

South Africa

Constitution of the Republic of South Africa, 1996
Civil Aviation Act 13 of 2009
South African Civil Aviation Authority Act 40 of 1998
South Africa UAS regulations 2015

M. Wanyonyi Rodgers, *The Law Regulating Unmanned Aircraft Systems in the United States, South Africa and Kenya*,
https://doi.org/10.1007/978-3-031-49927-2

The US

Air Commerce Act of 1926
Air Navigation Act 50 of 1920
Civil Aeronautics Act of 1938
Department of Transportation Act of 1966
Federal Aviation Act of 1958
FAA Modernization and Reform Act of 2012
FAA Reauthorization Act 2018
US Drone Aircraft Privacy and Transparency Act of 2013

M. Wanyonyi Rodgers, *The Law Regulating Unmanned Aircraft Systems in the United States, South Africa and Kenya*,
https://doi.org/10.1007/978-3-031-49927-2

Other Jurisdictions

EAC Civil Aviation Safety and Security Oversight Agency Act of 2007
United Kingdom Aerial Navigation Act of 1911

M. Wanyonyi Rodgers, *The Law Regulating Unmanned Aircraft Systems in the United States, South Africa and Kenya*,
https://doi.org/10.1007/978-3-031-49927-2

Internet Sources

Academy of Model Aeronautics, "National Model Aircraft Safety Code" https://www.modelaircraft.org/sites/default/files/105.pdf (Date of use: 1 August 2023)

American Bar Association "Aviation Regulation in United States" https://www.americanbar.org/products/inv/book/184862428/ (Date of use: 23 July 2023)

Andae G "Kenya flies behind peers in drones regulation" 2019-9-18 *Business Daily* https://www.businessdailyafrica.com/corporate/tech/Kenya-flies-behind-African-peers-in-drones-adoption/4258474-5278452-fvbplqz/index.html (Date of use: 6 August 2023)

Arjomandi M "Classification of Unmanned Aerial Vehicles" http://www.academia.edu/2055673/Classification ofUnmannedAerialVehicles2007 (Date of use: 10 August 2023).

Byrnes PT and Kalas MJ "FAA Admits UAS are a Severely Underfunded Mandate" https://www.jdsupra.com/legalnews/faa-admits-unmanned-aircraft-systems-i-37914/ (Date of use: 2 August 2023).

Carr EB "Unmanned aerial vehicles: Examining the safety, security, privacy and regulatory issues of integration into U.S Airspace https://www.e-education.psu.edu/geog892/sites/www.e-education.psu.edu.geog892/files/sp-Drones-long-paper.pdf (Date of use: 14 August 2023)

Caumont A "Start-Up" 28-11-2016 *Washington Post* 23 August 2023)

Electronic Privacy Information Center "Apple v. FBI" https://epic.org/amicus/crypto/apple/ (Date of use: 2 August 2023)

Ellen *et al* http://eprints.qut.edu.au (Date of use: 16 July 2023)

EUROCONTROL "Specifications for the Use of Military Unmanned Aerial Vehicles as Operational Air Traffic Outside Segregated Airspace" https://www.eurocontrol.int/publication/eurocontrol-specifications-use-military-unmanned-aerial-vehicles-operational-air (Date of use: 30 August 2023)

FAA "UAS operations in the US National airspace system- international operational guidance" http://www.uavn.com/images/AFS-400 (Date of use: 10 August 2023)

M. Wanyonyi Rodgers, *The Law Regulating Unmanned Aircraft Systems in the United States, South Africa and Kenya*,
https://doi.org/10.1007/978-3-031-49927-2

FAA "Advisory Circular" https://www.thebalancecareers.com/what-s-an-advisory-circular-and-why-should-youcare282774#:~:text=Advisory%20circulars%20can%20be%20directional,Standardization%20is%20one%20common%20reason (Date of use: 22 July 2023)

GNSS 'Transponder" http://www.lfv.se/ans/card (Date of use: 4 August 2023)

Goitom H "Regulation of drones: South Africa" https://www.loc.gov/law/help/regulation-of-drones/south-africa.php (Date of use: 2 August 2023)

Hagenauer B "Ikhana UAV gives NASA new science and technology capabilities" *2007-3-29 NASA Press Release* http://www.nasa.gov (Date of use: 2 August 2023)

Hofmeyr CD "Here is why South Africa's new drone regulations are ridiculous" https://businesstech.co.za/news/general/92072/here-is-why-south-africas-drone-regulations-are-ridiculous/ (Date of use: 8 August 2023)

https://www.afrocave.com/public-participation-kenya/ (Date of use: 4 August 2023)

https://airandspace.si.edu/stories/editorial/drones-doing-dirty-and-dangerous-jobs (Date of use: 22 August 2023)

https://aviationenglishway.com/2019/03/31/the-importance-of-an-effective-communication-in-aviation/> (Date of use: 4 August 2023)

https://www.baselineequipment.com/gps-land-surveying-equipment (Date of use: 19 August 2023)

https://www.businessinsider.co.za/absa-has-been-breaking-sa-drone-laws-and-is-about-to-put-on-an-illegal-spectacular-for-its-big-reveal-today-2018-7 (Date of use: 4 August 2023)

http://www.caa.co.za/Pages/RPAS/RPAS%20pilot%20licensing.aspx (Date of use: 7 August 2023)

http://www.caa.co.za/RPAS%20AICs/AIC%20007-2015 (Date of use: 10 August 2023)

http://www.cassoa.org/cassoa/> (Date of use: 21 August 2023)

http://de.calameo.com (Date of use: 9 August 2023)

Overview" http://www.cbp.gov (Date of use: 4 August 2023)

https://www.dhs.gov/news/2017/06/28/remarks-council-new-american-security-conference (Date of use: 6 August 2023)

https://www.droneitsa.co.za/remote-pilots-licence-rpl/ (Date of use: 7 August 2023)

https://www.easa.ac.ke (Date of use: 18 August 2023)

https://www.ecac-ceac.org (Date of use: 30 August 2023)

https://www.esrl.noaa.gov/gmd/grad/solcalc/ (Date of use: 4 August 2023)

https://www.FAA.gov.UAS (Date of use: 1 August 2023)

https://www.faa.gov/documentLibrary/media/Notice/N_JO_7210.889_Unmanned_Aircraft_Operations_in_the_NAS.pdf (Date of use: 1 August 2023)

https://www.faa.gov/news/updates/?newsId=84369 (Date of use: 2 August 2023)

http://www.faa.govNotice/N_8900.291.pdf (accessed 3 August 2023)

https://www.faa.gov/regulations_policies/airworthiness_directives/ (Date of use: 29 August 2023)

https://www.faa.gov/regulations_policies/airworthiness_directives/ (Date of use: 29 August 2023).

https://www.faa.gov/regulations_policies/rulemaking/ (Date of use: 15 August 2023)

https://www.iata.org/en/training/courses/state-safety-program/tcvg90/en/ (Date of use: 22 July 2023)

https://www.iata.org/en/pressroom/pr/2018-06-05-04/ (Date of use: 13 August 2023)

https://www.iata.org/en/pressroom/pr/2018-06-05-04/ (Date of use: 13 August 2023)

https://www.nps.gov/articles/unmanned-aircraft-in-the-national-parks.htm (Date of use: 20 July 2023)

https://www.icao.int/abouticao/History/Pages/default.aspx (Date of use: 11 July 2023)

https://www.icao.int/abouticao/assembly/Pages/. (Date of use: 11 July 2023)

https://www.icao.int/about-icao/AirNavigationCommission/Documents (Date of use: 11 July 2023)

https://www.icao.int/DownloadDocsFix/Organigramme_en.pdf (Date of use: 12 July 2023)

https://www.icao.int/environmental-protection/pages/ICAO_EU.aspx (Date of use: 4 August 2023).

https://www.icao.int/Meetings/anconf12/Document%20Archive/an02_cons%5B1%5D.pdf> (Date of use: 6 August 2023)

https://www.icao.int/safety/RunwaySafety/GRSS2011/Pages/PartnersandSupporters.aspx> (Date of use: 16 July 2023)

https://www.icao.int/SAM/Documents/2003/ANCONF11SEM/ANConf11PREP_Ip03.pdf (Date of use: 24 July 2023)

https://www.icao.int/safety/pages/usoap-results.aspx (Date of use: 22 July 2023)

https://www.icao.int/safety/SafetyManagement/Pages/Regional-Aviation-Safety-Groups-(RASGs).aspx (Date of use: 4 August 2023)

https://www.icao.int/Pages/default.aspx (Date of use: 12 July 2023)

https://www.icao.int/Security/Pages/default.aspx?p=12 (Date of use: 22 July 2023)

https://www.icao.int/WACAF/Documents/APIRG/APIRG%2022/WPs%20-%20FINAL%20ENG/WP%2051%20-%20%20U.S%20UAS%20Integration%20Update%20-%20FAA.pdf (Date of use: 15 July 2023)

https://www.Faa.gov (Date of use: 18 July 2023)

https://www.faa.gov/regulations_policies/advisory_circulars/index.cfm/go/document.information/documentID/74299 (Date of use: 22 July 2023)

https://www.gcaa.gov.ae/en/Pages/uas_old.aspx (Date of use: 2 August 2023)

https://www.govinfo.gov/content/pkg/GAOREPORTS-GAO-02-77/html/GAOREPORTS-GAO-02-77.html (Date of the use: 1August 2023)

http://www.hiller.org/ (Date of use: 19 July 2023)

https://www.hsdl.org/?abstract&did=746317 (Date of use: 1 August 2023)

https://legal.un.org/ilc/documentation/english/ASIL_1947_study.pdf (Date of use: 1 August 2023)

https://www.lmc.org/resources/drones-municipal-use-and-regulation/ (Date of use: 1 August 2023) https://www.microdrones.com/en/integratedsystems/mdlidar/mdlidar3000/?gclid=CjwKCAjwsMzzBRACEiwAx4lLG0I8cwr1VXYedXAB6U3PmzGwXLDhItULEHqj8uTMPcicAJTIuNwBgBoCxUIQAvD_BwE (Date of use: 19 August 2023)

https://mybroadband.co.za/news/gadgets/126654-12-things-you-need-to-know-about-south-africas-new-drone-laws.html (Date of use: 1 August 2023)

https://www.nationsencyclopedia.com/United-Nations-Related-Agencies/The-International-Civil-Aviation-Organization-ICAO-STRUCTURE.html (accessed on 11 July 2023)

https://www.oig.dot.gov/sites/default/files/FAA%20Oversight%20of%20Unmanned%20Aircraft%20Systems%5E6-26-14.pdf (Date of use: 2 August 2023)

http://www.president.go.ke/2017/12/12/speech-by-his-excellency-hon-uhuru-kenyatta-c-g-h-president-and-commander-in-chief-of-the-defence-forces-of-the-republic-of-kenya-during-the-2017-jamhuri-day-celebrations-at-the-moi-international/ (Date of use: 10 August 2023)

https://www.icao.int/safety/UA/UASToolkit/Pages/Narrative-Regulation.aspx> (Date of use: 16 July 2023)

https://www.kcaa.or.ke/about-us/consumer-protection (Date of use: 4 August 2023)

https://www.kcaa.or.ke/easa/about-easa> (Date of use: 1 August 2023)

https://www.statewatch.org/news/2013/mar/ecowas-dp-act.pdf (Date of use: 2 August 2023)

http://www.transportation.gov (Date of use: 30 July 2023)

https://uas.noaa.gov/Portals/5/Docs/Library/FAA-sUAS-Arctic-Implementation-Plan-2012.pdf (Date of use: 28 July 2023)

https://www.uasvision.com/2014/06/05/south-africa-civil-aviation-authority-bans-camera-uas/ (Date of use: 16 July 2023)

http://www.uavm.com (Date of use: 23 July 2023)

http://www.uniformlaws.org (Date of use: 18 August 2023)

https://www.icao.int/WACAF/Documents/APIRG/APIRG%2022/WPs%20-%20FINAL%20ENG/WP%2051%20-%20%20U.S%20UAS%20Integration%20Update%20-%20FAA.pdf (Date of use: 15 July 2023)

INFOSEC "Beware of the drone! privacy and security issues with drones" https://resources.infosecinstitute.com/privacy-and-security-issues-with-drones/#gref (Date of use: 23 July 2023)

Judson J "Future Unmanned aircraft to do the 'dull' and 'dangerous' work" 2018-3-26 *Defence News*https://www.defensenews.com/digital-show-dailies/global-force symposium/2018/03/26/future-unmanned-aircraft-to-do-the-dull-and-dangerous-work/ (Date of use: 22 July 2023)

Kesharwani T "Privatization in the Provision of Airport and Navigation Services" https://www.icao.int/Meetings/AMC/MA/1999/aps/01_kesharwani.pdf (Date of use: 13 August 2023)

Khyanyile N "Fun with a Warning" https://www.news24.com/SouthAfrica/News/fun-with-a-warning-20190204-2 (Date of use: 4 August 2023)

Mabika V "Privacy and Personal Data Protection Guidelines for Africa" 2018-8 *ITU* https://www.itu.int/en/ITUD/CapacityBuilding/Documents/IG_workshop_August 2018 Presentations/Session%207_Verengai%20Mabika.pdf. (Date of use: 30 July 2023)

Marcontelli D and Douglas S "Why the Use of Drones Still Faces Big Regulatory Hurdles" 2018-9-10 *Forbes* https://www.forbes.com/sites/oliverwyman/2018/09/10/why-the-use-of-drones-still-faces-big-regulatory-hurdles/#529c17ea1c0d (Date of use: 5 August 2023)

Mattingly P "FBI Chief admits Agency uses Drones in Domestic surveillance" https://www.washingtonpost.com/world/national-security/fbi-uses-drones-in-domestic-surveillance-mueller-says/2013/06/19/d51d40da-d925-11e2-a9f2-42ee3912ae0e_story.html (Date of use 11 July 2023)

McAuliff M "FBI's Robert Mueller: Drones are in use in US" 2013-6-19 *Huffingtonpost* https//www.huffingtonpost.com (Date of use: 12 August 2023)

Mngadi M "Two Lebanese brothers in court for Hezbollah drone export case" https://www.news24.com/news24/southafrica/news/two-lebanese-brothers-in-court-for-hezbollah-drone-export-case-20180226-2 (Date of use: 4 August 2023)

Mutai E and Otuki N "MPs annul drones rules over concerns of security, fines" 2018-6-18 *Business Daily* https://www.businessdailyafrica.com/corporate/shipping/KCAA-s-revised-drones-rules-set-for-Parliament/4003122-5135554-vc3c0p/index.html (Date of use: 29 July 2023)

Olingo A "Kenya now drafts regulations, joins Rwanda to allow drones into its airspace" 2016-4-17 *The East African* https://www.theeastafrican.co.ke/news/ea/Kenya-joins-Rwanda-to-allow-drones-in-its-airspace-/4552908-3162800-13jswqt/index.html (Date of use: 10 July 2023)

Otuki N "Kenya buys Sh1bn pilotless aircraft in war on Al-Shabaab" *2012-2-25 Business Daily* https://www.businessdailyafrica.com/economy/Kenya-buys-Sh1bn-pilotless-aircraft-in-war-on-Al-Shabaab .(Date of use: 4 July 2023)

Ozerov A "Drones for Railway Infrastructure Monitoring" 2019-12-16 *International Union of Railways* https://www.unescap.org/sites/default/files/Item8_UIC_0.pdf (Date of use: 16 July 2023)

Padgett "Using Drones in the Drug War" *2012-6-8 Time* http://www.time.com (Date of use: 15 July 2023)

Petcoff RP "Global Hawk Collects Reconnaissance Data During Haiti Relief Efforts" 2010-1-15 *US Air Force Press Release* https://www.af.mil/News/Article-Display/Article/118014/global-hawk-collects-reconnaissance-data-during-haiti-relief-efforts/ (Date of use: 4 August 2023)

Ragongo T and Caboz J "Was Absa's drone show illegal" https://myofficemagazine.co.za/was-absas-drone-show-illegal/ (Date of use: 7 August 2023)

ResearchGate "UAV collaborative and UAV applications: fire management -project overview" http://www.uav-applications.org/projects (Date of use: 15 August 2023)

Rodriguez K, Hernandez V and Jara C "The Inter-American Legal Analysis: The 13 Principles and the Inter-American System for the Protection of Human Rights" https://necessaryandproportionate.org/americas-legal-analysis (Date of use: 22 August 2023)

Secretary of Transportation "Unmanned Aircraft System (UAS) Compressive Plan: A Report on Nation's UAS Path Forward of September 2013" https://www.hsdl.org/?abstract&did=746317 (Date of use: 1 August 2023)

South African Civil Aviation Authority "South African Civil Aviation Authority Technical Guidance Material for RPAS Part 101" http://www.caa.co.za/Pages/RPAS/Remotely%20Piloted%20Aircraft%20Systems.aspx (Date of use: 28 August 2023)

South African Civil Aviation Authority "National Security Programme http://www.caa.co.za/Pages/Aviation%20Security/National-AVSEC-programme.aspx (Date of use: 9 August 2023)

Trible S "US open door to armed UAS exports" https://www.flightglobal.com/us-opens-door-to-armed-uas-exports/115939.article (Date of use: 16 July 2023)

Twala S "South African Civil Aviation Authority (SACAA)' (Canada, ICAO RPAS Symposium, 23 – 25 March 2015) https://www.icao.int/Meetings/RPAS/RPASSymposiumPresentation/Day%202%20Workshop%206%20National%20Regulations%20Sam%20Twala%20%20South%20African%20Civil%20%20Aviation%20Authority%20(SACAA).pdf> (accessed 8 July 2023)

US Department of Defense "Army Unmanned Aircraft Systems Roadmap 2010-2035" https://fas.org/irp/program/collect/uas-army.pdf (Date of use: 10 August 2023)

US Department of Transport "Federal Aviation Administration FDC. NOTAM 4/3621, Sporting Event Temp. Flight Restriction" https://www.faa.gov/uas/regulations (Date of use: 2 July 2023)

US Government Accountability Office "Unmanned Aircraft Systems" https://www.gao.gov/key_issues/unmanned_aerial_systems/issue_summary (Date of use: 9 August 2023)

Warwick G "Civil UAVs Need GPS anti-spoofing, but who pays. aviation week" http://www.aviationweek.com (Date of use:4 August 2023)